The Seamless Web

BY STANLEY BURNSHAW

André Spire and His Poetry
The Wheel Age
The Iron Land
The Bridge
The Sunless Sea
Early and Late Testament
Caged in an Animal's Mind
The Seamless Web
In the Terrified Radiance
Mirages: Travel Notes in the Promised Land
The Refusers
My Friend, My Father
Robert Frost Himself
A Stanley Burnshaw Reader

EDITED BY STANLEY BURNSHAW

Two New Yorkers
The Poem Itself
Varieties of Literary Experience
The Modern Hebrew Poem Itself

THE
SEAMLESS
WEB

By STANLEY BURNSHAW

WITH A FOREWORD BY
JAMES DICKEY

GEORGE BRAZILLER   NEW YORK

In Memory of Josephine Herbst

COPYRIGHT ACKNOWLEDGMENTS

BASIC BOOKS, INC.
    for quotations from *Preconscious Foundations of Human Experience* by
Trigant Burrow, edited by William E. Galt, Basic Books, Inc., Publishers,
New York, 1964.
    for quotations from *Metamorphosis* by Ernest G. Schachtel. Reprinted with
permission of the William Alanson White Psychiatric Foundation, Inc., and
Basic Books, Inc., Publishers, New York, 1959.

THE CLARENDON PRESS, OXFORD
    for quotations from *Doubt and Certainty in Science* by J. Z. Young, 1951,
by permission of the Clarendon Press, Oxford.

CORNELL UNIVERSITY PRESS
    for quotations from W. H. Thorpe, *Science, Man, and Morals.* © 1965 by
W. H. Thorpe. Reprinted by permission of Cornell University Press.
    for quotations from Frederick C. Prescott, *The Poetic Mind.* Reprinted
by permission of Cornell University Press.

DÆDALUS
    for quotations from "Science and Man's Nature" by René Dubos. Re-
printed by permission from *Dædalus: Journal of The American Academy of
Arts and Sciences,* Boston, Mass., Vol. 94, No. 1.

RANDOM HOUSE, INC.   ALFRED A. KNOPF, INC.

for quotations from *The Collected Poetry of W. H. Auden,* copyright 1940 and renewed 1968 by W. H. Auden. Reprinted by permission of Random House, Inc.

for the quotation from "Anecdote of the Jar," by Wallace Stevens, copyright 1923 and renewed 1951 by Wallace Stevens. Reprinted from *The Collected Poems of Wallace Stevens* by permission of Alfred A. Knopf, Inc.

SPRINGER-VERLAG NEW YORK INC.

for quotations from *Brain and Conscious Experience,* edited by Sir John Eccles, copyright 1966; reprinted by permission of Springer-Verlag New York Inc.: from Chapter 19, by W. H. Thorpe, and from Chapter 9, by W. Penfield.

THE UNIVERSITY OF CHICAGO PRESS

for quotations from *The Human Animal* by Weston La Barre, copyright 1954 by The University of Chicago. All rights reserved. Reprinted by permission of the author and of the publisher.

VANGUARD PRESS, INC.

for the quotation from "How Many Heavens" in *The Collected Poems of Edith Sitwell.* Copyright, 1949, 1954, by Edith Sitwell. Reprinted by permission of the publishers, the Vanguard Press, Inc.

THE VIKING PRESS, INC.

for the quotation from *The Complete Poems of Marianne Moore.* Copyright © 1959 by Marianne Moore. Reprinted by permission of The Viking Press, Inc.

YALE UNIVERSITY PRESS

for quotations from *Man Adapting* by René Dubos. Copyright © 1965 by Yale University. Reprinted by permission of the Yale University Press.

THE TOTAL ACT

by James Dickey

In our time—and encompassing all past time, and, I am willing to bet, future time as well—this book is the most eloquent and persuasive argument that exists for poetry as the one total act possible to us: the only process given to the human being in which he functions not only as an animal in a particular form, with certain specialized features, but as an entity in which all concomitants are one: a complex dynamism marshalling every resource available, and in its strivings toward memorable utterance also avid for those beyond availability, hinted but never given. *The Seamless Web* tells us that the poet speaks not merely as a human mind but as a *creature*; one whose humanity is only part of his endowment of being.

Burnshaw begins with an assessment of two ways of thinking: "those that seem to be involuntary and those that seem to be brought into play by the will." The "seem" is important, for what Burnshaw asserts is the essential and in some ways ungovernable interplay between these two types which in actuality are not capable of definitive separation; voluntary thinking is always to some extent involuntary, and the reverse. By means of a kind of scientific mysticism based on a great many technical sources—themselves fascinating—but moving also in a speculative realm beyond the enormous array of empirical evidence, Burnshaw puts himself solidly into position to ask the most important of all questions concerning the creative process: *Who* is doing the creating? This, and its corollary: What is meant when one says "I"?

In this book one skips nothing; "seamless" it is, indeed. The reasoning is so complex, and involves such a wealth of attested detail, that one can never risk dropping one of the threads, though it is often difficult to hold them all. The reader realizes early, however, that the journey toward Burnshaw's final evaluations is at least as important, for its information, its passing insights and the imaginative possibilities these suggest, as the conclusions they make possible. Then, too, the "way in" is so deceptively simple that one is likely to assume that the subsequent observations will be so, as well. They are not, but by the time the reader has passed the first primitive hurdle, the discussion of the terrors of basic animal self-preservation the author calls "the great Paleolithic fear, with its attendant internal preparations for struggle," he is fully into an encounter he realizes is not only likely to enhance and deepen his existence, but to change it.

For me, the most fecundating of Burnshaw's researches are those dealing with the effects on the human body of the various environments in which it exists: the Earth's magnetic field, the linkage of the body to the movement of the Earth and the moon, the tides of the ocean to the circulation of the blood and to blood pressure; the "Circadian rhythms" relating to pulse rate, urine volume, and body temperature; the electric changes in brain waves effected by those in the electromagnetic field of the planet; and—beyond, and always incoming night and day—cosmic rays, and by implication influences from unknown and infinite sources capable only of tentative measurement, and suggesting others that are not.

To my knowledge, never has instinct as it comes to an end in words been so convincingly tied to the whole of creation, and by such an inventive multiplicity of threads that one is drawn toward what amounts to a new kind of veneration for life, consciousness and their maintaining circumstances, and thus, in turn, to a form of contemplation that is in an entirely new sense religious.

Mallarmé, who might be looked on as the presiding spirit of *The Seamless Web*, tells us that "My thought thinks itself." Again, the Eskimo Orpingalik told an ethnologist that "We get a new song when the words we want shoot up out of themselves." Hyperintellectual or "primitive," Burnshaw's sources round to a common conclusion: we are beyond ourselves when we write: blood and the stars have got together on us. Or, "creativity is the work not of a six-inch cortical area of the human brain but of the total human organism": with Donne, "The Body Makes the Minde."

Nevertheless, in keeping with his pervasive emphasis on totality, Burnshaw does not leave out of account the role of conscious artistry. There has never been a more sure-handed manual of revision than this, a more useful assessment of the inventive power of rational focus: of "reason on fire."

On "native language and the condition of thought" Burnshaw also has much to say, and when one enters into this portion of his thought it is with a strong and positive shock of recognition that the reader recalls the author's theory of translation in his extraordinary *The Poem Itself*, which has given an extra dimension to the transliteration of poetry, and virtually created a new genre. He is especially at home in the limbo between languages that the translator find himself in, and the temptations, prohibitions, and possibilities that surround him there, when the choice of a word, say, depends not only on equivalence, and not on predictable connotation, either, but must be determined by or has a chance to draw upon the translator's own imaginative powers, and what vision he may summon: on resources not available to the original poet. As a personal note, it seems to me that this inventive limbo, in which, some of the time, and for some translators, it is better *not* to know the first language perfectly, is largely responsible for the "international style" that seems predominant in English-speaking poetry at this time. And it should also be apparent that the exploration—and not just the superficial exploitation—of this vast territory may well promise the most exciting discoveries since the Elizabethans. If the blank-verse line can be said to have helped Shakespeare become himself, we can also say—and already—with equal justice that "free" translation—the "imitation," the "version-from," the "suggested-by," and the "adapted-from," or even the "re-write"—have had a comparable influence on our own age and our own imagination. It would be excessive to say that Stanley Burnshaw's example alone has brought this about, but it has been and is a very powerful factor, and whatever emerges from this approach in the future will certainly bear his hand-print.

Having finished *The Seamless Web* the reader feels that he is not finished, and will never be. In the end the reader, especially if he is a poet or aspires to be, thinks not about the book but about himself and his resources, about what the universe has given him to funnel into his words: the words waiting in his own biorhythms, the Circadian cycles, the tides and the sun and moon, in cosmic rays and forces beyond all these, unascertainable but always incoming. One goes back through the book compulsively, then, re-assimilating everything, including the notes: *all* notes. Circadian cycle? Mystical, in essence. Instinct? Also. Birds? Perhaps the greatest mystics, with their celestial navigation, their homing capacities. Fish? Bees? All mystics. We? As well, in infinite complication and fascination. But also, by means of our language, with an opportunity to use all these things in a way that is ours alone.

In the end it is beautiful and simple: as simple as flight for the sparrow, as swimming for the trout. You think of God's advice to the millipede, the thousand-legs who asked the Universe that made him how to work all those legs. Does this one go here? If it does, what do I do, then, with *this* one? With all these others? God's advice is Burnshaw's: "Don't think, just walk."

Swing from the heels; get the Earth into it; your feet will tell you how. Also the tides. And the stars. Burnshaw's reliance on instinct and spontaneity, on "fusions of resemblance," releases metaphors at a rate the mortal poet would hitherto have thought impossible, before he became aware of all that feeds into them: of everything he has going for him. The central emphasis on the whole body and the environment it draws on as engendering the association, the mental picture, is something the poet acknowledges gladly, and moves *with*: in the present case—and under exactly this influence—has come the image of a javelin thrower just after the release. The body is off the ground, having just delivered everything with *everything*; the spear is in the air where it will go.

Prefatory Note

Says Paul Valéry, in a scriptural passage, "it is more useful to speak of what one has experienced than to pretend to a knowledge that is entirely impersonal, an observation with no observer. In fact, there is no theory that is not a fragment, carefully prepared, of some auto-biography. I do not pretend to be teaching you anything at all. I will say nothing that you do not already know. . . ." —And indeed my pages, wherever possible, have preferred to cite the most familiar examples. Nevertheless, in the discussions that follow, every reader will find a number of things to disagree with. What matters, how-ever, is the point of view that these pages propose. They see the "poet" as a creature concerned above all with keeping alive in his inner and outer worlds, whatever else he may seem to be focused on doing.

I use the word "poet" here in its broad, original meaning, to designate the "maker" of a work of art, whether he uses words or paint or stone or sound. At times the discussion applies to the sci-entist also, insofar as creative science is creative imagining. Hence

xii   PREFATORY NOTE

the omission of "poetry" from the title of this book which regards
the writer of verse as the archetype of the artist.

This volume is offered at a time when a good many people in
the West have begun to do more than discover that each of them
"has" a body. In the future course of this new awareness lies the
great hope: that the human creature, with his amazing capacity for
adapting to an earth which he alters, will not go on to adapt himself
out of existence.

To save the text from the disturbance of frequent digressions,
I have placed certain notes and comments at the close of each
chapter. Qualifying, complementing, adding, and at times debating,
they provide the obbligato to the central theme.

The writing of this book has entailed many debts, a great
number of which the Copyright Acknowledgments and Notes and
Comments make evident. Here I record my gratitude for help of
another kind: to Gregor Sebba and to Calvin S. Brown, for thoughtful suggestions and corrections; to René Dubos, for his reading of
the manuscript of Chapter 1; to Edward Dahlberg, for the Donne
quotation that I use for the same chapter; to Robert Greer Cohn,
Luciano Rebay, Hiram Haydn, Jackson and Marthiel Mathews, and
Edwin Seaver, for varied acts of assistance. So much for my recent
indebtedness. To speak of the earlier one would involve many books
and writers . . . among them the author of *L'Histoire de l'art antique*,
Elie Faure, whose reproductions of prehistoric paintings first led me
to question all I had learned—and would ever be told—about art.

S.B.

Contents

xiii

The Seamless Web

To be really man or nature
when thinking, one must think
with all one's body.

—MALLARMÉ

Introduction

"Who" Does the Creating?

In the pages that follow, I say, in the plainest prose I can command, what I believe poetry inclusively, comprehensively to be. And since my proposal differs from all other proposals, I offer its genesis at once:

Poetry begins with the body and ends with the body. Even Mallarmé's symbols of abstract essence lead back to the bones, flesh, and nerves. My approach, then, is "physiological," yet it issues from a vantage point different from Vico's when he said that all words originated in the eyes, the arms, and the other organs from which they were grown into analogies. My concern is rather with the type of creature-mind developed by the human organism in its long movement through time out of the evolutionary shocks which gave birth to what we have named self-consciousness.

So far as we know, such biological change failed to arise in any other living creature. So far as we can tell, no other species, alive or dead, produced or produces the language-thinking of poetry. We are engaged, then, with a unique phenomenon issuing from a unique physiology which seems to function no differently from that of other animals—in a life-sustaining activity based on continuous interchange between organism and environments.

How far beyond word-worn limits can such an approach to poetry lead? Before attempting to answer, one must get a clear view of the mode of thinking involved in creating a poem. Only then will it be possible to explore the essential function of poetry in human existence. Against such backgrounds, we may also begin to recognize the implications of calling poetry an "art." These considerations define the three parts of the present work.

Sir Herbert Read makes a pointed assertion in a recent discussion of creative originality: "From time to time along comes a special kind of craftsman, special because he possesses a particular vision of the world, a peculiar way of seeing the world, and this leads to a modification of the traditional forms of expression, to a *transformation*." The artist is "often unconscious of his discovery— it lurks in the background of his canvas. . . . It is not intentional, it is not *willed*." Thus, "we are thrown back on the individual—on the uniqueness of his mental disposition and the privateness of his experience. But this is where the difficulty arises, for it is not the sense of privateness, or the peculiarity of the personality, that the artist expresses when he is being most original." In support of his statement, Read adds: "I am well acquainted with Mr. Henry Moore's personality, and I am well acquainted with his sculpture. I cannot relate the two in any sense of expressive equivalence."[1]

Is this the task for a doctor of the Unconscious? Could he discover enough about the artist's sense of privateness and the peculiarity of the personality to get to the sources of his creativity? Before the analyst could begin, we should have to clarify all that "personality" must encompass, at which point he would have to with-draw—the point where all investigation confined to the cortex stops short. For the sources of an artist's vision involve aspects of biological response and processes of accumulation and release to which no investigation has as yet found access. Long before it became socially admissible to talk about the "wisdom of the body," William James as well as Pierre Janet had observed that the brain is not the only bodily organ which thinks.

Yet if psychology is in fact the "science of man in his entirety," as Pierre Janet declared it to be, does it not offer the best available means for understanding poets and perhaps also the genesis of poetry —especially in the territory opened up by Freud? No other science embraces so much of the creative personality, and none has devoted itself so intensively to phenomena of art. It would seem almost fool-hardy not to take the "Unconscious approach," since so many of its findings coincide with the observations of poets on their own creative experiences, from the time of Plato on.

An ungrateful response, however, cannot be avoided. Although it has often brought confirmation and correction, this approach as a whole has not advanced far beyond the line at which explaining amounts to attempts at describing. Freud's own avowals are much to the point. "[T]he nature of artistic achievement is inaccessible to us psychoanalytically," he said in 1910, adding three years later that it is "not a question for psychology."[2] Moreover, in his *Autobiography* he reaffirms his conviction that his science "can do nothing toward elucidating the nature of the artistic gift, nor can it explain the means by which the artist works," only to restate it with finality at the opening of his essay on Dostoevsky: "Unfortunately analysis has to lay down its arms before the problem of the creative writer."

One ought to be convinced, yet such a devoted disciple as Ernest Jones disagrees with his master's declaration that "Whence it is that the artist derives his creative capacity is not a question for psychology." While acknowledging that the sources lie deeper than any unconscious fantasy—that they are "more remote from our in-stinctual life than any other human interest, with the possible excep-tion of pure mathematics"—Jones maintains that "remoteness need not connote impenetrability." And he may prove to be right. At some future time psychoanalysis may come up with an elucidation "in entirety" that will show its founder to have been wrong. But if this happens, the language it must use and the assumptions it must propose will be likely to dismay even the hardiest reader. We have already experienced enough of the first to know what to count on. Even in Ernst Kris's often brilliant discussion of esthetic ambiguity, we run into such a passage as:

Central to artistic—or indeed any other—creativeness is a relaxation ("regression") of ego functions. . . In fantasy and dream, in states of intoxication and fatigue, such functional regression is especially prominent; in particular it characterizes the process of inspiration.

And the accompanying footnote makes clear that " 'functional regression' is here and in the following used equivalent with topographical regression." Though Kris regards creativity as "self-regulated regression," much of what he offers in his *Psychoanalytic Explorations in Art* has vivid interest. But he too warns that "the quest for what is specific to the psychological processes connected with art, its creation and its re-creation, constitutes a problem that we can hardly hope to solve."

And yet the "Unconscious approach" still strikes many people as indispensable, despite the disclaimers and despite the fact (in the words of Philip Rieff) that "Every work of art is to Freud a museum piece of the unconscious, an occasion to contemplate the unconscious frozen into one of its possible gestures." Moreover, before one could study the creative process from the psychoanalytic point of view, the word "Unconscious" would have to be defined. Whose version to use? It is not possible to proceed without involving the picture of the Unconscious as detailed by Freud, and here the difficulties are overwhelming. For no matter how one tries to think of the mental processes that Freud describes, one ends in reifications. The master himself has all but made this inevitable with his penchant for picturesque terms, despite his own warnings against graphic representations of psychoanalytic hypotheses: the Unconscious is "a cauldron of seething excitement"; the ego is "like a cortical layer with which a particle of living substance surrounds itself"; etc. Most problematical of all is the visual aid that he used for clarifying the interrelations of the three "divisions" of the mind: Unconscious, Preconscious, Conscious, along with the other famous three: Id, Ego, Superego.

It hardly helps to be told that the domain of the Unconscious consists, in large part, of instinctual forces or energies (Id) where two forces are in conflict: the libido (Eros) and the death- or destruction-wish (Thanatos). Freud tells us that "the interaction of the two basic instincts with and against each other gives rise to the whole variegation of the phenomena of life, and at once we think of locating them in some structure of the organism. Indeed, the names for mental aspects or forces have become so real that we tend to see them vividly objectified when we read about the "different regions of the mind," the "deeper layers of the ego," the "widening of its field of vision," and its taking over new "portions of the id," or when Freud concludes with the famous "Where id was, there shall ego be."

It is not churlishness that leads one to suspect reifications, nor ungratefulness that insists on the limits of psychoanalysis. Kris himself points out that Freud's "findings and the subsequent inquiries of a generation of psychoanalysts were mainly concerned with one issue . . . to fathom the id in its onto- and phylogenetic nexus." Though nobody justly questions the implicit interest of psychoanalysis for art, even far-reaching "understanding" of a writer or painter can be no more at best than an aspect. The work, said Otto Rank, "can never be compared with its author or with the artist as a psychological type." One is reminded of another sentence—by a writer, Pierre-Jean Jouve, whose own work was nourished by psychoanalytical meditation: "Poetry constantly surpasses its origins."

If in these pages I depend often on testimony from people who have done creative work, it is because it illuminates processes of composition vastly more, both in general and in particular, than do all the discussions of psychoanalysis. And it will not be in the least surprising to find that writers from Plato and Sophocles, through Shakespeare, Goethe, Melville, Henry James, and Proust, have (as Kris says) "contributed views which in many ways coincide with what psychoanalysis has ascertained by another method." Nor that Freud himself, when urged to publish his theories of sexuality, made a reply characteristic of an artist: "If the theory of sexuality comes, I will listen to it." These and similar findings go to confirm the first-hand testimony. However, if I avoid employing "the Unconscious" for explaining or illuminating, it is not in order to deny that there is such a "thing." So little agreement exists as to what the term actually means that to use it is to aggravate bewilderment in an area sufficiently menaced by confusions of much more than terminology. The broad currency of other portraits of the Unconscious in competition with Freud's—Jung's (archetypal), Maritain's (musical), Lacan's (verbal), to name only three—sharply reduces the possibility of obtaining any consensus.

Finally, when attempting to follow what occurs in the composing of a poem, one's terms should be neutral of values. Unfortunately this ideal does not accord with any psychoanalytic system, each of which inevitably erects some kind of metaphysical vantage point which implies a system of values. Freud's has been the most influential; even if Brown's *Life Against Death*, Marcuse's *Eros and Civilization*, or similar essays had never been published, *Civilization and Its Discontents* would have made the Freudian thesis an un-evictible component of modern philosophic thought.

In the pages that follow I shall be referring to two "ways" of thinking: those that seem to be involuntary and those that seem to be brought into play by the will. In discussing what happens in the course of composing a poem—the entire course, down to the last redaction—I shall limit myself to these two, bearing in mind always that "voluntary" and "involuntary" are unpretentious adjectives which correspond to two clearly dissimilar ways in which, for most of us, our brains *appear* to behave.[3] To mistake them as substitutes for "logical" and "alogical," for example, is to abuse and misconceive. My terms have nothing in common with dualisms of any variety; every dualism, no matter where it appears, needs to be scrutinized for what it may (wittingly or not) conceal, reduce, or oversimplify. Furthermore, in no possible sense are "voluntary" and "involuntary" processes proposed here as the thinking of two separate brains or minds within a single organism—which is what the Freudian view, for example, proposes ("The unconscious is the true psychical reality; in its nature it is just as unknown to us as is the reality of the outer world, and it is just as imperfectly communicated to us by the data of consciousness as is the outer world through the information reaching us from our sense organs. . . . In what is psychically real *there is more than one form of existence*").

"Voluntary" and "involuntary" do not split man in two. They are purely observational names for two of the manners in which we think; to imply anything more would involve impossible questions of Free Will which, happily, is not our subject. If each should at some time be shown to subsume other mental ways, "voluntary" and "involuntary" nevertheless would retain their unique virtue of being manageably distinguishable—for which one can give great thanks.

Although such terms imply a method for viewing the behavior of the brain in its moments of creativity, their use suggests nothing conclusive of how voluntary and involuntary processes come into play or where or why. In itself, it does not begin to answer the question rising out of Read's confessed inability to relate Moore's personality with his creative productions. It does not, in sum, say anything about the artist himself or what is meant by personality or originality or mind. The terms voluntary and involuntary describe observable processes brought into operation by other processes. To look for what Read could not find—expressive equivalence between a person and his productions of art—we must consider conditions which initiate the processes that discharge themselves in the creation of a poem. Hence, before attempting to follow the acts of composition, I ask a source question: *Who* is doing the creating?

NOTES AND COMMENTS

Unless otherwise indicated, the place of publication is New York • Prefatory Note quotation: Paul Valéry, *The Art of Poetry*, Bollingen Foundation, Pantheon Books, Inc., 1958, p. 58.

1. Herbert Read, *The Origins of Form in Art*, Horizon Press, Inc., 1965, p. 26.

2. For this paragraph and the two that follow, see Ernst Kris, *Psy-*

choanalytic Explorations in Art, Schocken Books, Inc., 1964, pp. 253, 31, 105, 105f., 23, 318; Philip Rieff, *Freud: The Mind of the Moralist*, Doubleday & Company, Inc., 1959, p. 121; Ernest Jones, *The Life of Sigmund Freud*, Basic Books, Inc., 1955, vol. 2, p. 403; also *The Modern Tradition*, Richard Ellman and Charles Feidelson, Jr., eds., Oxford University Press, 1965, pp. 563 ff.; Otto Rank, *Art and the Artist*, Alfred A. Knopf, 1932.

3. See note 36, Chapter 1.

I

Language-Thinking

1 · "The Body Makes the Minde"

To believe with John Donne that "the body makes the minde" is to take into account everything that might affect the body: forces separate or in fusion, from without and from within, whose existence we have only started to recognize, whose nature and number may lie past our powers of perceiving. So immense are the possible combinations of external forces alone that it seems ludicrous to discuss them in terms of what we now know or in time hope to know. The more promising course has been to learn our bodies and then from within to look outward. And we have come upon one finding with which all that may be discovered will have to accord: *the entire human organism always participates in any reaction*. To be sure, the body is made up of qualitatively different structures, each associated with specific functions. However (to use the careful, condensed language of Dr. Kurt Goldstein), "A specific location is characterized by the influence which a particular structure of that area exerts on the total process, i.e., by the contribution which the excitation of that area, by virtue of its structure, makes to the total process." Which is to say that the particular quality which the functioning of any localized part contributes to the organism's performance does not exist by itself and cannot exist outside the total relation.[1]

A newcomer to experimental biology is startled to discover that actually the same poisons can produce very different reactions in the same body tissue (depending on many factors and on the respective situations), and that this is quite similar to the effect of nerve stimulation. Like most of us he has been led to think of his body as an assemblage of organs or specialized structures held together in an envelope called the skin. Yet if he follows the verified findings he will see why, in each case, specificity arises from the particular total situation in which the localization is embedded. For him the statement that a human being is a whole, acting always and reacting always as a whole is not lofty philosophic humanism but clinical plain-talk about the behavior of the nerves, tissues, and bones.

Observers of bodily motion end with similar conclusions, their technical term being "multidimensional responses." A person makes postural movements which support and position his body in space and transport movements which propel his body, limbs, or extremities from one point in space to another or, in the case of speech musculature, propel the syllable pulses. He also performs manipulative or articulative movements by which his hands, feet, eyes, and speech apparatus make the fine adjustments that are superimposed on his larger (postural and transport) movements. What must be noted, however, is that his most skilled movements cannot be made without the support of the larger movement components. If, as K.U. and M.F. Smith have found, the latter "maintain orientation and attention and establish the over-all response pattern within which the skill is executed," "this is no less true of the implicit responses [such] as thinking than of overt psychomotor skills." In fact, "it is impossible to understand or analyze the organization of highly complicated human skills, *including symbolic skills*, except in the context of multidimensionality."[2]

The innocent parenthetical phrase I italicize drops us squarely into the middle of an ancient battle: between body and mind. While the issue seems to have fled from practical discourse—television commercials talk confidently of psychosomatic ills—it nevertheless keeps conjuring up irreconcilable entities in all but the most cautious discussions; and even there one sees shadows of virtual belief in their existence as discrete realms. The presumed dichotomy though dead seems unable to die. Yet once the relationship between somatic and mental processes is recognized as being exactly the same as that among all somatic processes in their single indivisible totality, the so-called psychophysical problem evaporates. Such words as mind and emotion "as commonly used cannot possibly refer to attributes located in fragments isolated from the body or associated with special chemical reactions," says René Dubos. "They denote activities of the integrated organism responding as a whole to external or internal stimuli."[3] Often enough "psychological" and "physical" seem indispensable as terminology but unless the data they help to describe are evaluated in the light of their functional significance for the entire body, they will end up designating what simply does not exist. "We are always dealing with the activity of the whole organism," states Goldstein, "the effect of which we refer at one time to something called mind, at another time to something called body." Hence, rather than depriving the psychical or the physical of their respective uniqueness, the emphasis merely explains why uniqueness cannot derive from independent segments of the body acting independently—why kicking a football is no more a purely physical act than reading a musical score is a purely mental one.

This is not to say anything different from what poets have at times remarked, in exalted or "objective" terms. The favored example of the first is from Emily Dickinson, of the second from A. E. Housman:

If I read a book and it makes my whole body so cold no fire can ever warm me, I know it is poetry. If I feel physically as if the top of my head were taken off, I know this is poetry.

Experience has taught me, when I am shaving of a morning, to keep watch over my thoughts, because, if a line of poetry strays into my memory, my skin bristles so that the razor ceases to act. This particular symptom is accompanied by a shiver down the spine; there is another which consists in a constriction of the throat and a precipitation of water to the eyes; and there is a third which I can only describe by borrowing a phrase from one of Keats's last letters, where he says, speaking of

Fanny Brawne, "everything that reminds me of her goes through me like a spear." The seat of this sensation is the pit of the stomach.

More significant generally—and closer to the biologist's particulars —are the views of another modern, the late André Spire, who saw poetic experience as somatic accumulation and release and the action of the organism as a parallel to the poem.[4] Distinguished by its word-order and other expressive structures, every poem (of the kind Coleridge would call "essential") exemplifies in an especial manner the involuntary physical activities that accompany all affective speech. Hence, in the writing of verse, the order and other forms of its language—with the more or less strong stresses, undulations, sudden stops, repetitions, modulations, and the like—are an "echo" of the movements within the poet's body: the poem's language is their external and communicative aspect. Conversely, in the reading of a poem, the motions and attitudes of the muscles in all the bodily structures—not only those of the face (especially the mobile and sensitive muscles associated with responses of sight and taste) but equally those hidden from view—"translate" into physical motion the psychological impressions and ideas and feelings evoked in the reader.

Spire's intuitions, like many others, have been confirmed by the laboratory. (To quote Goldstein again: "Numerous investigations have shown that, simultaneous with the perceptual phenomenon, a great variety of additional somatic events take place. . . . [We] are justified in assuming that a certain muscle tension corresponds to every sense impression.") But Spire goes further, being also concerned with the meaning of the bodys' natural way of paralleling a poem. These actions set into motion by the feelings cannot, of course, be thought of as mechanically imitative since the body is not a machine. Rather, because the poem evokes an "organismic" experience which takes the form of a correspondence or parallel, it must be regarded as an internal metaphor.[5] And for the organism it is this metaphor that constitutes the "true" poem.

Forces: External and Internal

To gain an even sketchy understanding of the human organism, one must keep constantly in mind the fact that it still possesses a paleolithic past. Very much more cannot be done; we know hardly anything of the way in which traits, needs, urges retained from evolutionary experience condition our behavior today. So far as innate responses are concerned, they are still, says Dubos, the ones that had developed aeons ago to adapt mankind to the conditions that then prevailed but which have long ceased to exist. Since paraphrase invites distortion, I quote his own words:

Many aspects of human behavior that appear incomprehensible, or even irrational, become meaningful when interpreted as survivals of attributes that were useful when they first appeared during evolutionary development and that have persisted because the physical evolution of man came to a sudden halt about 150,000 years ago. Phenomena ranging all the way from the aberrations of mob psychology to the useless disturbances of metabolism and circulation that occur during verbal conflicts at the office or at a cocktail party are as much the indirect expressions of the distant biological past as they are the direct consequences of the stimuli that were their immediate cause.

Furthermore,

man has also retained from his evolutionary past certain needs that no longer have a place in the world he has created, yet must be satisfied. . . . Ancient civilizations were aware of the profound effects that hidden physiological needs exert on human behavior. . . . In several empirical ways, they developed procedures to let the occult components of man's nature manifest themselves under somewhat controlled conditions. As shown by E. R. Dodds, in *The Greeks and the Irrational*, the Dionysian celebrations, the Eleusinian mysteries, and many other myths and rituals served as release mechanisms for the fundamental human urges that did not find adequate expression in the rational and classical aspects of Greek life. Even Socrates found it wise to participate in the Corybantic rites.[6]

No analogous outlet, so far as I know, has ever been proposed for the fight-or-flight response that is still very much with us—the body's astonishing capacity for anticipating danger and for mobilizing its resources almost at once. The great paleolithic fear with its attendant internal preparations for struggle was no less than an adaptive necessity in the wild. In civilized existence, however, the same physiological and metabolic changes that were crucial when the need for physical effort was imminent may cause severe disturbances of vitally important functions. The once adaptive responses have become problems for civilized man.[7]

There is yet another complicating factor in normal behavior, one peculiar to man as the symbol-making, symbol-using creature *par excellence*. Living forms respond, says Dubos, in a manner which is determined not only by the nature of the stimulus itself but also by the indirect reactions that it mobilizes in them. This chain of indirect response is of greatest importance in man because of his propensity to symbolize everything that happens to him, and then to react to the symbols as if they were actual environmental stimuli.

Hence everything we perceive and interpret by thinking processes "become translated into organic processes."

This conclusion goes far beyond ordinary notions of how the "mind" can affect the "body." Does it mean that the only stimuli which are not altered or qualified by mental processes are those of which mental processes are not aware—such as might be exerted by climate or landscape or geography without even entering a person's mind? What of the relationship of the mother's mental life to the embryo growing in her womb: does it affect the intrauterine environment which itself can affect anatomical structures, physiological functions, and even more? Obviously even before asking questions of this kind, it is necessary to define "awareness" and the relationship between these mentally unaltered or unqualified stimuli and a person's thought. And then thought itself must be defined! Cosmic rays and others of unknown origin constantly drill human bodies—which is to say that stimuli incessantly flow within them from the world outside. What are their effects upon the organism? How are they expressed in human responses? Certain animals not only feel the earth's magnetic field but can even distinguish its direction. Do magnetic fields have any comparable meaning for man, whose retina, for some strange reason, records their presence?

Though we seem to know little about much in the blooming, buzzing confusion of bodily existence, the gap shows signs of narrowing.[8] We have learned that a human being's internal environment varies with the season: for one thing, his hormonal activities, for another, his blood pressure—in temperate lands its peak is in spring, its trough in late summer. Not only is the behavior of certain animals linked directly to the cycles of the moon but statistical data now suggest lunar periodicity in human reproduction also. Man's responses to any situation are not the same in the spring as in the fall:

his body fluctuates according to certain rhythms linked to the movements of the earth and of the moon in relation to each other and to the sun. "The high tides of the oceans," says Dubos, "may have their counterpart in the high tides of our blood stream."

In ways that were never suspected, man depends on the fact that Earth turns on its axis once every 24 hours. His body reflects the "circadian rhythm" in pulse rate, urine volume, body temperature, all of which are in phase with the time of his maximal physical activity. And as the circadian cycle progresses, his body's condition changes. He has been told only recently about the biological clock of his organism—told, nothing more. But how explain the operation of this chemical system which is corrected by temperature, runs continuously, receives the signals of the time each day from the natural rhythm of daylight and darkness?[9] How, for that matter, explain the behavior of the fiddler crab, which ignores all changes in environment? Take him from his native habitat on the Atlantic and put him into a laboratory under controlled conditions and he will do exactly as he did on the shore: he will darken his skin at the time when it would be sunrise there and he will run around at the same time he would be running around his beach. The daily cycle of the sun governs the color of his skin; the lunar rhythm of the tide, his bodily motion. Circadian rhythm has been found to persist even in regenerating tissues: perhaps the biological clocks can be "located" by cytologists. If they find the rhythm of the cell to be formed in the turning of the spheres, the words of Freud will begin to sound more like a seer's than a scientist's: "In the last resort, what has left its mark on the development of organisms must be the history of the earth we live in and of its relation to the sun."

The Brain as Machine

Against this background of hidden immensities, computers seem less than miracles. None of them bears in its circuits remembrances of a paleolithic past, nor are its rhythms linked to the cosmos. Only in the most reductive sense might it be called a user of symbols. Pull one switch and the inanimate mass comes to life; pull another and it dies. And despite the human actions it can perform with superhuman speed, it is only a makeshift model. As the 17th century compared man to a clock, the 20th compares him to a calculating machine. But the comparison does more than compare; it implies the credo of faith at the base of our biology and medicine: the conception of live human bodies as machines endowed with structures and functions. The calculating machine is not of course "like" the mind, nor even "like" all that is meant by the brain, being inherently deprived of essential aspects.[10] Meanwhile it serves its employers wonderfully. If (to use Bronowski's epitome), the characteristic invention of the First Industrial Revolution was the power machine that does the routine work of man's muscle, that of the Second—through which we are passing—is the control mechanism that does the routine work of man's brain. And since the bulk of such work is mechanical, it does it incomparably better than could its makers, whose calculations are subject to disturbance by ideas, hence also by feelings, for, as one of its advocates quaintly reminds us, there is considerable evidence that it is "illegitimate to separate thought completely from feeling."[11] The computer itself has no such scruples—as yet (though A. M. Turing's theoretical robot might simulate many).[12]

In a remarkable book called *The Nature of Explanation*, the British scholar K. J. W. Craik presents man's nervous system as a calculating machine capable of modeling or paralleling external events. Without departing very far from the classical laws of mechanics or Euclidean conceptions of space, he suggests that the basic feature of human thought and methods of explaining (that is, its "neural machinery") is its power to parallel or model external events, to imitate. It "has only to produce combinations of excited arcs, not physical objects; its 'answer' need only be a combination of consistent patterns of excitation—not a new object that is physically and chemically stable." Thus "thought models, or parallels, reality— its essential feature is not 'the mind,' 'the self,' 'sense data,' nor propositions but symbolism . . . As for symbolism, it is the ability of processes to parallel or imitate each other." We get a concrete picture of the theory from the author's later statement that "the organism carries 'a small-scale model' of external reality and of its own possible actions within its head."

There are qualifications, of course. "It may be that a mind does not function only in this way; but this is *one* way that 'works,' in fact the only way with which we are familiar in the physical sciences." Craik sees no reason to suppose that the processes of reasoning are basically different from the mechanism of physical nature. However, "human memory and learning have a vivid, conscious aspect, and an astonishing elasticity and power of grasping principles which no machine has hitherto imitated and which may be in the power of conscious processes alone." Nevertheless, as he makes quite clear, consciousness plays no part in this theory—and he is in respectable company in omitting it, since "the existence of consciousness as an attribute of organized matter has never been either proved or disproved." His theory has also some "bleaker consequences," as he puts it. "What becomes of purposes and ideals and creative thought?" he asks. An excellent question. . . .

Despite the enormous publicity their findings receive in the press, scientific explorers of the human brain have little to say with certainty. If (to quote Lancelot Whyte) theirs is one of "the three basic ignorances" that mark the scientific scene today, they are not to be blamed for lack of zeal or ingenuity. The object they study is probably the most complicated six inches on earth: the supposedly 15 billion cells in the cortex, tens of thousands of nerve cells in the spinal cord, with millions of receptor fibers converging upon them— the center of the retina of each human eye, for example, has nearly a half-million sensitive cells, each connected with a single nerve fiber. Obviously observers cannot learn much about brain processes unless the subject under study can converse with them while his cortical areas are exposed. Brain anatomists have even succeeded in arranging such dialogue; they have invented astounding techniques. Nevertheless, a plain account of what all investigators of the brain surely know consists largely of warnings, qualifications, disclaimers. "We cannot yet say that we have a clear model by means of which we can speak of how the cortex works," says J. Z. Young in his *Doubt and Certainty in Science: A Biologist's Reflection on the Brain.* "The details [of the cortical system] are of hardly imaginable complexity, and we have only begun to unravel them . . . the patterns of interaction are very imperfectly known to us."[13]

While certain specific findings about localized processes have the marks of certainty, the conclusions they imply remain speculative. What is worse, we are given very little explanation of some of the most interesting aspects of thought. Of memory, for example. Information presumably reaches the brain in a type of code of impulses passing up the nerve fibers, then it is stored. But where? by what process? K. S. Lashley, who came to doubt the existence of circumscribed memory circuits, proposed a theory of mass-action effects ("equipotentiality"). But if multiple circuits holds the answer, their claim has yet to be proved. The same must be said of all other neural explanations as well as those of biochemists. As for the marvelous ability of the human and animal brain to make generalizations, virtually nothing can be stated with confidence: it has neither been explained by any process nor tracked down to any location.[14] Finally, as Young assures us, "we are so ignorant about the brain that we do not know properly how the input fibers are related to the cortical cells." He might have added: we do not know how even a reflex works.

Nevertheless, a few verified conclusions have startling implications. "The activity of nervous conduction is accompanied by electrical changes"; electrical brain-waves are in some way a sign of brain-cell activities. Note, however, that "the waves are most clear when the brain is idling—for instance, when a person is asleep or day-dreaming. Then, apparently, large masses of cells are working in unison. When the person wakes or begins to think, the electrical charges become more complicated." Stimuli—from without the organism or from within—irritate the brain into action; and instantly it goes to work to "dispose" of the disturbance, so that the cells may "return to their regular synchronous beating." If the brain is unable to accommodate the stimulus, to reconcile it with its habitual pattern of response, great activity arises, all directed toward reducing the disturbance. In the language of Young: "The situations that we call painful or unpleasant are those in which we cannot fit the input of nerve-impulses to our set of rules." Moreover, "the body and brain seek every possible means of avoiding any situation that sets up those impulses." In some way of which we are ignorant "the brain initiates sequences of actions that tend to return it to its rhythmic pattern, this return being the act of consummation, or completion. The brain runs through its rules one after another, matching the input with its various models until somehow unison is achieved."

Unison, regular synchronous beating, lack of disturbance; these surprising terms describe the condition for which the brain naturally strives: a life of untroubled rhythm. And like the organism of which it is a part, it mobilizes all its resources for this purpose—of making what Carlyle in another context called truce with necessity. Once a truce has been achieved, the brain can resume the harmonious state of idling that it desires.

But, as we have seen, not without resorting to its "rules"—those ways of dealing with situations which it has learned in the course of its existence and which it has then organized as its own. For this is no one-way process of being taught. Though each human being must learn from others how to see, the brain "is not by any means a simple recording system like a film. Many of our affairs are conducted on the assumption that our sense organs provide us with an accurate record, *independent of ourselves* [my italics]. What we are now beginning to realize is that much of this is an illusion; that we have to learn to see the world as we do." Perception is no longer understood as a passive relationship between the viewer and what he views. So much does the process involve action on the part of the viewer that elements entirely outside the objects and events before him will influence and sometimes even determine what is seen. As the art critic Ernst Gombrich remarks, "The innocent eye sees nothing."[15]

It is in the course of dealing with all that disturbs its harmony that each brain develops its very own organizing "laws." For, as Young maintains:

The effect of stimulations, external or internal, is to break up the unison of action of some part or the whole of the brain. A speculative suggestion is that the disturbance in some way breaks the unity of the actual pattern that has been previously built up in the brain. The brain then selects those features from the input that tend to repair the model and to return the cells to their regular synchronous beating. . . . If the first action performed fails to do this, fails that is to stop the original disturbance, then other sequences may be tried. . . . During this random activity further connexions and action patterns are formed and they in turn will determine future sequences. As the child grows, therefore, the brain acquires a series of ways of acting, of laws, as it were. . . .
The cortex of the new-born baby . . . is in the main a blank sheet of possibilities. But the very fact that it becomes organized minute by minute, day by day, throughout the years, reduces progressively the number of possible alternative ways of action.

It goes without saying that each brain sets up its own characteristic rules as a consequence of its twofold uniqueness: genetic endowment and life experience. Its ways of dealing with stimuli borne
on the almost innumerable nerve fibers from the exteroceptors and
interoceptors become the rules or laws of its particular behavior—
of its thought. Though it is impossible to see how this happens within
the brain, it is, as Young would remark, "certain that changes, however small, in such a delicate meshwork will affect the probability of
future action." The resulting cortical uniqueness will be constantly
subject to change—so long as the brain is able to develop new ways
for dealing with stimuli. Young is led to conclude that the form that
we give to "the plain, commonsense world of hard material facts . . .
is a construct of our brains." The statement may at first seem inadequate in its failure to take special account of the un-plain world
of imagination, which can ultimately be traced to the same common-
sense source. Yet the seeming omission is necessary to Young's own
construct of the brain, which in fact provides for all that the mind
might attempt, with its common *and* uncommon sense.

Though "a really useful and interesting brain is always starting
off on new ways," this grows more difficult as one grows older: "the
randomness . . . becomes gradually used up." "The brain ceases to
be able to profit from experiment, it becomes set into patterns of
laws."[16] The point may have bearing on the plight of the physicist,
who stops expecting to make important discoveries once he has
passed age thirty, but what of the poet? When I asked the eighty-
eight-year-old Spire to show me some of his writing, he replied,
"At my age one finds himself always re-doing the same poem." Yet
Goethe wrote his "Trilogie der Leidenschaft" when he was seventy-
four and Spire himself lived on to disprove his own words with the
poem of his ninety-sixth year.

Brain "and" Body

While we are always dealing with the activity of the whole organism,
to use Goldstein's phrase, it is occasionally necessary to refer to "the
effect of something called the mind" at one time and at another to
that of "something called the body." And, as might be suspected, the
relationship between them has bearing upon creativity.

That the highest neural centers of the brain can produce sharp changes in somatic behavior is no longer questioned, even while scientists keep making zealous attempts to explain precisely what occurs. Hypnosis, for example, has become an accepted medical technique, with well-authenticated if empirical applications. For non-medical investigators, to judge from the amount of their researching and theorizing, hypnotic phenomena scintillate with possibilities. Yet hardly less dramatic are some of the effects of placebos, and not only in relieving pain or anxiety (even sham surgery has been proved to bring on a placebo result). Moreover, the findings have been measured in terms of various functions of pulmonary, gastrointestinal, urogenital, adrenocortical systems. No ground remains for the doubting Thomases to stand on.

Certain other changes in somatic behavior appear even more mystifying, and since nobody has been able to explain the accompanying processes, we attribute the effects—like those of hypnosis and placebo—to the influence exerted by "suggestion" and by the cerebral cortex. The most scientific thing we can do is to exclaim when a yogi succeeds in deliberately altering his pulse rate and blood pressure. As for other documented cases—such as those of death by suggestion, of the will-to-live, of the will-to-die—nobody as yet has produced satisfactory explanations. So we content ourselves with marveling at the complexity of psychophysical interrelations, and with supposing that we may yet learn how they work and why.

Unlike some of these phenomena, changes in thinking produced by somatic processes are an ancient story. How ancient nobody knows, though it is likely that the body's ability to alter states of mind has long been exploited. History and ethnology give reports of varied types of ecstatics, and at least some of them might have discovered dependable methods for inducing extraordinary states of mind. In any event, it seems certain that a good many human beings have been deliberately swallowing toxic substances—such as the magical mushrooms of the Guatemalans, the cactus juices of the Southwestern Amerindians—for hundreds, perhaps thousands, of years. With wholly differing procedures, flagellants of Christian Europe and practitioners of the Far East could also attain to extraordinary conditions of awareness. Though no one has taken inventory of all the phenomena, the known effects are believed to range from exalted visions of the Deity to pragmatic insights which can even help to cure alcoholism. What all of them hold in common is qualitative alteration in thought process, for the most part temporary but at times beyond reversal.[17]

Certain of the effects have been accounted for biochemically. According to some theorists, as every newspaper-reader knows, lysergic acid diethylamide (LSD), when taken internally, may compete with serotinin (one of a number of bodily substances intimately involved with brain behavior) for a particular enzyme. Since each chemical reaction in the body is controlled by its own enzyme, this competition is almost certain to produce a change. However, no two organisms have the identical constitution or identical ways of responding; hence nobody can predict the outcome of the competition with serotinin in a specific case—whether the thought processes will be mildly or severely affected, whether the taker's brain will be temporarily or permanently altered.

A different biochemical explanation—which, like the foregoing, has gained some acceptance—accounts for the effects of a drug obtained from a certain cactus plant. The mescaline molecule is chemically close enough to the body's adrenalin to be able to interfere with a specific enzyme (amine oxidase) which the body normally uses to get rid of an overproduction of adrenalin. Hence mescaline eating may cause too much adrenalin to accumulate within the body, and when it does hallucinations arise.

In recent years "psychedelic" (mind-manifesting) experiences have been lavishly described in all species of books and periodicals. While differing in particulars, they are universally marked by extraordinary assertions, often of bliss: everyday objects are discovered to be ineffable both for what they are in themselves and for what they signify and suggest. A scientist would have to remark that in contrast to normal perceptions, those of the mescaline eater, for example, with their bizarre overtones, are distorted—inappropriate to the "real" universe. Primitive Indians, however, see mescaline as leading them into a universe beyond the real one. Aldous Huxley speaks of the possibility of a "temporary self-transcendence," "a genuine religious experience." But however described or adjudged, the state of magnified awareness is accompanied by ineffable clarity, wondrous simplicity, feelings of complete harmony with the universe. What the scientist defines as merely abnormal, the participant defines as supernormal.[18]

Is it possible that something in the organism of a creative artist —something of which he is not aware (for example, particular combinations of compounds)—may also at times result in biochemical reactions of the kind that cause him to respond in comparably abnormal-supernormal ways? We are told that bodily adrenalin can easily be altered to form a slightly changed compound (adrenochrome) which in turn can produce many of the symptoms observed in mescaline intoxication. Since the organism is capable of forming its own hallucinogens, might adrenochrome, or something comparable, form "spontaneously" within an otherwise "normal" human body? My adverb does not suggest any lack of causality but the absence of any known stimuli, external or internal, from the accounts of such people as Newton and Pascal, for example, who also experienced abnormal-supernormal states. Moreover, in a basic sense all works of art are reports of magnified awareness, of abnormal-supernormal states of vision in which quite ordinary objects or events suddenly take on ineffable import for the artist because of what they are in themselves and what they signify:

> To me the meanest flower that blows can give
> Thoughts that do often lie too deep for tears.

In terms of what an outsider would have to refer to as "process," what could be the difference in kind between Wordsworth's report and Baudelaire's in his *Fusées*:

Dans certains états de l'âme presque surnaturels, la profondeur de la vie se révèle tout entière dans le spectacle, si ordinaire qu'il soit, qu'on a sous les yeux.

"The Wisdom of the Body"

To " 'look into our hearts and write,' " says T. S. Eliot, "is not looking deep enough; Racine or Donne looked into a good deal more than the heart. One must look into the cerebral cortex, the nervous system, the digestive tracts."[19]

Within his enclosing skin, each man is an interior sea. And like

the ocean itself, this invisible world contains "all of us that is *alive*"
—the enormous multitudes of microcosmic living elements (cells)
which compose our muscles, glands, brains, nerves, and other structures. All of us that is alive are water inhabitants, inhabitants of a
fluid matrix, and whenever danger of its loss arises, agencies within
the body act swiftly to reduce the danger.

A century ago the French physiologist Claude Bernard declared
that "the stability of the interior environment is the essential condition of free and independent life," for "all the vital mechanisms,
however varied they may be, have only one object: that of preserving constant the conditions of life in the interior environment." No
more pregnant sentence was ever framed by a physiologist, said
Haldane. No more inspiriting enlargement of such a conception
could be desired than that of Dr. Walter B. Cannon, whose thought
and words make up the preceding paragraph.[20]

Drawn from first-hand laboratory experiences, Cannon's *The
Wisdom of the Body* often reads like a book of marvels:

When we consider the extreme instability of our bodily structure . . .
its persistence through many decades seems almost miraculous. The
wonder increases when we realize that the system is open, engaging in
free exchange with the outside world, and that the structure itself is
not permanent but is being continuously built up again by processes
of repair.

The astonishing fact is that

Organisms, composed of material which is characterized by the utmost
inconstancy and unsteadiness, have somehow learned the methods of
maintaining constancy and keeping steady in the presence of conditions
which might reasonably be expected to prove profoundly disturbing.
If changes threaten, indicators at once signal the danger, and corrective
agencies promptly prevent the disturbance or restore the normal when
it has been disturbed.
The corrective agencies act, in the main, through a special portion of
the nervous system which functions as a regulatory mechanism. For
this regulation it employs, first, storage of materials as a means of adjust-
ment between supply and demand, and, second, altered rates of continuous processes in the body.

By storing and releasing material supplies, by altering the rate of
continuous processes, by mobilizing natural defences against injury—
all within a very wide margin of safety—the normal human organism

protects itself for decades against perturbations. The agency responsible for preserving this homeostasis, for protecting the cells in all their parts whether from within or from without, is the controlled fluid matrix (water modified by the addition of salt and thickened by an albuminous or colloid material).

To read through Cannon's volume is to discover not only unimagined complexities of the world within each man, woman, and child but also specific ways in which it acts to maintain the balance essential for continuing existence—in Bernard's language, for "free and independent life." How, for example, it assures constancy of the water content in the blood; of the salt content; of the blood sugar; of the blood proteins; of an adequate supply of oxygen (which it cannot store as it can food and water). How, in the face of enormous variations both within and without, it achieves constant body temperature. In some organs, one is surprised to learn, the margin of safety drawn on in emergency situations can amount to five, ten, even fifteen times the quantity actually needed. Perhaps most impressive of all is the part played by the sympathetic division of the autonomic system, which goes about its work *independently of voluntary thought*, since every change in the outer world, in fact every considerable move in relation to the outer world, demands undelayed processes in our inner world.

At the very beginning of a disturbance, sentinels (automatic indicators) set the corrective processes into operation without otherwise being told to do so:

If the blood pressure falls and the necessary oxygen supply is jeopardized, delicate nerve endings in the carotid sinus send messages to the vasomotor centers and the pressure is raised. If by vigorous muscular movements blood is returned to the heart in great volume, so that cardiac action might be embarrassed and the circulation checked, again delicate nerve endings are affected and a call goes from the right auricle, that results in speeding up the heart rate and thereby hastening the blood flow. If the hydrogen-ion concentration in the blood is altered ever so slightly towards the acid direction, the especially sensitized part of the nervous system which controls breathing is at once made active and by increased ventilation of the lungs carbonic acid is pumped out until the normal state is restored.

All such processes go on by themselves—we are not even vaguely aware of most of them—for the good reason that the organism cannot afford to wait for voluntary decisions from the brain if it is to maintain the requisite stability in relation to both internal and external worlds. On the contrary, it is precisely what these processes do on their own initiative that frees the higher centers of the brain to go about their particular interests, in a quite different mode of "thought." If "higher" and "lower" as applied to thought structures denote only complexity and distance from the ground, a revision seems in order in our notions of human wisdom. As the last few paragraphs suggest, the bodily processes responsible for assuring the organism's security discharge their tasks through most remarkable modes of response. For swift and exact knowledge of when to begin, what to do, and when to stop, the cleverest brain would be hard put to match this lower body's wisdom.

> Numberless are the world's wonders, but none
> More wonderful than man

cries the chorus in the great ode of *Antigone*,[21] celebrating man's highest thought "rapid as air," his "clear intelligence, force beyond measure." But among the wonders he possesses, what outrivals his unsung inner sea that guards the gift of his life?

No one can understand the organism's response to a disturbance without being impressed by a magisterial fact: both brain and "body" do whatever they can to dispose of it quickly—a thought, rarefied air, a bleeding blood vessel. The brain, when its rhythmical unison is broken by an upsetting idea, at once activates its resources so that it can return to its synchronous beating. The fluid matrix, when something disturbs its balance, moves its processes in the same direction of stability. To be thus peaceably at one with the worlds within and without is the guiding dream of the organism, the goal toward which it strives in all its parts and as a whole.

Because this ideal state of internal constancy cannot always be attained, the organism learns both to adapt itself and to maintain adaptedness against the pressures of ever-changing environments. Physiological and biochemical homeostasis do not, however, account for all the processes through which man's organism responds adaptively. The world is still ignorant of how these unknowns operate; perhaps it will never find out.

Meanwhile other "talents" have emerged which suggest how

much more might be learned about human nature. One scientist brings evidence for a remarkable sensitivity of the skin even to speech. Another finds "a differential effect of colors" to be not limited to the eye but also holding for light stimulation of the skin in general, though to a much smaller degree (green and blue leading to a changed position of the arms in the direction opposite from that induced by yellow or red). A number of blind people under study accurately assess not only the distance of objects in their environment but also the size and the composition. Will a built-in sense of distance eventually prove to be latent in the sighted as well? What of the "eyeless vision" extensively studied by Soviet scholars?—of the reputed ability of one of their citizens to distinguish colors through her fingertips?—of the Michigan housewife with seemingly comparable skill? . . .[22]

Enough unanticipated phenomena have been encountered to start what one psychologist calls "a renaissance of interest in the role of kinesic and paralinguistic information as it contributes to the total process of communication." Both studies—the first, of bodily movements relevant for transmitting information (such as gestures); the second, of vocal behaviors (such as tone of voice) having similar relevance—belong to the larger field of "semiotics," now being subjected to research. Not an hour of scientific training, however, is needed for identifying modes of "phatic" communication—those manifestations which convey information about a person's physiological or emotional state. As Weston La Barre remarks:

Many mere males have noted in bewilderment the acute phatic prescience of a mother when her child is concerned: she somehow knows when it is hungry and when it has had enough; when it is thirsty and when it is soiled; when it is tired, ill, or merely in a bad temper. Close emotional concern, endlessly repeated contexts, the infant's idiosyncrasies of expression, and the mother's own organic receptors all give her a large and continuing intelligence about the child. The phatic closeness of lovers also commonly reaches fantastic extremes of precision. . . . The great social burden that even phatic verbalization still bears in humans is quite enormous.[23]

The startling extent to which silent gestures and cues can replace verbal communication came to light sixty years ago when a

German psychologist set out to explain the feats of Clever Hans, the famous horse belonging to a Mr. van Osten.[24] Hans had apparently mastered the cardinal numbers from 1 to 100 and the ordinals at least to 10, but this skill was the least of his accomplishments. He could also add, subtract, divide, and multiply with integers and fractions. He could tell time to the minute, count the windows on distant houses, the number of street urchins climbing on the neighborhood roofs, and so on. He also had musical gifts, including absolute pitch and the ability to tell whether two tones simultaneously sounded made a third or a fifth. Hans had been trained by his owner to convert his replies into numbers and to tap them out with his foot, even when questions were written down on pieces of cardboard. An investigating committe of thirteen trained observers certified, after observing Hans in action, that the horse had not received any signs or cues from anyone. The conditions, in fact, precluded trickery.

One investigator, Oskar Pfungst, found not only that Hans was clever but that his performance did not depend on his trainer's presence since virtually anyone could ask him a question and very probably receive the correct response. But it was only after altering the conditions between questioner and horse that Pfungst could begin to see what was passing between them. A slight forward inclination of the questioner's head gave the signal for Hans to start tapping whether a question had been asked or not, and the rate of tapping seemed to depend on the angle of the questioner's head. When Hans reached the right number of taps, the questioner tended to straighten up, thereby providing Hans with the cue to stop. The horse proved responsive to the most minute upward motions of the head, even to a raising of eyebrows or a dilation of nostrils, any of which could stop him from tapping. Pfungst was able to demonstrate that anybody could start Hans's tapping and that anyone else could stop it merely by employing these cues.

The most unexpected among the findings came not from the response of the horse but from the behavior of the questioners. Even after he had thoroughly mastered the system, Pfungst discovered that despite his efforts to withhold them he was continuing to give signals to Hans. In order to verify his explanation of the horse's performances, Pfungst set up a new experiment. He took the part of Hans and invited other people to ask questions, to which Pfungst-as-Hans would now tap out the answers. Of the 25 questioners, 23 unintentionally cued Pfungst. None had been told what was being investigated and one of them, a psychologist trained in introspection, was unable to discover how he was sending out signals.

A number of related experiments have been made, and though some failed to locate the precise elements in the communication system, all have been explained on the same theory: that subjects are able to perceive subtle nonverbal cues at levels ordinarily found to lie below the threshold. As Robert Rosenthal sums up the entire phenomenon, Pfungst's findings as well as subsequent ones "may be interpreted to mean that not only does the experimenter unknowingly evoke expected responses from his subject but that the subject also unwittingly evokes appropriate cues from his experimenter."

The body not only can "speak" without depending on words or other sounds but its urge to communicate tends to be too powerful to be checked by the will. One body can "speak" to another body and be "heard" even when the speaker is deprived of his full expressive means, of voice and ear. What we have been watching here holds a new dimension of the involuntary processes. If the communicative behavior of the "exterior" organism points to more than the "interior" body wisdom adduced by Cannon, it is because of the difference in occasion. No threat to the body's integrity is involved. The insistence on communicating that underlies the behavior of the signalling "speaker" does not rise out of any immediate need for preserving his organism, though the need it fulfills may, in the long terms of creature survival, be just as great.

One cannot, in this general connection, help recalling what Janet remarked about human thought: that it "is not the function of any particular organ"; that "the brain is only a switchboard." The senses, to take only one set of structures, edit their messages before the latter reach the brain. The eye, for example, sees not points of light, for it is arranged to read the shape of things into what it sees. As Jacob Bronowski puts it, "the sense impressions do not come to the brain as blank signals, but as elaborately prearranged and biased messages." "A single nerve fiber . . . does not so much inform the brain as instruct it, by sorting its messages in advance . . . by judging for itself what is irrelevant and discarding it, without leave from the brain."[25] Long before the investigations were undertaken that made this statement possible, Janet had declared that "we think as much with our hands as with our brains, we think with our stomachs, we think with everything." We cannot think otherwise, each of us being the organism that he is, carrying on a variety of behaviors for sustaining existence, many of which never reach into our level of awareness.

From what has been brought into view in the foregoing several pages, it is certain that much of the time we are being thought. Reflexivity is the only language we possess for suggesting the ways by which the organism and its environment maintain their existence without the aid of what we call a directing consciousness. Creature and world flow into each other on their own, without need of commands. Left to themselves, each gives and takes what it needs. And living as we do in dependence upon processes that guard and maintain our existence, we might well regard the relationship as a kind of mystical exchange; for this is the picture that the descriptions ultimately reveal. Much of the time, perhaps most, we are being lived.

"Who"?

"A man is born into the world with his own pair of eyes, and he is not at all responsible for his vision," wrote Stephen Crane, who then went on to burden him with responsibility "for the quality of his personal honesty." The extended implication—that everyone is "responsible" for what he makes of the capacities he was born with— seems unarguable. It is that indeed and imperatively more to British and American ethologists, many of whom would dispense with all notions of the "innate." By contrast, their European colleagues cling to "genetic endowment."[26] And they put forth powerful arguments for assuming (as one of them phrases it) that "certain mechanisms of behavior must themselves be refractory to any modificatory changes for the simple reason that they *do* contain the phylogenetic programming of learning processes." Not that they would disagree, for example, with the assumptions in Camus' remark that "After a certain age every man is responsible for his face." Their experiences, rather, compel them to insist that even before an entity of protoplasm first encounters society, its responses will have been predetermined to a significant degree.

I have not encountered any possible reason for doubting that the genetic uniqueness of every newborn organism makes for differences in response and *consequently* for differences in development—emotional, mental, physiological, whatever aspect be considered. This does not mean, however, that the organism can long continue to respond with the full capacities with which it was born; on the contrary, from the very beginning (in the womb) some are inhibited, others diminished, yet others lost in the natural courses of interaction with an environment that presses and modifies.[27] Hence the organism comes to respond with the functional remnant of its original totality —the remnant made functional within the influences and accidents of all it encounters. Since for each person these are as unique as his genetic endowment when he enters the world, the nature of Crane's and Camus' "responsibility" changes: from a solidly based demand to an ethic conventionally fashioned of stern as-ifs.

Any composite of "a person" which is faithful must glow with elements conveniently ignored by our habit of making each "I" the master of all it was given. For the organism, participating in every action and reaction, working toward continuously stable interchange with its environments, and driving to dispose of whatever disrupts its balance, always proceeds *as an entirety* "on its own," regardless of what may be happening in the structure usually looked upon as its director.[28] Which is to say, its brain, though "the brain" is itself composed of a number of structures, some of which think by themselves (spinal cord, medulla oblongata, cerebellum, hypothalamus). Only in one small area, the six square inches of the cerebral cortex, can be found the type of thinking we describe as voluntary—and this thinking, like every other event in the universe that is the person, is a bodily process.

How can such a material event be converted into an idea? Stimuli produce biochemical changes which give rise to nerve impulses which, in their turn, produce specific responses—so runs the current explanation. Though this general picture will possibly be replaced by another, we may remain sure that in normal human beings the sequence will always be the same as the outcome in thought will always differ. So each person, as he grows and learns and changes, makes his own ways of thinking out of the functional remnant of the capacities he was born with *and* out of all that his organism encounters. Or, if one prefers, each person is a unique constitutional entirety only some aspects of which become available for others to behold.

Herbert Read in referring to one of these aspects as "personality" was thinking of the directly perceived self of a man as it appears to his friends, which differs from the same man's self as adduced from his creations. Whether the first be known to acquaintances or only to intimates, it must be clearly more "outer" than the second. Hence, to expect in these two aspects an equivalence is to ignore the unlikeness of the occasions that bring each forward. As readily equate a certain "outer self" busily negotiating insurance contracts with the same man's (more inner) "creative self" at work on a "Peter Quince at the Clavier."

What, then, can be said of occasion and creativity? (The very question reflects what Young remarked of the way each person organizes his brain. Westerners look at once for causal relations. Since it lies at the basis of our science and reason, we do not question causality itself, as others whose brains have been differently organized would do.) Like anyone else, a creative artist inhales the surrounding world and exhales it. Whatever is taken in is given back in altered condition or transformed into matter, action, feeling, thought. And in the case of creative persons, an additional exhalation: in the form of words or sounds or shapes capable of acting upon others with the force of an object alive in their surrounding worlds.

Such an object arises out of characteristic cycles of accumulation and release. At certain moments, words or sounds or shapes demand escape from the creative person. The organism becomes burdened. When it cannot find relief, it becomes literally overburdened. The interruption in the cycle produces an over-accumulation, a dysfunction of the organism, which manifests itself in a variety of states, from vague excitement or tension and irritability to malaise, severe discomfort, even pain. (Robert Frost speaks of "lovesickness"; Schiller, Newman, T. S. Eliot, of "burden"; Byron of "rage.") Persons other than artists may of course go through similar cycles, but with a poet the accumulation becomes associated and involved with a specific kind of verbal expression that affords relief. He may accumulate and release poems throughout his life; for a limited period or periods, regularly, irregularly; he may stop for years, then resume writing, or never resume writing.

The pattern of any single poet has no significance within the total view of a unique psychophysical constitution which cannot maintain normal balance without discharging the burdens it accumulates periodically.[29] The poet must get the disturbance out of his system to enable it to regain the requisite stability in relation to its surrounding world until the next disturbances accumulate and reach for release. This is his normal mode of functioning, for which he deserves neither credit nor blame. Within the mass of humanity, he belongs to the creature sub-type which quite literally must ex-press that which builds up within. So it appears when viewed simply as animal behavior. Creativity consists of one more cyclic excretion of the organism, having nothing to do with esthetic goodness or badness. It has to do only with constitutional need which discharges itself into what becomes a thing we call art.

Such an approach has the virtue of clearing the way for a new context in which to view creative "temperament" both with and without the eye of scientists. For while they keep repeating how little has been discovered of human thinking as detailed interreactions, scientists take for granted its involvement with individual biochemistry. And they are able to predict—as noted before in connection with drugs—outcomes of interfering with normal biochemical arrangements. Meanwhile some experiments with nonhuman animals have produced impressive responses as a consequence, in one instance, of altering the organism, and in another, of altering the environment.

Representative of the first is the work of James L. McGaugh with some of the various drugs that facilitate learning. For example, an optimal dosage of metrazol, when injected into the brain of mice, was shown to produce a 40% improvement in learning ability. Not that specific effects were predictably the same; quite the contrary, in some subjects, it altered "attentiveness," in others, the capacity to vary the attack on a problem; in still others, persistence, or immediate memory, or long-term memory. "Different drugs work differently for different strains, different individuals, different intellectual tasks, and different learning components"—the comment comes from David Krech.[30] Taking what may seem a complementary approach, he and his colleagues have been studying the effects of "enriched" versus "impoverished" educational environments on the brain of the rat. In accordance with their expectations, not only did the cortex of the stimulated subjects (as compared with that of their fellows) expand and grow deeper and heavier but the postulated chemical changes also occurred, showing increased levels of activity in two enzymes (the one involved in trans-synaptic conduction of neural impulses, the other found primarily in the glia cells).

What these experiments may signify for our view of creativity cannot, I think, be dismissed. And surely instead of consigning it to the dust-bin of irrelevance, one does better to consider two facts: not a single rodent family has become extinct since the first appearance in Eocene times; and the rat operates basically with the same methods that are used by man.[31] In any event, the investigations make clear that whatever interference can achieve—from without (by the action of environment) or from within (by the action of drugs)—must depend on the constitution of the specific brain that is being stimulated. It depends, that is, on specific chemical status—on constitutional uniqueness. As to whether analogous changes in human thinking are possible, for answering this question we have at least hints—negative, positive, and uncertain. We know, for example, when something obvious is lacking in the organism—when a child is born with a body which cannot produce a specific enzyme. Abnormal substances accumulate, mental deficiency follows.[32] We also know when something obvious is added to the organism—when a substance is taken into the body which interferes with a specific enzyme. Abnormal substances accumulate; mental "magnification" follows. Finally, we know that the body itself can produce biochemical changes which lead the brain into abnormal-supernormal activity. In all three cases, the outcome depends on the specific chemical status of the person who is observed—and what does specific chemical status depend on but the "twofold matter" of genetic endowment and functional remnant of the original totality —the remnant made functional (as noted earlier) within the influence and actions of all it encounters?

One could say that this twofold matter "describes" creative temperament if it did not equally describe every other kind. Its comprehensiveness, however, has worth, for it points to creative difference as one of degree which, in its largeness, distinguishes the artist as a type. His twofold matter has indeed developed into behaviors that set him apart: the cycle of burden and release, the ability-and-need to transform the world he inhales into objects which act upon others with strange forces of thought and feeling. What potentialities he began with at birth and how they were fostered as he grew remain unknowable, though it is easy to believe that the first in some measure forms a part of every human birthright. If in his case it was present in vastly greater amounts than in most others, then artists are surely born. If, however, in the course of his development, the extent and nature of the original capacity was shaped by what it experienced, then artists are surely made. In this view, all artists are born *and* made—and both, by the workings of chance, which recovers these plain phenomena under the same sure mystery they had and will always have. Though some poets stumble on ways for releasing their creativeness, they cannot alter the fate that gave one more or less potentiality than another, as they cannot select for themselves the crucial early and subsequent influences that would foster best the gift they were born with. And to all these reasonings in terms of amount and extent, must be added that other unknowable which gives to the work of each authentic poet its cachet, setting Goethe apart from Hölderlin, Hardy from Eliot, Horace from Catullus.

Similarly these reasonings say nothing of literary excellence or of why such a thing as creativity has had to evolve. But at this point the former would lead us away on a sidetrack and the latter would force us to quote the whole of Part II of the present book. We do better to question the passivity underlying the simplified explanations attempted above. Nothing more need be said of endowment or intrauterine influence since both (as of now, at least) stand beyond reach. It is the seeming determinism of all that ensues that may be questioned. But if poets are very much made in the course of their experiences, this making involves the identical twofold direction that controls all other makings of the human organism: the ways in which we organize our brains, our habits, our gestures, our other selves. The verbs, whether active or passive, bespeak interraction. Nevertheless, a very great part of all that is associated with creativity bears the certain mark of involuntariness. And the fact has been recognized for centuries by poets and others, some of whom have viewed it with acceptance mixed with desperation. In any event, as it responds to the forces surrounding it, the action characteristic of the creative self is a reflex. Although, as J. B. S. Haldane points out, "Reflex, drive, and purpose shade into one another in men," many writers emphasize the reflexivity of creative processes. "My thought thinks itself," says Mallarmé. "What a delight to drown one's gaze in the immensity of the sky and sea . . . all those things think through me, or I through them (for in the vastness of reverie, the I quickly loses itself)," says Baudelaire. "One no longer dreams, one is dreamed," says Henri Michaux eighty years later. Or, as we put it today, "I do not write, I am written."

"Who," then, "is doing the writing?" The question must in part be meaningless if "awareness" (which implies a directing agent) is, as many are convinced, no more than a construct of human brains: an assumption we have taught ourselves to make as part of the picture we compose of ourselves. Certain brain scientists tell us that the "reticular activating system [an arrangement of interconnected nerve cells in the brain stem] is the source of a special pattern of electrochemical nerve impulses that must be *received* by the brain if we are to be aware of what is going on." This system, then, can regulate degrees of awareness; but what regulates the system and determines its action? Apparently at the very moment when our attention is engaged by one phenomenon, a second will come along and seize our attention, making us far more aware of its presence than of the first. Why? Because, says Dean E. Wooldridge, "the appearance of an object of overriding interest generates a new electric signal that serves to turn down 'volume control' of the nerve system registering an object of lesser interest."[33]

Change in awareness, it would seem, is something that happens to the brain as a result of change in stimulation. Attention, awareness, is "turned on, high" by something that commands one's attention by reason of its "overriding interest." The stimulus-object forces itself upon us, literally seizing our attention. Rather than that we can always select from a field of stimuli, certain among them impose their presence upon us and fill up our awareness. Objects, events in the surrounding world can speak to us and make us heed.

But is all awareness involuntary? The notion seems absurd; from our experience we feel convinced that at least much of the time we can willfully focus our thought and when attention wanders, bring it back and hold it there—perhaps even when something of greater interest appears. Chemists of the brain may be able in their terms to prove this false, but the brains we have created for ourselves think otherwise. And as we live, we proceed by the rules of our brains— as we must, being also their creatures.

As one of them, I have no difficulty in believing that I am being thought most of the time, that my attention is being directed, that only in between such moments do I find myself focussing my thought. For, except at such an instant as this one, I do not think about how I think, nor stop to ask what is voluntary, what involuntary, or how the two processes shuttle back and forth. When I stop to behold what is occurring, I realize that they must, my organism being what and as it is. I know when, as a consequence of my forcing, my brain has added up a column of figures and when, by no effort, it goes its own way in reverie. I know when my mind, deeply absorbed, has suddenly been pulled away by a flash of thought.

What kind of "I" is implied here? From these sentences and from all that has been said in this chapter, it obviously has nothing in common with the stereotyped notion of a directing agent in steady charge of all the activities of the organism and responsible for its action. On the contrary, much—perhaps most—of the time this thinking "I" is reflexive: how else account for what takes place when "I happen to think of an idea," when a thought "occurs to me," when a notion "comes into my head" as constantly happens?

But even such an "I" may be unreal, only a manner of speaking—
something we have taught ourselves to assume in order to be able to
discuss ourselves. "We use the convention," says Young, "that
placed in some way within us there is an agent who is said to act as
we describe other men acting. This habit of postulating active creatures within bodies, the habit of animism," is directly traceable to
the ways in which we have organized our brains—as indeed it must
be—and for all its convenience in communicating, we might perhaps
be better off without it. But as Young says elsewhere (in discussing
the work of a fellow scientist who also believes "that the soul is
imaginary and that what we call our minds is simply a way of talking
about the functions of our brains"):

However much we learn later, we probably never lose the modes of
receiving information and acting upon it that were appropriate to our
earliest communications. When we were babies the human face was the
all-important source of welfare, and all actions in the world around us
came to be described according to it. Perhaps none of us can completely
escape this fundamental source of animism because it is the way in which
our brains must work.[34]

There is obviously much more to be learned even of this limited
facet of the subject and, by implication, vastly more than is considered even in *Brain and Conscious Experience*, the compendious
record of a world-wide symposium held at the Pontificia Academia
Scientiarum a few years ago. For consciousness involves "the one
great philosophical question that embraces all others"—as Erwin
Schrödinger says—the one that Plotinus expressed by his brief *Who
are we?* But have we any right, asks another philosopher-scientist,
"to expect a solution to such fundamental problems when the efforts
made have been trivial relative to the extreme nature of the problem?"[35] It is easy to forget that human impotence before baffling
questions does not cancel out their existence. Continuing investigations have been unable to "solve the problems" of memory, to discover a structural basis, yet nobody declares memory to be an illusion
or merely a way of talking about the function of our brains. The
inability to account satisfactorily for consciousness does not prove
that consciousness does not exist, that it is no more than a way of
talking about the function of our brains.[36]

What should we use in its place that would serve us better? If we follow Young, we enter a plane of reality which has no room for the very machine-model on which so many proposals depend, for the organism does not maintain a static structure, as the comparison with any machine implies—the computer today or the telephone switchboard fifty years ago. In fact, as Young reminds us, "living things consist of no steady fabric of stuff . . . individual chemical atoms remain in the cells only for a short time." The cells die out. If the stuff of which the organism is made disappears, what is preserved? A pattern? Living patterns "are kept intact only by their continued activity." The "basic unit of biology is a non-material entity, namely an organization."

Organization? Pattern? Are these the best words for describing the something that is an organism which remains constant so long as the dying cells are succeeded by cells that live? Could other terms more faithfully denote this something and also suggest the uniqueness of each of these "nonmaterial entities" that make up the species, Man? Perhaps such a scheme as "Voluntary⟷Involuntary Process" (with its arrow denoting interreaction) might suggest the range of each human being's behavior as it maintains itself in interchange with the world? But even this ungainly description lacks reality. It is only another way of talking—a form, "a construct of our brains," like every other reality that we "know." Yet if "the form that we give to the plain, commonsense world of hard material fact is a construct of our brains," this "Voluntary⟷Involuntary Process" is not less real than others. Both the material world and this "I" are forms of our thinking. Whether or not they "actually" exist, we behave as if they existed because we must.

"The body makes the mind"—what else could make it? Yet men have been splitting themselves into two for thousands of years. Descartes was not the first, the religions may not be the last; and even those who scorn the dualism cannot quite wipe from memory the shadow of "mind active" versus "matter inert." Dealing with the latter only, scientists can hardly discern a sure line between "living" and "dead"; yet some philosophers perceive it vividly with the light of the principle of metabolism; while for others the distinguishing characteristics of man are continuous with the properties of natural objects. For philosophy is, as ever, bursting with logically proved demonstrations that destroy one another. If the body makes the mind, and what we have found can be trusted, all such irrefutable proofs are arrangements of words each of which mirrors a particular way in which the rules of a brain have been organized; they depend on the vantage point and what one is seeking.[37]

The same must be said of the arrangements of words I offer. My vantage point—neither an angel's nor a worm's—does not rise above the levels of the earth on which we exist. I do not (like the materialists) reduce matter to something phantasized by the mind. Looking at our question "Who is doing the writing?" I proceed from the manifest fact that every poem that is born comes out of a living person and I follow it to the action of unburdening by which his living organism releases poems. We are ready to look at the processes of unburdening.

NOTES AND COMMENTS

1. Kurt Goldstein, *The Organism*, Boston, Beacon Press, 1963, foreword by K. S. Lashley ("one of the great classics of the century, not only in psychology but also philosophy and biology"—A. H. Maslow), pp. 260, 270; also pp. 338-340. • "The organismic doctrine, developed since around 1920, [emphasizes] the organized structural pattern of living systems. An organism is a complex system of relations with a characteristic form of ordering and of change. . . . This relatively new school . . . is the collective product of many minds. . . . Whitehead, d'Arcy Thompson, Child, Goldstein, Bertalanffy, Needham, and Woodger are among those who have contributed to it. . . ."—Lancelot Law Whyte, *Internal Factors in Evolution*, George Braziller, Inc., 1965, pp. 32 f.

2. K. U. Smith and M. F. Smith, *Cybernetic Principles of Learning and Educational Design*, Holt, Rinehart and Winston, Inc., 1956, pp. 50-51.

3. René Dubos in *The American Scholar*, Spring 1965.

4. André Spire, *Plaisir Poétique et plaisir musculaire*, S. F. Vanni, 1949. See below p. 190. See W. V. O'Connor, *An Age of Criticism*, Chicago, Henry Regnery Company, 1952, p. 166.

5. "Organismic" grates on my ears; it may also grate on the reader's (though Whitehead, Herbert J. Muller, and Whyte use it without apology). "Organismal" is no better. "Organistic," while linguistically decent, has impossible denotations.

6. René Dubos from "Science and Man's Nature" in *Daedalus*, Winter 1965, p. 233, and *Man Adapting*, New Haven, Yale University Press, 1965, pp. 28, 34, 29, 7, 14, 49.

7. ". . . much of our aggressiveness probably springs from behavior selected when man was living in small groups, probably in constant competition with each other. The same is probably true of much of our sexual behavior and explains many of the difficulties and dilemmas that we find in our marriage laws and in our sex laws in general."—Sir Francis Crick, *Of Molecules and Men*, Seattle, University of Washington Press, 1966.

8. "If my reader can succeed in abstracting from all conceptual interpretation and lapse back into his immediate sensible life at this very moment, he will find it to be what someone has called a big blooming buzzing confusion, as free from contradiction in its 'much-at-onceness' as it is all alive and evidently there."—William James, *Some Problems of Philosophy*, Longmans, Green, 1911, p. 50. The "blooming, buzzing confusion" (the phrase appeared earlier, in James's *Principles of Psychology*, 1890, vol. 1, p. 488) may be different for each creature. For example, many of the colored markings on the flower which indicate the position of the sources of sugary substances are invisible to us yet clearly visible to a bee, with its ability to perceive ultra-violet "color." The "essential" of the flower is one thing to a man, another to an insect. See also Vitus B. Dröscher, *The Magic of the Senses: New Discoveries in Animal Perception*, Dutton, 1969.

9. See S. D. Beck, *Animal Photoperiodism*, Holt, 1963. On effects of the so-called "jet lag," see *N.Y. Times Magazine*, April 17, 1966, pp. 33 f.

10. "[C]omputers work on a binary system and are extremely accurate. Our brains, on the other hand, show no signs of working on a binary system, and in addition are very inaccurate. . . . Elements of the brain act to some extent in parallel, whereas much of the working of computers occurs in series."—Crick, *op. cit.* ". . . not only do important steps of [human] thought occur without language, they cannot be put into language after they have occurred."—Donald Hebb, *A Textbook of Psychology*, Philadelphia, W. B. Saunders Company, 1958, p. 211.

11. K. J. W. Craik, *The Nature of Explanation*, Cambridge University Press, 1952, pp. 86, 56, 57, 59, 61, 53, 99, 120.

12. A logical machine operating on a set of axioms by making formal deductions from them in an exact language, named after the late British mathematician A. M. Turing • "We cannot now conceive any kind of law or machine which could formalize the total modes of human knowledge," says J. Bronowski (*The Identity of Man*, Doubleday, 1966). A machine, by his definition, is an entire procedure of three steps, the first being the instruction or input. Then "the physical machinery obediently carries out the instructions and turns them into actions." The third step is the result or output. In the second step—between the

information that the senses send to the brain, and the instructions or other decisions that issue from it—"in this grey region, the brain manipulates the input and draws conclusions from it. During this process, the brain presumably uses some symbolism which translates and codifies its conceptions of the outside world. We do not know what this symbolic language is. . . ." "The Logic of the Mind," *American Scientist,* March 1966, p. 2, Phi Beta Kappa-Sigma Xi Lecture, American Association for the Advancement of Science, Dec. 29, 1965.

13. J. Z. Young, *Doubt and Certainty in Science,* Oxford, 1960, pp. 45, 60, 88, 50, 82, 87, 86, 56, 67, 116, 68, 66-8, 70, 86, 107, 70. The well-known "exploratory" drive of the organism which leads it to seek "unknown" experiences does not (as will become plain in our later discussion) in any way contradict what Young says of the brain's drive toward regaining its regular synchronous beating.

14. See Joseph Altman, *Organic Foundations of Animal Behavior,* Holt, 1966, pp. 357 ff. Also "Pills to Help Us Remember," by Isaac Asimov, *N. Y. Times Magazine,* Oct. 9, 1966, for popularized discussion of the biochemical speculation. Of interest: J. V. McConnell, "Memory Transfer through Cannibalism in Planarians," *Journal of Neuropsychiatry,* 1962, pp. 3, 542-548.

15. For the effect of mental set on perception, see Jerome S. Bruner and C. C. Goodman, "Value and Need as Organizing Factors in Perception," *Journal of Abnormal and Social Psychology,* 42, 1947: 34. Also Chap. 9, note 17, p. 303 below. For the effect of native language upon mental set, see pp. 115 ff. • In her introduction to Lucien Lévy-Bruhl, *How Natives Think,* Ruth L. Bunzel remarks: "Collective representations are those intimations of reality which are given to the individuals by virtue of his membership in a group; hence they include all elements of his symbolic system. The individual's views of the nature of his universe are given to him, impressed upon his consciousness by ritual and myth, and are not subject to question. They are the basic premises according to which he *organizes his inner and outer worlds*" (my italics). Washington Square Press, 1966, p. xii.

16. Young, *op. cit.,* p. 70.

17. Hypnosis: see Stephen Black, *Mind and Body,* London, William Kimber, 1969, Chapters 11-14, which summarize the author's experimental research. • For popular discussions, see J. N. Bleibtreu, "LSD and the Third Eye," *Harper's Magazine,* Sept. 1966, pp. 64 ff.; Aldous Huxley, "Drugs that Shape Men's Minds," in *Collected Essays,* Harper & Row, 1959; Isaac Asimov, "That Odd Chemical Complex, the Human Mind," *N. Y. Times Magazine,* July 3, 1966. See also Frank Barron, *Creative Person and Creative Process,* Holt, 1969, pp. 146-159.

18. No matter what descriptive terms are used, the question of "abnormal-supernormal" takes a medical turn. Dostoevsky writes of the state which preceded his seizures: "For a few moments I experience

such happiness as is impossible under ordinary circumstances and of which other people can have no notion. I feel complete harmony in myself and in the world and this feeling is so strong and sweet that for several seconds of such bliss, one would give ten years of one's life; indeed, perhaps one's whole life." The description and judgment can be matched by reports of religious mystics and drug-takers; from those whose abnormal-supernormal states arose "spontaneously" and others whose states were deliberately induced. Dostoevsky's "case" has been diagnosed as psychomotoric epilepsy; etc. A clue to the state of contemporary public bias appears in the widespread preference for "psychedelic" (mind-manifesting) over terms which imply pathology (psychotomimetic), on the one hand, or self-deception (hallucinogenic), on the other.

19. T. S. Eliot, *Selected Essays,* Harcourt, Brace & World, Inc., 1950, p. 250.

20. Walter B. Cannon, *The Wisdom of the Body,* 2nd ed., W. W. Norton & Company, Inc., 1963, pp. 27, 59, 38, 20, 23, 303, 313, 239, 267, 288. All these responses are addressed to immediate dangers to the organism. For observations on long-term effects, see René Dubos, *So Human an Animal,* Charles Scribner's Sons, 1968, pp. 146-148.

21. Dudley Fitts's translation.

22. F. A. Geldard, *Science,* 1960, 131, 1583-1588. Goldstein, *op. cit.,* pp. 264 f. Experiments of researchers from Harvard and Yale were reported to have demonstrated that the skin of a wide variety of animals is able to see, through responses possibly similar to those of the eye (N. Y. Times, Dec. 15, 1966, p. 28). See W. N. Kellogg, *Science,* 1962, pp. 131, 399-404 and *International Journal of Parapsychology,* Autumn 1965, devoted to "Parapsychology in the Soviet Union."

23. Weston La Barre, *The Human Animal,* University of Chicago Press, 1954, pp. 161-167 *passim.* See also B. Malinowski, "The problem of meaning in primitive languages," in C. K. Ogden and I. A. Richards, *The Meaning of Meaning,* Harcourt, 1923, 9th ed., pp. 296 ff.; E. T. Hall, *The Silent Language,* Doubleday, 1959.

24. I am following very closely Robert Rosenthal's introduction to his edition of *Clever Hans,* by Oskar Pfungst, Holt, 1965, often using his phrases. In a note, Rosenthal observes: "Mr. von Osten, unlike scientific antagonists, had everything to lose and nothing comparable to gain by having his Hans investigated. He must indeed have been completely honest and sincere and the findings in this book grieved him deeply, nor could he accept them. Within a few months he died." Says Pfungst: "It is in the highest degree improbable that Mr. von Osten purposely trained the horse to respond to certain cues. It is also improbable that he knew that in every test he was giving signals."

25. J. Bronowski, *The Identity of Man,* Natural History Press, 1966, pp. 30-35, referring to the work of James Olds and H. K. Hartline.

There is more than enough justification for regarding "mind" as the totality of processes by which the human organism maintains itself in relation to the world in which it lives.

26. See Konrad Lorenz, *Evolution and Modification of Behavior*, Chicago, 1965, pp. 101-106, which refer to ethologists and psychologists. (I am speaking of genetic endowment at the time of birth.)

27. Permanent effects of early experiences: Urie Bronfenbrenner, "Early Deprivation in Mammals and Man," in *Early Experience and Behavior*, G. Newton, ed., Springfield, Ill., Charles C. Thomas. For "determination" of behavior and interference with the acquiring of new experiences, see Dubos, *American Scholar, op. cit.*

28. The brain is not always looked upon as its master; certainly not in the flight-or-fight response. As the textbooks say:—the spinal cord is often called the switching center for the common reflexes. At its upper end, the medulla oblongata, or brain stem, performs the same type of function for more complicated activities, such as keeping the muscles in balance when a person is standing. The cerebellum, or "little brain," also takes care of the organism in motion—when we reach for a cup or a pair of scissors, we neither go too far nor too short of the object; etc. See: *Primates*, P. C. Jay, ed., Holt, 1968, on the "limbic system," common to the brain of all mammals, which "makes the animal want to do what it has to do to survive and reproduce" (fn. p. 447). • "Although no one can disagree with this traditional view [of the unusually great development of man's cerebral cortex as the prime factor in the development of human intelligence], it could nevertheless be asked if there may not be more of the brain involved in the shaping of man's unique intelligence. Along with his cortex, other parts of his brain have become larger, not the least his limbic lobe. Is it not conceivable that man's intelligence is founded also in a more differentiated responsiveness of precisely the same nervous structures in the limbic lobe which in more primitive forms appear to subserve crude affects?"— Walle J. H. Nauta, *N. Y. Times Book Review*, April 20, 1969, p. 43.

29. Periodic accumulation does not necessarily result only from things that happen to the poet. The creative personality also tends to stimulate, even to produce, the disturbance without being aware of doing so. See p. 56 below. • "A poem is 'expressed' in the most vivid sense of that word: it is pressed out of the poet, forced out of him."—George Whalley, *Poetic Process*, London, Routledge & Kegan Paul, Ltd., 1953, p. 167.

30. See "The Chemistry of Learning" by David Krech, *Saturday Review*, Jan. 20, 1968, for details. In the Krech experiments, all the rats had access to the same food.

31. See p. 160.

32. The phenylalaline is normally converted into tyrosine by an enzyme. The disease is phenylpyruvic oligophrenia.

33. "How the Machine Called the Brain Feels and Thinks," by Dean E. Wooldridge, *N. Y. Times Magazine*, Oct. 4, 1964. • "The greater the biological relevance an object has to us the more will we be attuned to its recognition. . . ."—E. H. Gombrich in *Aspects of Form*, Lancelot L. Whyte, ed., London, Humphries, 1951, p. 216.

34. J. Z. Young, *N. Y. Review of Books*, April 6, 1967, p. 18.

35. Sir J. C. Eccles, ed., *Brain and Conscious Experience*, Springer-Verlag, 1967, pp. xv, 327.

36. The relation between memory and nucleic acids and proteins as well as electrical circuits may have suggested a "structural basis" by the time this book has appeared. No such "solution" is likely to be found regarding free will, determinacy, and behavior. See George Wald, "Determinacy, Individuality, and the Problem of Free Will," in *New Views of the Nature of Man*, John R. Platt, ed., Chicago, 1965: "Behavior may all be determined, but it is surely not all predictable; and I think that the essence of our free will lies in that unpredictability [p. 36]. It is this essential unpredictability of animal behavior that led an exasperated physiologist some years ago to state what came to be called the Harvard Law of Animal Behavior: 'Under precisely controlled conditions, an animal does as it damn pleases.' [p. 40] There is a kind of indeterminacy that involves human behavior—and probably also to a degree the behavior of other animals—that is somewhat analogous to physical indeterminacy [pp. 40-41]."

S. A. Barnett, *Instinct and Intelligence*, Prentice-Hall, Inc., 1967, pp. 195–196, 29, remarks: ". . . it is not enough to brush off the whole concept of voluntary behavior, or even the idea of mind. It is more useful to ask what real features distinguish the behavior colloquially called voluntary. . . . As brains become larger, so behavior becomes more adaptable. The input from the senses is combined, by means we do not know, with the results of *previous* activity. Much of the brain of the most complex animals seems organized for autonomous activity. One part excites another, without waiting for any special information from the external senses." • I should not in the least be surprised to learn, one day, that some kinds of involuntary thought are simply the swiftest modes of human reasoning through processes of connection evident in the slower modes. I suspect that they are, and that their very swiftness helps them from going astray, as deliberate thought so readily can do, by weighing alternative courses.

37. See my *Caged in an Animal's Mind*, Holt, 1963, p. 44, last stanza; also A. Quinton, "The Large Questions," *N. Y. Review of Books*, July 7, 1966. • The implications of the foregoing pages—of the fact that creativity is the work not of a six-inch cortical area of the brain but of the total human organism—constitutes the subject of this book.

2 · Composition: Collaboration

For an hour, even two, a reader can be fascinated by first-hand accounts of the creative process, differing as it does from poet to poet, often from poem to poem. Yet after a time the variety fades into likeness. And the story palls as the differences begin to consist mainly in the terms for unknowns. Unable or unwilling to see a poem as the joint creation of a man and his universe, the explainers ascribe its parentage to the one or the other. So the ancients speak of the divinity without, the moderns of the power within—Greek "enthusiasm" and Roman "afflatus," Elizabethan "frenzy," Romantic "imagination," and twentieth-century "Unconsciousness." Meanwhile the act of composition remains as surprising as ever to the poet, who knows only one thing for certain: that he is *being used*.[1]

Since no one can observe from outside what occurs in the mind, any attempt to say how or by what must depend on available reports, all of which confirm more or less what has long been suspected. In a popular current formulation: "A short poem, or a passage of a long poem, may appear in its final form at once; or it may have to go through the transformation of a dozen drafts" (Eliot). Now if "at once" means that the short poem or passage arrives in its completed form, composition exists as two different experiences: one in which the poet simply takes down dictation; another, as a process of revision. In either case, however, it begins as dictation, with the poet listening to something that speaks to him: he listens and sees the words. They command his attention. They break through and into his awareness; they will not be ignored. They are using him as their recorder.

Being thus seized, he changes his outward behavior. When Freud, busily writing the last chapter of his book on dreams, was interrupted to come to a meal, he walked, says his daughter, as if in a trance, oblivious of his surroundings.[2] Similar behavior has been noted in any number of artists, for the concentration of such a state may be so intense as to make the worker seem to himself and to others to be in a trance. In itself the concentration, the transport, the waking dream gives no assurance of the outcome. "I imagine," said Edwin Arlington Robinson, "that the worst poetry in the world has been written in the finest frenzy of inspiration; and so, probably, has the best."

Best or worst cannot matter to the person held in this heightened excitation who knows he is being borne along in a steady unfolding. At the inception, at least, the journey is unpredictable. Inspiration has a purpose of its own of which the host becomes gradually aware, though a sudden flash may at any time reveal the course or hint at its direction. Alberto Moravia "never knows" what the work he is writing "is going to be" until he is "under way." What Yeats began as a political poem ended in "Leda and the Swan." Frost repeatedly speaks of a voyage of discovery ("I have never started a poem yet whose end I knew"). Keats could express even stronger surprise than Eliot's (the poet "does not know what he has to say until he has said it") or Ransom's (poets "later wonder what they've done and look at it to see").[3] To Keats, what he had written in describing Apollo in *Hyperion* seemed to be more the production of another person than his own—which points back to dictation and the language-thinking it uses. During the creative act the poet was both hearing and being "told"; both concentrating and being held in a trance-like state; both discovering and being made to discover—my verb-forms denote the reflexive character of the experience. And yet, if the poet can be said to be writing the poem while it is writing him, his active work is only a passive response to the words that command him to listen. During such concentrated moments, "It is not I who think but my ideas who think for me" (Lamartine), "Words rise up unaided and in ecstasy" (Mallarmé).

(With a reader who objects that these statements do not apply to everything called "poetry," I quite agree. They most surely have no bearing on the species that Juan Ramón Jiménez calls "voluntaria" —works composed deliberately, out of a decision to make a poem. The present book, as a serious inquiry, deals only with the type of poem that demands to be born—what Jiménez calls "necesaria.")[4]

Vision

In his review of Shelley's *Posthumous Poems*, Hazlitt remarked that the author "mistook the nature of the poet's calling, which should be guided by involuntary, not by voluntary impulses." The sentence is almost incredible, coming as it does three years after publication of *A Defence of Poetry*, for not only did Shelley not mistake the poet's calling but he was, so far as I know, the first to have insisted unrelentingly on the magisterial role of involuntary thought in composition:

Poetry is not like reasoning, a power to be exerted according to the determination of the will. A man cannot say, "I will compose poetry." The greatest poet even cannot say it. . . .

Poetry differs in this respect from logic, that it is not subject to the control of the active powers of the mind, and that its birth and recurrence have no necessary connexion with the consciousness or will.

This belief was not of course new. Yet it is worth noting that for a century following (though not necessarily because of) the publication of *A Defence*, esthetic theory showed astonishing unanimity in excluding volition from creativity. Kant, Schopenhauer, Coleridge, Bergson, Croce—the list can be expanded by a great many others including the unlikely author of *The Philosophy of Composition*. Poe had fooled a generation of more than receptive French writers with his fanciful account of the writing of "The Raven" only to reverse himself later: "With me poetry has not been a purpose but a passion, and the passions should be held in reverence: they must not—they cannot at will be excited."

Strangely enough his admirers were not discomfitted, not even Valéry, the most exacting of the younger generation, whose career as a poet may also be regarded as a laboratory for examining the work of the mind in the making of a poem. The "case" of Valéry is worth mentioning not only for intrinsic interest but also because it appears at a point in time which he himself might have called the intersection of the Age of the Unconscious with the Age of Science.

In one of the brief entries in "A Poet's Notebook," he stops to deride a certain X who "would like to believe that a metaphor is a communication from heaven":

A metaphor is *what happens* when one *looks in a certain way*, just as a sneeze is what happens when one looks at the sun.

In what way?—You can feel it. One day, perhaps one will be able to *say* it precisely.

Do this and do that—and behold all the metaphors in the world. . . .

Did such a prospect attract Valéry as poet? The entry is sketched in wistful modes and, most probably, with ironies. Any answer depends on how one understands the conflict between Valéry's passion to master his mental processes and his dependence as poet on their behavior. It depends, moreover, on what one makes of all his striving, after Valéry came back to literature from his twenty-year study of mentation. Since in the years of the return he produced his best verse, had he actually remade his mind into a tool of controlling precision? Was the observer in him at last overwhelmed by the creator?[5]

Whatever truce he had arranged between these two drives, the peace that followed was at best uneasy, for up to the last there are rumblings of resentment against the caprices of the brain. And he seems obsessed by a need to disclaim responsibility, as though the poems bearing his authorship were not entirely his own. His remarks about "The Graveyard by the Sea" are typical. "Thus, it was by *accident*," he declares with italics, "that the form of this work was fixed [because an editor] coming to call on me, found me at one 'stage' of my *Cimetière marin* [and] he did not rest until he was allowed to read it and, having read it, until he could snatch it away." The editor took it, and that settled the matter. Hence, Valéry was able to say that the poem "*as it stands*, is *for me* the result of the *intersection* of an inner labor and a fortuitous event." (Coleridge, in another context and without recourse to the language of geometry, conveys comparable detachment about "Kubla Khan"; but who would insist here on kinship between an exemplar of Romanticism and its dedicated foe?) "Spontaneity," says Valéry in the same passage, "even when excellent or seductive, has never seemed to me sufficiently *mine*. I do not say that 'I am right,' but that that is how I am. . . . The notion of Myself is no simpler than that of Author: a further degree of consciousness opposes a new *Self* to a new *Other*."

A lifetime of maturing thought had elapsed between the foregoing statements and Valéry's early essay (1889) "On Literary Technique," yet the direction of the writer's desire is the same. The "totally new and modern conception of the poet" holds the wonder of an ideal for the writer of eighteen anticipating the almost religious bias-to-be of the scientific twentieth century. For young Valéry, the poet was "no longer the disheveled madman who writes a whole poem in the course of one feverish night; he is a cool scientist, almost an algebraist, in the service of a subtle dreamer." Much of the faith in the omnipotence of science drops away as the man grows older, yet the passion to dominate the disheveled processes remains as strong or grows more insistent. And although Valéry never succeeds to the point where he can dispense with what lies (as he says) "at the depth where treasures are always buried," he disparages inspiration at every opportunity. So he carefully explains that "our personal merit—after which we strive—consists not so much in feeling these inspirations as in seizing them, and not so much in seizing them as in examining them." Why? Because "the true value of such inspirations does not depend on the obscurity of their origin, or on the supposed depth from which we are simple enough to believe they came, or on the exquisite surprise they cause to ourselves; it depends rather on their meeting our needs, and, in the final analysis, on the conscious use we make of them. . . ."

The emphasis and insistence are typical—and so pervasive as to have led Eliot to remark that of all poets, Valéry has been the most completely conscious of what he was doing. True or not, this is the picture given us to believe—and composed by the same Valéry who elsewhere declares that "there is no theory that is not a fragment, carefully prepared, of some autobiography."

The warning will not be ignored by anyone aware of the seemingly willed complexity of Valéry's statements. For although their effect has been to put overwhelming emphasis on testing and conscious revision, on conscious judgment and analysis, they never actually deny the sources of involuntary thought. An example:

those imperious verbal illuminations which suddenly impose a particular combination of words—as though a certain group possessed some kind of intrinsic power. . . . I nearly said: some kind of *will* to live . . . a will that can sometimes force the mind to deviate from its plan and the poem to become quite other than what it was going to be and something one did not dream it could be.

One wishes to hear more, so attractive is the passage and also characteristic, though not of his treatments of this uncontrollable aspect of creativity, which normally bristle with deprecations. Valéry is of course compelled to acknowledge the existence of—and his dependence upon—inspiration, but he seems to take contemptuous delight in couching his admissions in nimbly subordinated clauses ("after being charmed by those divine murmurings of the inner voice") or phrases ("in the service of a subtle dreamer") or in florid irony. What posture could be more respectable, what tone more congenial, to an Age of Science? No wonder that Valéry's mind, viewed from where we stand, seems to epitomize the prevalent attitude of his era with its true-believer's faith in achieving ultimately self-conscious control. In his own way, Valéry fought as desperate and doomed a battle as the different one of his master, Mallarmé. Hence it is but occasionally that one stumbles on a total confession of his poet's dependence on involuntary thinking: "We must simply wait until what we desire appears, because that is all we can do. *We have no means of getting exactly what we wish from ourselves.*"

If the passage seems to cancel the effect of his contrary pro-
testations, it is not unique in so doing. Yet the weight of each word
bears down with enough finality to make of these sentences an em-
blem for "conscious artistry." But before considering this "secondary" stage of creativity, one must look at specific examples of the
"first."

"We get a new song," an Eskimo poet, Orpingalik, told an
ethnologist recently, "when the words we want to use shoot up of
themselves." Orpingalik made no mention of the source other than to
say that "songs are thoughts sung out with the breath when people
are moved by great forces." The thoughts "are driven by a flowing
force—they can wash over him like a flood, making his breath come
in gasps and his heart throb." But then, he adds, something may
"keep him thawed up. And it will happen that we, who always think
we are small, will feel still smaller. And we will fear to use words.
But it will happen that the words we need will come of themselves."[6]

The Eskimo poet was explaining himself to a person who may
have remembered similar sentences, such as: "The idea simply comes"
(Eliot); "It will come if it is there and if you will let it come" (Ger-
trude Stein); "A poem upon Mount Meru came to me spontaneously" (Yeats). The whole of "Cargoes" came into Masefield's head
one Sunday morning "on the spur of the moment." "My ideas come
as they will, I don't know how," said Mozart. Frost's "Two Look
at Two" and "For Once Then Something," were "written with one
stroke of the pen." Wordsworth "began ["Tintern Abbey"] upon
leaving Tintern, after crossing the Wye, and concluded it just as
[he] was entering Bristol in the evening. . . . Not a line of it was
altered, nor any part of it written down till [he] reached Bristol." A
few words "floated into my head," says Siegfried Sassoon, "as though
from nowhere. . . . I picked up a pencil and wrote the words on a
sheet of note-paper without sitting down. I added a second line. It
was as if I were remembering rather than thinking. In this mindless,
recollecting manner I wrote down 'Everyone Sang' in a few
minutes." And so on and so on.

Some reports contain warnings—direct or indirect—against
forcing or other interfering. "When your Daemon is in charge, do
not try to think consciously. Drift, wait, and obey" (Kipling). "All

truly poetic thought begins to sing by itself, unless the poet is clumsy enough to prevent it from singing" (Spire). The thing to do is "to let each impression and each germ of feeling come to completion quite in itself . . . beyond the reach of one's own understanding" (Rilke). "Conscious writing can be the death of poetry" (Marianne Moore). And so on and so on.

At times there is stress upon trance, generally when the writer has been greatly surprised by its power. But not always. Tennyson frequently experienced a kind of waking trance; his "individuality itself seemed to dissolve and fade away into boundless being." It was "not a confused state, but the clearest of the clear, the surest of the sure, the weirdest, utterly beyond words." Contemporary remarks sound more matter of fact, with concern for broader aspects. Though "The nucleus of every poem worthy of the name is rhythmically formed in the poet's mind during a trance-like suspension of his normal habits of thought" (Robert Graves),[7] the trance-like suspension may occur in all shades of intensity. "In a light trance" (to continue with Graves) "the critical sense is not completely suspended; but there is a trance that comes so close to sleep that what is written in it can hardly be distinguished from ordinary dream-poetry; the rhymes are inaccurate, the phrasing eccentric, the texture clumsy, the syntax rudimentary, the thought connexions ruled by free association, the atmosphere charged with unexplained emotion." But the very opposite can also occur in the sleep-like state—or so it seems from Coleridge's preface to "Kubla Khan."

Whatever the degree or nature of trance-like suspension, a poem is rhythmically formed in the writer's mind. The poem itself—which is to say, the language-thinking—begins as rhythm and often only as rhythm. At least two of Valéry's poems came in this wordless compulsive form:

"Le Cimetière marin" began in me by a rhythm . . . of 10 syllables, divided into 4 and 6. . . . I had as yet no idea with which to fill out this form. Gradually a few hovering words settled in, little by little determining the subject. Another poem, "La Pythie" first appeared as an 8-syllable line whose sound came of its own accord.

"I know," declared Eliot, "that a poem, or a passage of a poem, may tend to realize itself first as a particular rhythm before it reaches expression in words, and that this rhythm may bring to birth the idea and the image." Goethe said much the same thing; Schiller speaks of a "musical mood." A documentary complement to these avowals is reported by J. Isaacs, who found in one of Shelley's notebooks an entry where the first draft of one of his finest poems consists only of a rhythmical scheme held in place by a sequence of completely meaningless syllables.[8]

"Involuntariness" has been so marked in the foregoing discussion that the word itself seldom was called for. At some point, however, its use is essential: no other phenomenon is significantly common to all reports of creativity with their differing manifestations and personal hosts. "Involuntary" epitomizes the testimony of the philosophical positivist George Eliot and the mystic Blake; of the painter (Picasso), the composer (Mozart), the scientist (Poincaré). The novelist did her best writing when something "not herself" possessed her and made her feel "her own personality to be merely the instrument." The poet took down "from immediate dictation, 12, or sometimes 20 or 30 lines [of *Milton*] at a time, without premeditation and even against [his] will." Creativity arrives, it "simply comes." It comes in the sudden flash that gave James *The Ambassadors,* in the fleeting vision that brought Stravinsky *Le Sacre du Printemps,* in the visible dance that resolved for the half-sleeping Kekulé the atomic structure of the benzene ring. And so on and so on. It comes—and even the greatest artist cannot will its arrival.

This dependence, while acceptable to some, inspires others to experiment with stratagems. Goethe (like Bertrand Russell) finally learned the futility of trying: "My counsel is to force nothing and rather to trifle and sleep away all unproductive days and hours, than on such days to compose something that will afterwards give no pleasure." Herrick entitled a poem "Not Every Day Fit for Verse." Burns observed that on the two or three times in his life when he "composed for the wish rather than the impulse," he failed, just as Frost was never able "to worry" any poem into existence. "What is one to do when thoughts cease to flow and the proper words won't come?" asked Freud; "one's productivity depends entirely on sensitive moods." Yet dependence may at times become unbearable and anything seem better than waiting. One writer puts his feet in ice water, another lies down on a couch (Heine), a third exposes his head to heat (Shelley), a fourth dresses in the robes of a monk

(Balzac), a fifth makes regular use of a pint of beer (Housman), a sixth tries jazz and liquor (Hart Crane), a seventh tobacco (De la Mare), an eighth the odor of rotted apples (Schiller). Mozart finds it easier to compose after eating a good dinner, Prudhomme after abstinence. . . . These methods (if the word can be used) would have been arrived at inductively, only later becoming an act of choice, like the taking of drugs. And of the latter, nothing need be said, so renowned is its use among artists. Yet I have heard of few well-known works other than Henri Michaux's poems and drawings which were actually created while drugs were controlling the mind. On the other hand, Utrillo is reported to have painted some of his best landscapes while in a perpetual alcoholic haze; the more he drank, the greater his productivity.

Roughly comparable in outcome is auto-suggestion according to some who have used it with effect. Nowadays the subject cannot even be mentioned without citing Rimbaud and his "Alchemy of the Word":

> Poetic old-fashionedness figured largely in my alchemy of the word.
> I grew accustomed to pure hallucination: I saw quite frankly a mosque in place of a factory, a school of drummers made up of angels, carriages on roads in the sky, a parlor at the bottom of the lake; monsters, mysteries. The title of a vaudeville conjured up horrors before me.
> Then I explained my magic sophisms with the hallucination of words!

Sometime later he remarked to his sister: "I would have become crazy and besides . . . it was bad." The Surrealists, on the contrary, saw nothing wrong with auto-suggestion, whatever the form. And I see nothing essentially different from their behavior in the kind of self-preparation undertaken by Valéry, who used to rise very early indeed: "Sometimes I find myself (at dawn) in a state of intellectual [mental] availability and general preparation. Like a hunter ready to pursue the first prey that comes along. . . . Delectable sensation of being ready. . . ."[9]

"Re-vision" and "Conscious Artistry"

If at the outset of this book I had not forsworn psychoanalytic language, at this point I should probably be quoting Kris where he talks of the "driving of the unconscious toward consciousness [which] is experienced as an intrusion from without." But I should also be adding the statement from John Locke that defines consciousness simply as "the perception of what passes in a man's own mind." Locke's formulation still serves so long as one realizes what it is that can pass and usually does pass in a man's own mind. The what is not limited to thoughts he intended to think or chooses or wishes to perceive. On the contrary, it includes—in addition to the thoughts he attends to—many other kinds of thinking which flow into his perception uninvited by his will. To put it concretely, one can sit down with the intention, the hope, and the wish to complete an unfinished poem and before long perceive that what passes in the mind are ideas that "simply come" interspersed with other ideas drawn out of notes, books, and other premeditation. And that all these various kinds of thought will keep flowing in and out intermittently. As a consequence, one discovers as he sees what he is doing that the process by which a poem is revised comprehends vastly more than is generally conveyed by the curious term "conscious artistry."

The quotation marks are essential. Even a makeshift—such as "unconscious⟷conscious artistry"—is not adequate. As Graves remarks in "A Poet's Investigation of Science":

Objective recognition of the poem as an entity as a rule induces a lighter trance, during which the poet realizes more fully the implications of his lines and sharpens them . . . (granted the truthfulness of the original draft, and the integrity of the secondary elaboration).[10]

Rather than soberly controlled deliberateness, "conscious artistry" denotes a state of heightened feeling during which the writer concentrates on his poem as it changes toward enhanced self-expression. The fact that it changes while the writer perceives what passes in his own mind tells nothing of who or of what does the changing. But this question cannot be asked without first considering its context.

All poems, before they are released to the world, including those written whole at one stroke, are subjected to "conscious artistry"; whether everything or nothing be altered from the original, the work is given "objective recognition as an entity." It is tested by the author and, if found wanting, changes will be made—to be supplanted by yet other changes including, occasionally, the very words that at first had seemed wrong. Testing-and-altering may be completed in time or may continue indefinitely without ever bringing the wanted satisfaction. The poem may be abandoned, or part of it kept as a fragment, or the whole reluctantly acknowledged at some later moment as the best that might ever be achieved. *The outcome of "conscious artistry" is no more controllable than that of the trance that created the draft.*

Secondly, the poet who at one time writes original drafts in final form may at another write original drafts that come to demand innumerable re-visions. Blake, who said about one of his Prophetic Books: "I may praise it, since I dare not pretend to be any other than the Secretary; the Authors are in Eternity," showed a meticulous capacity—in the poems preserved in rough draft—for making alteration upon alteration, rearrangement after rearrangement, deletions, additions, and inversions. Of the 396 poems in the final *Leaves of Grass,* more than nine-tenths had been subjected to some sort of re-vision ("The Prayer of Columbus" to almost twenty). Moreover, certain lines that now ring for the reader with the inevitable sound of inspiration were not given at their first dictation in final form. The "Ode to a Nightingale" originally began: "My Heart aches and a painful numbness falls." "Out of the cradle endlessly rocking" was "Out of the rock'd cradle" (in both the 1860 and 1867 editions). . . .[11]

If one must say of "conscious artistry"—as of the creative process as a whole—that it differs from poet to poet and from poem to poem, a few examples can readily show why. According to Symonds' *Shelley,* Trelawney found the poet alone in a wood near Pisa, holding in his hand a manuscript of one of his lyrics:

a frightful scrawl, words smeared out with his fingers, and one upon another, over and over in tiers, and all run together. . . . On my observing this to him, he answered, "When my brain gets heated with a thought, it soon boils, and throws off images and words faster than I can skim them off. In the morning when cooled down, out of the rude sketch, as you justly call it, I shall attempt a drawing."

Rafael Alberti, at the period of composing *Sobre los ángeles,* gradually withdrew from friends, coffee-talk, the city he lived in:

A "guest of the clouds," I fell to scribbling in the dark without thinking to turn on a light, all hours of the night, with unwonted automatism, febrile and tremulous, in spontaneous bursts, one poem covering the other in a script often impossible to decipher in broad daylight. . . . Rhythms exploded in slivers and splinters, angels ascended in sparks, in pillars of smoke, spouts of embers and ashes, clouds of aerial dust. Yet the burden was never obscure; even the most confused and nebulous songs found a serpentine life and took shape like a snake in the flames.[12]

The opening lines of "Oenone" as printed in 1833 had apparently satisfied Tennyson:

> There is a dale in Ida, lovelier
> Than any in old Ionia, beautiful
> With emerald slopes of sunny sward, that lean
> Above the loud glenriver, which hath worn
> A path through steepdown granite walls below
> Mantled with flowering tendriltwine . . .

Nine years later he republished them as follows:

> There lies a vale in Ida, lovelier
> Than all the valleys of Ionian hills.
> The swimming vapour slopes athwart the glen,
> Puts forth an arm, and creeps from pine to pine,
> And loiters, slowly drawn. On either hand
> The lawns and meadow-ledges midway down
> Hang rich in flowers, and far below them roars
> The long brook falling thro' the clov'n ravine
> In cataract after cataract to the sea . . .

Re-vision has at times added an entire passage long after a poem had been published as complete. Five years went by before Allen Tate made the wind-leaves refrain part of his "Ode to the Confederate Dead," eight years before Wordsworth inserted a second stanza into the 1807 printed version of "The Daffodils" ("Continuous as the stars that shine . . .").

To take a quite different example. Three years before his death, while conversing with Frost about "A Minor Bird," I happened to ask when he had revised the final couplet. It had never been different, he assured me; it was always:

> And of course there must be something wrong
> In wanting to silence any song.

Having by chance saved the tear-sheet from a 1925 issue of the students' magazine of the University of Michigan, where Frost had been in residence, I was able to show him the earlier version:

> And I hold that there must be something wrong
> In ever wanting to silence song.

Frost shook his head, wondering. He could willingly forget other revisions: " 'Birches' was two fragments soldered together so long ago I have forgotten where the joint is." Here, however, was something else; for although any alterations in some degree reflect the life of a writer's mind, certain ones among them reveal the shift in direction of his total vision.

I entitle this section of the chapter "Re-vision," with a hyphen that might have been placed there by Bryant, who spoke of the poet's need "to summon back the original glow." Perhaps if the word were taken with due stress on the prefix, writers would not at times feel constrained to fight off confusions:

There's no way to revise a poem . . . without taking the very same situation, shutting our eyes, and submitting it again to the imagination to see what's there: To see if better little aspects, little angles, of that experience won't turn up. It's hopeless if you go out into the woods, say, and say well, I'll rewrite this poem. You sit down and ponder but the thing won't come back, and you don't know what you're looking for, really.[13]

John Crowe Ransom's spontaneous answer to a question, together with Graves's more studied statement, should be enough to lay the ghosts that conceal the actualities of "conscious artistry." But they live on, especially in the bland superstition that creativity requires two qualitatively different stages, the second one practically dominated by the will.

Except for those fortunate works composed in final form at one stroke, every poem is a draft demanding two types of action: (1) creating pieces and entireties of language to replace or to add; (2) judging, choosing from the existing "givens." That both actions also may occur during the initial session of composing is unmistakably evident in any number of original drafts. We ask, then, whether any qualitative differences result from the differences in their times of occurrence. One answer appears in the statement of Graves that (the subsequent) "objective recognition of the poem as an entity as a rule induces a lighter trance, during which the poet realizes more fully the implications of his lines." He is, at least at the start of a session of re-vision, not oblivious of his surroundings: he is alert to perceive what passes in his own mind. Yet the moment he gets back into the poem, he will again be suffused by the "original glow"; though the trance be lighter, it will still take charge of his mind.

In the course of reconstituted vision, how does he create what is needed? The "most objective" poet ought to supply the "least subjective" answer—Valéry, whose own poems, as he declared, were composed of both lines that he was given and lines that he had to make. How was he able to make what had not been given? After typical digressions, he comes to the point (my italics):

When we think we have completed a certain thought, we never feel sure that we could come back to it without either improving or spoiling what we had finished. It is in this that the life of the mind is divided against itself as soon as it sets to work. Every work requires acts of will (although it always includes a number of components in which what we call the *will* has no part). But when our will, our expressed power, tries to turn upon the mind itself and make it obey, the result is always a simple arrest, the maintenance or perhaps the renewal of certain conditions.
In fact, we can act directly only upon the freedom of the mind's processes. We can lessen the degree of that freedom, but as for the rest, I mean as for the changes and substitutions still possible under our constraint, *we must simply wait until what we desire appears, because that is all we can do.*[14]

His master, Mallarmé, had said much the same thing more briefly, and if literary history is dependable, no one devoted more time or zeal to "conscious artistry." To quote Robert Greer Cohn, who quotes Mallarmé's key phrase:

Like an over-eager huntsman, the greedy grasp of the will could only frighten the delicate prey, get in the way; the best chance of success was to gently stalk and lie in wait, "céder l'initiative aux mots."

To yield the initiative to the words—what better definition of involuntary language-thinking in obtaining what is needed in re-vision. Might it also play a part in the other act—in the judging, choosing from existing givens? The participles point to a slow, cold process epitomized by the word *analysis*. But the direction misleads. Analytic thought can determine what the words, whatever their syntax, are likely to say to a reader; it can signal the need for change —and that is all. Analysis takes things apart. To judge and to choose calls for more than a talent for dissecting.

What is required? Jacques Hadamard, in *The Psychology of Invention in the Mathematical Field*, approaches the subject with essentially the same assumption I stated a few pages back: that every composition demands two types of action: creating and choosing. The key question—it applies equally to scientist and poet—consists in asking *How* such choice *can* be made? Is there some connection, some rule, to be deduced from the experiences of the scientist during the creative process and the validity of his choice as later verified? Hadamard, like other investigators, leans heavily on the analyses of Poincaré (especially in the celebrated lecture before the Société de Psychologie in Paris and the essay on "Mathematical Creation"):

How can such choice be made? The rules which must guide it "are extremely fine and delicate. It is almost impossible to state them precisely; they are felt rather than formulated. . . . The privileged unconscious phenomena [the givens that are chosen] are those which, directly or indirectly, affect most profoundly our emotional sensibility. It may be surprising to see emotional sensibility invoked à propos of mathematical demonstrations which, it would seem, can interest only the intellect."

But in fact it is not surprising in the least, says Hadamard, adding:

That an affective element is an essential part in every discovery or invention is only too evident, and has been insisted upon by several thinkers. . . . But with Poincaré, we see something else, the intervention of the sense of beauty playing its part as an indispensable *means*.[15]

Choice is "imperatively governed" by the sense of beauty.

If neither mathematician attempts to define the components ("the feeling of mathematical beauty, of the harmony of numbers and forms, of geometric elegance"), it is obviously because (as Poincaré emphasizes) there is more to this "true esthetic feeling that all real mathematicians know than [can be] formulated"—just as there is more to its analogue in poetry than can be analyzed. In both fields (to keep to the words of scientists and poets), the governing criteria are felt; they cannot be stated; they are known by the results they bring. Which at once calls to mind Frost's remark: "If the sound is right the sense will take care of itself." And Valéry's refinement of the statement: "An intimate alliance of sound and sense, which is the essential characteristic of poetic expression, cannot be achieved except at the expense of something—which is none other than the thought"; "a true poet will nearly always sacrifice [thought] to form (which, with its organic necessities, is, after all, the end and the act itself)."[16] Choice, to sum up, is determined by "emotional sensibility," by "esthetic criteria": *by responses that make themselves known,* that "govern imperatively." We can go no further—nor need we, having learned, as Valéry elsewhere declares, that "direct volition is useless."

Wherever relevant I have cited Valéry and Frost—also Eliot— not only because each has written and spoken extensively on creativity, and not only because, as contemporaries, they are nearer to us in attitude than earlier poets. I have done so for a larger reason. Placed on a spectrum, Frost and Valéry lie at opposed extremes with Eliot shifting between. Frost warned readers against "studying" a poem too much. He also warned writers that though a poem may be worked over once it is in being, it cannot be ordered into existence: "Its most precious quality will remain its having run itself and carried the poet with it." Valéry expressed contrary attitudes, yet on the issues central to creativity, their testimony scarcely differs. Similarly with Eliot's, on what the poet can and must do. The idea "simply comes." "We must simply wait until what we desire appears." ... ("It could be asked," writes the neuroanatomist W. J. H. Nauta, "how man can know the value of a thought—no less than that of food—if not by some internal physical response to it.")

The will, it would seem from the foregoing pages, plays no part at all. The poet is merely borne along as he makes, as he chooses. If at times he resorts to analysis, it is only to help him untangle lines in confusion. Obviously any such model of compliance omits the all-too-human in a writer, which sees itself as a person living among persons: listened to, disagreed with, admired, contemned, spurned. In the ongoing practices of re-vision, the demand of self-images can bring on wreckage, notably when driving the poet to resist being borne along on thoughts, choices, impulses, desires he would dis-avow. In other situations, when determined on specific outcomes, self-images can urge him to overrule spontaneous judgments; to bend the involuntary course of his poem according to ways à la mode; making it accord with plurisignation, deliberate ambiguity, por-tentous vagueness; bringing in slang, scientific plaintalk, anti-rhythm; and so on and so on. One can readily locate other hazards and pre-dict that their outcome also will depend on volition.[17]

By far less direct is its influence on a writer's development; in-deed, volition may merely reinforce the natural reactions reflected in a writer's "periods." The assumption of "development" is often opened to question; yet though every author writes only one work, most poets who continue to produce through a lifetime mark a course of some kind: the successive chapters differ. Yeats is the bril-liant instance—"the greatest remaker," as Horace Gregory calls him, from the earliest rewriting of his plays until the last few months of his life. A poem started with a vision.

From there onward he began the process of remaking toward greater clarity of the original vision and completion of the poem. Then, at progressive stages of his life, he would reshape certain of his poems to unify them with the body of his work. . . . [T]he final versions never failed to be improvements of the first.[18]

Yeats's development is unique—and so, in much less remarkable ways, is that of every other poet in the course it traces; in the change, for better or for worse (as in Wordsworth, probably Browning, Wallace Stevens—judgment of value depending on the appeal of the writer's altering vision to that of the reader-critic).

The question here, however, is not of literary excellence but of the possible effect on the poetry of the writer's self-images as related to his vision and mediated by his will. Guesswork is all one can pro-duce out of all the evidence. Yeats was, as Gregory says, "the greatest remaker of his poems and *of himself*." Unlike Frost, who could seriously wonder at the re-vision he had forgotten of "A Minor Bird," Yeats was steadily concerned with the altering movement of his mind as embodied in all his words:

> The friends that have it I do wrong
> Whenever I remake a song,
> Should know what issue is at stake:
> It is myself that I remake.

Keats, in the preface to his *Endymion*, referred to its "mawkishness": he was already reaching out toward a new "mature imagination of a man." A quite different example: Whitman with apparently minor re-visions changed the meaning of his "Song of Myself." " 'Myself,' [says Malcolm Cowley] is 'my personality,' and Whitman had originally been writing about a not-myself, a representative figure who, by achieving union with his transpersonal soul, had realized the possibilities latent in every man and woman."

Though relationship be assumed between a writer's view of the world and his failure to complete a re-vision, it can obtain only with poems belonging to an outgrown self. His inability to bring others to completion must have different reasons. Valéry was so dissatisfied with what he called solutions to technical problems that he said more than once that a poet ought to be allowed to spend his whole career writing variations on a single theme.[19] And when he insisted that "a work is completed only by some accident, such as exhaustion, satisfaction, the necessity of giving up, or death," he brought no more light than did the Romantic Lamartine, whose attitude was not much different. In fact, he confused it a little. For Accident No. 2 is what accounts for the lines that in one place he refers to as "given" and in another as those "for which we must simply wait"—the same satisfaction that Yeats described with "a poem comes right with a click like a closing box." Valéry's Accident No. 3 states the true question. Mallarmé did not publish "Hérodiade" during his lifetime. Eliot, however, put several "Unfinished Poems" into his definitive volume. Doubtless any number of *Collected Poems* also include such work without the qualifier. The last lines of "Two Tramps in Mudtime" never satisfied Frost:

> Only where love and need are one,
> And the work is play for mortal stakes, . . .

Shortly before his death he was "still wondering whether there should be a mark of punctuation. . . . The 'work is play' bothers me."[20]

An artist does what he can. The inevitably right words for completing a poem may simply not exist—or they may lie outside his orbit. He takes no real satisfaction when a passage left unfinished or abandoned happens especially to stir a reader as it invites him to imagine for himself all that might have been said (as may also happen in translations with alternative words, each of which suggests more than what a single word might encompass). This type of accident—if the word can apply—is the last thing wanted by an artist, though he knows that a sketch may hold a magic lost to the canvas. Going as far as he can, he may "simply wait" for the choice to appear that will make the poem come right with a click like a closing box.

Discussions of creativity are always in part discussions of taste, so tightly are the two entwined in the functional remnant of all that a poet and a reader were born with. Even to a hasty glance, it stands forth as the crucial decider, the unseizable power that an artist is most likely to trust in his final choice. And relative though it must be (who would have it otherwise?), enough consensus exists to make readers startle at Crashaw's description of Magdalene's eyes:

> Two welling baths, two weeping motions,
> Portable and compendious oceans . . .

or at Arnold's almost unspeak-able question:

> Who prop, thou ask'st, in these bad days, my mind?

or at Meredith's picture:

> I dreamed a banish'd Angel to me crept:
> My feet were nourish'd on her breasts all night.

No one needs to prove that "O the bleeding drops of red" is better than "Leave you not the little spot" in Whitman's threnody, or "perilous" seas than "keelless" and "shipless" in Keats's ode. Patmore referred to the " 'careful luck' of him who tries many words, and has the wit to know" when he has been "supplied unexpectedly with those which are perhaps even better than he knew how to desire." Apt though it is, I prefer Frost's "passionate preference" to epitomize the action of taste as it engages the poet's entire being, entire mind.

For the mind that creates the poem out of both vision and re-vision is able to draw on the totality of its thinking-and-feeling capacities (however we separate them—to see them better—into categories). Even analysis can be brought into play and, as the pressures of the person's self-imaging show (at the poet's risk), also the will. At this point it must therefore be apparent that my symbol Involuntary⟵⟶Voluntary means that these observable processes, while contrasted at the extremes, give way to subtle transitions in the middle registers. With the old dichotomy between conscious and unconscious thinking "now clearly too crude to be sustained," we are faced (adds Norman Mackenzie) "by a great variety of modes of thought, each with its own functions for the organism." For it is, of course, all one mind, however unlike its manifestations, however various its capacities, to compose, dissect, choose, wander, concentrate, and so on. And since the poet is able to proceed upon the freedom of the processes of the mind, composition must be an act of their collaboration.[21]

If poetry does not come as naturally as leaves to a tree it had better not come at all, said a poet whose worksheets are a monument of "conscious artistry." Anyone for whom this still holds the slightest contradiction is unlikely ever to understand the creative process.

The Well, The Coral Reef, Africa

Is there a "type of person" who engages in creative imagining?

My judgment is as active while I am actually writing as my imagination. In fact all my faculties are strongly excited and in their full play.—John Keats

What use is my mind? Granted that it enables me to hail a bus and pay my fare. But once I am inside my studio, what use is my mind? I have my model, my pencil, my paper, my paints. My mind doesn't interest me.—Edgar Degas

The first man believes, at the same time, that poetry must come as naturally as leaves to a tree and the second that poets make sonnets out of ideas:

Contradictions? The author of the following passage was entirely at home with the current theories of knowledge at his time:

"What," it will be Question'd, "When the Sun rises, do you not see a round disk of fire somewhat like a Guinea?" O no, no, I see an innumerable company of the Heavenly host crying, "Holy, Holy, Holy is the Lord God Almighty."

When Blake was asked where he saw all his visions, he pointed to his head:

Innocence? Goethe combined great intellectual power with astonishing naivete. For Newton science was much less important than a surprising kind of theology.[22] Freud was willing to credit what he was told whether it was likely or not:

Foolishness? "Great poetry," Baudelaire exclaimed, "is essentially stupid; it believes, and that is what makes its glory and force." It believes because it has to believe, possibility being the condition of all imagining.

And artists believe in themselves. Even when suffering physical wretchedness and reader apathy, they are likely to keep on striving—less out of reasoning choice than constitutional necessity to bear forth the burdens seething within them:

Where? In "the deep well of unconscious cerebration" according to Henry James. F. C. Prescott says it is "a coral reef, older, deeper, larger than the island." Jean Paul, disagreeing with both, calls "the immense realm of the Unconscious, this real interior Africa in every sense." Though most writers grow solemn when contemplating the mystery, I prefer—as did F. W. H. Myers—to forego the hushed tone. The first to have conceived the subject scientifically, he defined the not-conscious as "a rubbish-heap as well as a treasure house." And how could it be otherwise if, as is assumed, everything that enters the brain leaves an imprint, a mark, of some kind? The least confusing term for referring to these traces is memory. And that they do not in fact disappear is powerfully urged on us, perhaps less by dreaming and other imagining than by types of hypnosis that enable one to remember what no amount of willing recalls. If, as Ribot made clear and seems beyond question, an individual's "conscious personality is never more than a small fraction of the physical personality," how can anyone hope to understand most of what exists as thought, especially when even the process of remembering has not been explained?

We know only that literally millions of neurons are involved in the recall of any memory. Since this is the working effect of a trace, can we wonder that experts regard the profusion of interconnections among the cells as beyond human power of imagining—at least 10 billion neurons, each receiving connections from perhaps 100 others and connecting to still 100 more? The transmission of a "wavefront" may sweep over 100,000 neurons in a single second (it can operate not only on nearby cells but also on distant parts of the cortex); the entire wavefront can advance through as many as 1,000,000 neurons in a second. In the midst of all this electrochemical arithmetic, Sir Charles Sherrington's famous figure brings delighting relief, with its picture of the brain as an "enchanted loom where millions of flashing shuttles [the nerve impulses] weave a dissolving pattern, always a meaningful pattern, though never an abiding one; a shifting harmony of sub-patterns."

Through all this incessant activity, the brain, ever in love with peace, with synchronous beating, appears quite capable of disposing of anything disruptive. Nevertheless, in the midst of the general calm, certain signals will enter which can neither at once nor in time be accommodated. Soon or long after their first impact has been managed by the brain, they may develop into a burden.[23] That stimuli of this kind sometimes enter into the enchanted loom, is a normal hazard of a person's interreaction with the world; that they might manifest themselves through all types of later eruption into awareness, is equally to be expected. They erupt very often in dream, and if safely disguised, enable the dreamer to continue sleeping, though what they actually embody may burden him long after waking. They erupt very often in intuitions seizing the mind in broad daylight with unexplained feelings—of pain or pleasure, of fear or exaltation—to come.

And so on . . . including creativity, which ranks as less common because its mode of eruption is less common, being part of the bodily cycle earlier described as accumulation released in imaginative thought. Here the stimulus that comes from outside and that signals the brain can stir up a world within, which in time will out through behaviors peculiar to the "type of person" they affect.[24] Or, if one prefers, the disturbing element together with all it has disturbed will ex-press, emerge, come forth, declare itself while the host looks on. What appears in this initial self-ejection must at least surprise him in his double role of participant-observer borne on a voyage. Although it may never have passed through his mind as more than a flash, if at all, the disturbance will at times have made itself known as a seething within the organism. But the irritability, malaise, tension (the "burden" referred to before) may not spend itself completely at the moment it pours into consciousness—most poems are not completed at a single stroke. More time will be required before the brain can again return to its synchronous beating . . . to be entered again by another signal which in time may give rise to another burden and cycle . . .

Leaving out of account their divinities, the ancients now appear to have been thinking in the "true" direction, heretical as this may seem to an Age of Scientism. Traced to its initiating sources, "inspiration" fairly defines what the organism does when it *breathes* something *into* itself, the signal from without that is transformed within as response. Once lodged there, it starts a series of motions; and whatever its nature or the time it requires, the signal-response works inexorably toward achieving the answer-relief for itself and for its host.

This sequence of (gathering, widening, deepening, self-resolving, self-discovering) processes is the first great meaning of creativity as a function *of* the organism. Part II of this book will attempt to make clear the complementary meaning of this creative imagining, as it functions *for* the organism.

NOTES AND COMMENTS

1. Pablo Picasso: "When I paint, my objective is to show what I have found, not what I was looking for. . . . A painter paints to unload himself of feelings and visions. . . ."—*Artists on Art*, Robert Goldwater and Marco Treves, eds., Pantheon, 1945, pp. 416 ff.

2. See Ernest Jones, "The Nature of Genius," Freud Centennial Lecture, April 23, 1956, N. Y. Psychoanalytic Institute and Society. The Robinson sentence I owe to Louis Untermeyer.

3. A poem, as understood in this book, is language-thinking, not the feeling, the flash, or other experience that precedes the arrival of words. • T. S. Eliot, *On Poetry and Poets*, Farrar, Straus & Cudahy, Inc., 1957, p. 107. J. C. Ransom, *Conversations on the Craft of Poetry*, Cleanth

Brooks and Robert Penn Warren, eds., Holt, 1961, p. 19. • "I feel that I am in an awfully good period now, and I must keep it going. I can tell, as never before, what to *say* in any certain part of a particular poem; it just comes to me, and I put it down. . . . It is with very great pleasure that I sit down each morning to see what the hell I'm going to say today. Believe me, it surprises me more than it ever could anybody else."—Letter to me from James Dickey, Nov. 21, 1965.

4. As an ideal a necessary poem is one which not only demands to be born but is felt by the reader, after he has experienced it, to have been a necessity for him also. (The inception provides no test: a poem may become necessary once it is under way, even though its getting under way was a voluntary process.) Since I speak of authentic and successful poems, an explanation is in order. I regard as authentic a poem which has the sound of the writer's voice only, which strikes an experienced reader as an adequately realized object in accordance with its own implicit assumptions (attitude, tone, feeling, language, belief, etc.); hence one which, for such a reader, may take on independent existence as an object added to his landscape. Such a poem, though successful within its own terms, may fail in its effect upon a reader who finds himself dissenting too strongly from some of its assumptions.

5. The "real subject matter of most of [Valéry's] poems is a presentation of the states of mind which promote composition," says Norman Suckling, *Paul Valéry and the Civilized Mind*, Oxford, 1954, crediting the remark to Mlle Emilie Noulet. • " 'Tenter de vivre!' That, I think is toward the end of *Le Cimetière marin*. But it's really of no account. Almost a cliché. At any rate: an utterance that was spontaneous, painless—therefore . . . *fatherless*. To my mind, *pater is est quem labor demonstrat.*"—*Self Portraits: The Gide/Valéry Letters, 1890-1942*, Robert Mallet, ed., Chicago, 1966, p. 321. • Note elsewhere: "Inspiration is that hypothesis that reduces the author to the role of observer." "At the basis of every thought is a sigh." See Paul Valéry, *The Art of Poetry*, pp. 180, 144, 315, 143, and "The Course in Poetics: First Lesson," Jackson Mathews, trans., in *The Creative Process*, Brewster Ghiselin, ed., New American Library, 1955. See also Jean Hytier *The Poetics of Paul Valéry*, Anchor Books, 1966, especially Chaps. V, VI, VII.

6. Orpingalik, quoted in *Diogenes*, No. 12, pp. 5-6. Compare: "Song bursts forth spontaneously from its own native spring—so immaculately that countless rhythmical groups of images are reflected in all directions."—Mallarmé, letter to Charles Morice, undated, in Bradford Cook, *Mallarmé*, Baltimore, Johns Hopkins Press, 1956, p. 105. Also Stephen Spender, *World Within World*, Harcourt, Brace & World, 1951, pp. 223, 228.

7. Robert Graves, *The Common Asphodel*, London, Hamish Hamilton, Ltd., 1949, p. 1. Compare Tennyson's words with Dostoevsky's (p. 43). Frank O'Connor: "One writes in a sort of dream, and I can

only hope that when I wake, I shall be satisfied with what I have dreamt." • Paul Valéry, *The Art of Poetry*, p. 80. T. S. Eliot, *Selected Essays*, p. 276.

8. J. Isaacs, *The Background of Modern Poetry*, E. P. Dutton & Company, Inc., 1952, p. 102. For examples of involuntary processes in scientific creation, see below pp. 176 ff. • "[Blake's] method of composition, in his mature work, is exactly like that of other poets. . . . The idea, of course, simply comes, but upon arrival it is subjected to prolonged manipulations." T. S. Eliot, *Selected Essays*, p. 276.

9. See Robert Gibson, *Modern French Poets on Poetry*, Cambridge, 1961, "a connected anthology of pronouncements on poetry by the poets themselves" (this quotation appears in French on p. 232).

10. Graves: *Saturday Review*, Dec. 7, 1963. The poets' "liability to be possessed by the creations of their own brains is limited and proportioned by the artistic sense," says James Russell Lowell, "and the imagination thus becomes a shaping faculty, while in less regulated organizations it dwells forever in the Nifelheim of phantasmagoria and dream." Lowell's view is close to Charles Lamb's, which stresses the "hidden sanity which still guides the poet in the widest seeming aberrations"; the poet "is not possessed by his subject but has dominion over it." It is close to the view of Lionel Trilling, who declares in his essay on "Freud and Literature" (*The Liberal Imagination*, The Viking Press, 1951, p. 45): "the poet is in command of his fantasy, while it is exactly the mark of the neurotic that he is possessed by his fantasy." I take this to mean that the poet knows—when he stops to think of it or if he stops to think of it—that he is engaged in composition, for it is in this sense only that he might be regarded as "in command" of his fantasy. Obviously Coleridge was not in command of his fantasy when writing down the lines of "Kubla Khan," nor was Henri Michaux when producing his drawings and poems under the control of narcotics. And what of the "short poem, or [the] passage of a long poem, [that] may appear in its final form at once" (p. 48)? Conceptual, discursive, logical reason—which is to say "the working reason"—"plays a secondary part in the fine arts. . . . As soon as it gets the upper hand, the work is but a corpse of a work of art."—Jacques Maritain. As Eliot remarks, "The bad poet is usually unconscious where he ought to be conscious, and conscious where he ought to be unconscious" (*Selected Essays*, p. 10). See the discussion of Mallarmé's "Demon of Analogy" in Guy Michaud, *Mallarmé*, N.Y.U. Press, 1965, pp. 41 f.

11. "[M]ost poets resemble Beethoven whose notebooks bear witness to the false starts, the groping after clarity, and the organized strivings to discover what one desires to say."—John Press, *The Fire and the Fountain*, Oxford, 1955, p. 233.

12. Rafael Alberti, *Selected Poems*, Ben Belitt, ed./trans., California, 1966, p. 65.

13. John Crowe Ransom, Brooks and Warren, *Conversations on the Craft of Poetry*, p. 24. • It should be unnecessary to point out that

re-vision consists of far more than ever happens to get recorded on paper. To report from my own experience during the weeks when *In the Clearing* was in page-proof, at least one crucial change was being tested in the mind of Frost—and in our discussions—without either of us having even scribbled down the possible alteration (which, as it turned out, was finally discarded). What written drafts omit may be more interesting and telling than all they contain. They give no more than a partial view of any specific re-vision. Which is not to deny the often enormous interest of what even this partial picture can show.

14. Paul Valéry, "The Course in Poetics: First Lesson," pp. 101 f. Robert Greer Cohn, *Towards the Poems of Mallarmé*, California, 1965, p. 3.

15. Jacques Hadamard, *The Psychology of Invention in the Mathematical Field*, Princeton University Press, 1945, pp. 30 ff. See also below, p. 176. What Poincaré refers to in saying that the movements of the mathematicians' mind in creation are guided by esthetic considerations (with which, incidentally, other mathematicians have agreed) "is not feeling in the sense of emotional excitement, but an affective response to an intellectual order still eluding rational grasp."—Brewster Ghiselin, in *Scientific Creativity*, Calvin W. Taylor and Frank Barron, eds., John Wiley & Son, Inc., 1963, p. 359. Barron's summary of the research carried on at the Institute of Personality Assessment and Research of the University of California lists five qualities found typical of "the more highly regarded young scientists," two of which read: "(4) unusually appreciative of the intuitive and non-rational elements in their own nature; (5) distinguished by their profound commitment to the search for esthetic and philosophic meaning in all experience." (p. 386). ". . . creative scientists are similar to artists in the importance they give to esthetic qualities in their theories. On the Barron-Welsh Art Scale, the more original scientist differs from the less original in preferring the asymmetrical figures that artists too prefer. Gough even found that the Art Scale was the single best predictor of his criterion ratings of scientific creativity."—Frank Barron, "The Psychology of Creativity," in *New Directions in Psychology II*, T. Newcomb, ed., Holt, 1965, p. 88. See also J. D. Watson, *The Double Helix*, Atheneum, 1968. • "The trouble with taste, of course, is that in the end one has to trust it."—L. C. Knights, *N. Y. Review of Books*, Dec. 19, 1968, p. 27.

16. Valéry, "Cantiques Spirituels," *Œuvres*, p. 455. "Direct volition is useless" (Valéry, *Tel Quel*, I, p. 150). That other writers also believed that the demands of sense should be subordinated to those of sound, is evident in Gibson's citations from Baudelaire, Leconte de Lisle, Laforgue, Claudel, and Flaubert. He adds: "Valéry's much-vaunted 'vers calculés' are seen, then, to be no more under the poet's control than the disparaged 'vers donnés,' " *op. cit.*, pp. 253 ff. Nauta quotation, *op. cit.*, p. 43.

17. "It was part of our purposeful labor, in those days, to fill our poems with somewhat studied puns which could be said 'to work on

several different levels.' "—Howard Nemerov in *Poets on Poetry*, Basic, 1966. Isidor Schneider reports analogous fashionableness as of thirty years earlier. But long before, some among the French Surrealists were willfully striving to put together two objects as remote as possible from each other in striking and sudden ways ("les mettre en présence d'une manière brusque et saisissante"—André Breton). Among the "other" hazards: in re-vision, not knowing when to stop; soliciting or taking advice. "It is nearly impossible to make the RIGHT suggestion for emending another man's work. . . . At most one can put one's finger on the fault and hope that the man himself will receive inspiration from the depths of his own personal Helicon."—Michael Reck, *Ezra Pound*, McGraw-Hill, Inc., 1967, p. 2 (quoting Pound). "Elizabeth used to entreat Browning invariably to cancel his own alterations. She told a friend that he never altered without damage."—Maisie Ward, *Robert Browning and His World*, Holt, 1969, p. 15.

18. Horace Gregory, review of *The Variorum Edition of the Poems of W. B. Yeats*, *N. Y. Times Book Review*, Dec. 22, 1957. A different kind of example: Tennyson's "The Lotos-Eaters." Lockhart reviewed the volume in which it first appeared. Twenty years later the poem was published in final form. Tennyson had either deleted or altered every line to which Lockhart had objected. • Richard Ellmann, *Yeats: The Man and the Masks*, Dutton, 1958, p. 186.

19. See Gibson, *op. cit.*, pp. 254, 271. "A poem . . . is a closed system in all its parts, in which nothing can be modified"—Valéry's ideal definition, to Charles DuBos. Elsewhere he says—echoing Mallarmé—that to complete a work consists in making everything that reveals or suggests its workmanship disappear. • In the thirteenth lecture of his "Course in Poetics" he invokes "two quite different factors, satisfaction and the impossibility of going further," Hytier, *op. cit.*, p. 243 n.

20. Frost was concerned essentially with the word "play," he told Keith Jennison: "What RF wanted out of 'play' was the gambler's word."

21. Compare: "Some thinking and some dreaming enter into all our mental procedures: the extremes are sharply contrasted, but give way to delicate transitions in the middle registers."—Joseph Jastrow, *The Subconscious*, Houghton Mifflin & Co., 1906, p. 446. • Norman Mackenzie, *N. Y. Times Book Review*, June 12, 1966.

22. Innocence? Newton, for many people the greatest scientific genius of all, spent much time experimenting in alchemy, searching for the philosopher's elixir and the means for transmuting metals into gold, in an age when alchemy had long passed its prime. "He followed Bishop Ussher in dating the creation from 4004 B.C. . . . From the Book of Daniel he deduced that the tenth horn of the fourth beast must refer to the Roman Catholic Church and confidently predicted its downfall in the year 2000." Newton's case was not unique. A "remarkable epidemic

of belief in the cruder aspects of spiritism . . . infected several of the leading English physicists early this century."—Ernest Jones, "The Nature of Genius." • Foolishness? "A great poet, too, spells a great intellect, and such an one is fairly sure to have the faculty of delight in abstract thought. Is it necessary to cite the acute analytical thinking in Yeats's and Shelley's letters, the flawless forensic armour of Milton's Satan, the discursive vigour of the *Paradiso*, or the logical fisticuffs of Shakespeare's comic characters?"—Owen Barfield, *Poetic Diction*, London, Faber & Faber, Ltd., 1928, p. 108.

23. Sherrington's figure: see Goethe's *Faust 1*, lines 1922-1928. • The poet "is oppressed by a burden which he must bring to birth in order to obtain relief . . . to gain relief from acute discomfort. . . ." T. S. Eliot, *On Poetry and Poets*, p. 107. • Assuming the reader to have assimilated Chapter 1, I do not add cross-references to supporting data (i.e., the brain ever strives toward synchronous beating) or to qualifications (i.e., the brain can be stirred into activity also by stimuli arising from within the body). That the entering stimuli can be of every possible kind hardly needs stating, or that a writer's mind can be powerfully and uncannily affected by images and similar creations of other writers. Hence, I have not included in the text instances of literary borrowings (of which the borrower may or may not be aware), similarities (or passages that reflect similarity, whether arising out of influence or not), and coincidences. I give a few examples here, for such interest as they may have.

BORROWINGS (OF WHICH THE BORROWER MAY OR MAY NOT BE AWARE):

(a) Shelley: "Poets are the unacknowledged legislators of the world." Compare *Rasselas*, where Imlac describes the poet: ". . . he must, therefore, contemn the applause of his own time, and commit his claims to the justice of posterity. He must write, as the interpreter of nature, and the legislator of mankind, and consider himself, as presiding over the thoughts and manners of future generations [etc]."—Samuel Johnson, *Works*, Hill and Powell, eds., Oxford, I, p. 222.

(b) T. S. Eliot: "objective correlative" (as cited in countless critical essays). The "phrase [was] formulated by a half-forgotten classicist, Washington Allston," says Harry Levin, *Contexts of Criticism*, Cambridge, Harvard University Press, 1957, p. 259. "Eliot himself was surprised when he learned about the origin of the phrase. . . . But the actual phrase comes from the lectures on art, posthumously edited by R. H. Dana and published—as I remember—around 1850" (p. 16).—Personal letter to me. See also Bruce R. McElderry, Jr., "Santayana's and Eliot's 'Objective Correlative,'" *Boston University Studies in English*, III, 1957, pp. 179-181.

SIMILARITIES:

(a) Masefield: "Sea Fever," published in 1910, widely anthologized. Compare Arthur Symons' "Wanderer's Song," reported to have been written before 1910. The opening stanza:

I have had enough of women, and enough of love,
But the land waits and the sea waits, and day and night is enough;
Give me a long white road, and the grey wide path of the sea,
And the wind's will and the bird's will, and the heart-ache still in me.

(b) Frost: "Stopping by Woods on a Snowy Evening." Compare the quatrain in a draft written by Keats, dated 1819:

Keen fitful gusts are whispering here and there
Among the bushes, half leafless and dry;
The stars look very cold about the sky,
And I have many miles on foot to fare.

(c) Housman: *A Shropshire Lad, passim.* Compare the poem by Samuel Johnson:

Hermit hoar, in solemn cell,
  Wearing out life's evening gray,
Smite thy bosom, sage, and tell
  What is bliss? and which the way?

Thus I spoke; and speaking sighed;
  Scarce repressed the starting tear;
When the smiling sage replied:
  "Come, my lad, and drink some beer."

COINCIDENCES:

(a) Unamuno, writing in 1923 of Pirandello:

"In fact, from the little I have known till now of the Sicilian writer, I've seen as in a mirror many of my most intimate attitudes. More than once I have said to myself, "I could have written those very words!" And I am almost certain that just as I knew nothing of Pirandello's, he knew nothing of mine. One senses his originality, and it is because I sense him to be original that I recognize myself in him. A writer never recognizes himself in an imitation, no matter how ably done."

What I have at first felt to be coincidence at times turns out to be affinity, remote or impressive (e.g., between some poems by Juan March [1397?-1437], as translated by John F. Nims, and some by the English Metaphysicals). What I have elsewhere called a poetry of "appropriated effects" has nothing in common with the present subject, since it issues from deliberate use of words or images created by an earlier writer (e.g., Eliot's "To purify the dialect of the tribe" in *Little Gidding* and Mallarmé's "Donner un sens plus pur aux mots de la tribu" in *Le Tombeau d'Edgar Poe,* see p. 276). Hopkins regarded these effects as "a disease of education, literature is full of them; but they remain a disease, an evil," *Letters,* i, p. 206. See "The Three Revolutions of Modern Poetry" in my *Varieties of Literary Experience,* N.Y.U., 1962, pp. 163 f.

24. The event that triggers the release of the accumulation within, like so much else in creativity, shows endless variety. *Werther* had been occupying Goethe for about two years without assuming form, when he

received startling news of his friend Jerusalem's suicide. "At that instant the plan of *Werther* was found; the whole shot together from all directions and became a solid mass, as the water in a vase, which is just at the freezing point, is changed by the slightest concussion into ice." Valéry talks of benefiting from "the lucky accident"; Milton asks the gentle Muse to favour "With lucky words . . . my destin'd Urn"; and so on. But "accident" is meaningless and misleading here. Whether an accident of circumstance, however, can influence the result or the process of ex-pression (the course of dictation in the onset of creativity) raises different considerations. According to their own reports, Coleridge, Tennyson, and Yeats had experiences at both extremes: at one time, writing poems at a single stroke; at another, producing passages bearing the curious name of "prose drafts." Compared with the *ideal* normality of the first, the second seems clearly dysfunctional, suggesting interferences, anxieties, the basic trouble Eliot remarked of "the bad poet" (note 10 above). A certain amount of confusion, however, may often accompany original dictation—plain mistakes in hearing. In any event, the confusion attending the onset (whatever its amount) may be followed by great lucidity during re-vision.

(At this point I may add that, with the exception of what Coleridge reported of the writing of "Kubla Khan," I have personally experienced some of the varieties of creativity described in the foregoing pages. I have written [a] entire poems at a single stroke and never afterwards changed; [b] entire poems in an hour or two with subsequent changes of a half-dozen words or phrases and [c] of deletions only; [d] I have later added a passage to a poem I had considered complete; [e] I have continued to re-vise poems at intervals during ten, twenty, thirty years, resulting in completion, [f] sometimes in failure. Examples appear on the following pages of my *Caged in an Animal's Mind*, pp. [a] 17, 62, 84, 124, 141; [b] 64, 70; [c] 36, 87; [d] 54; [e] 90, 107, 149.)

3 · The Ways in Which Poems Speak

The world did not need to be assured by Samuel Johnson or anyone else that it is harder to say what poetry is than what it is not. Quite obviously it is not a news report, recipe, brief, state constitution, or any other set of words assembled for conveying facts or events or agreements in ways that leave no room for uncertainty. A business firm's articles of incorporation are not poetry, nor is a dictionary entry. And yet, as Emerson was careful to point out, bare lists of words in themselves are sometimes enough to set off the imagination. Moreover, the line for demarking poetry from prose grows problematical when applied to certain clusters of words removed from their setting in a poem. At times these isolated fragments fulfil not only the requirements of the linguist's "emotive utterances"—they not only express and evoke.[1] They also inform, interrogate, and direct, which is what the linguist's other type of utterances—the "rational"—will do. Thus:

Informing

 Whose dwelling is the light of setting suns
 After life's fitful fever he sleeps well
 And in His Will is our peace
 The unplumb'd salt, estranging sea
 I will show you fear in a handful of dust
 And all his island shivered into flowers
 I saw eternity the other night
 The slow, smokeless burning of decay

Questioning

 O body swayed to music, O brightening glance
 How can we know the dancer from the dance?
 And was the Holy Lamb of God
 On England's pleasant pastures seen?
 Art thou poor, yet hast thou golden slumbers?
 Or are we live remains
 Of Godhead dying downwards, brain and eye now gone?
 What wilt thou do, God, when I die?

Direct-Exclaiming

 Absent thee from felicity awhile
 Make me thy lyre!
 Batter my heart, three-personed God!
 Mine, O thou lord of life, send my roots rain!
 Get with child a mandrake root

Compared with these, the fragments that follow—also drawn at random from well-known poems—are in themselves neither evocative nor expressive. Each when read in isolation does little more than inform or interrogate or direct. None leaves larger room for uncertainty in a hearer's mind than do snippets from ordinary conversation, journalism, or correspondence. Of "emotive utterance" they make feeble examples indeed for a person innocent of their contexts:

Informing

 My heart aches
 We passed the setting sun
 The lights in the fishing boats at anchor
 When icicles hang by the wall
 He ate his supper in a room/Blazing with lights
 It is time that I wrote my will
 My sash is lowered when night comes on

The sea is calm tonight
I, too, dislike it
There are three conditions which often look alike

Questioning
Is my team ploughing?
How many are you, then?
"Is there anybody there?" said the Traveller
Are these ideas right or wrong?
Why so pale?
Does the road wind uphill all the way?

Directing-Explaining
Grow old along with me
Bring me my scallop-shell
Let us go and make our visit
For God's sake hold your tongue
You come too.
Give a man a pipe he can smoke
No, no! Go from me.

A reader making his first encounter with these groups of words in isolation, as I have presented them, has every reason for assigning them to non-literary sources. Once they are restored to their native habitats, the mistake ceases to be possible, for the total nature of their impact changes. While retaining their communicative power as rational utterances, they also regain the expressive-evocative powers they had been deprived of by being isolated. Acting upon the reader from where they live within the poem, they speak in both ordinary and extraordinary ways, however irreconcilable these ways would appear in a partial view of the mind. A reader, once he has entered the poem, never stops to think of demarcations of any sort, caught up, as he is, in experiencing its seamless totality in a wholly effortless response.

Common and Other Kinds of Sense

To understand the ways by which poetry speaks, the brain has to wrench itself out of the grooves it has been using throughout the last 2,000 years. It faces the troubling necessity of trying to realize how it can think when it can draw on all its capacities. I say "troubling" because we have been led into organizing our brains by dichotomies, into thinking of our thought as producing either common (discursive) sense or its "opposite," rather than into common sense *and various other kinds* of sense. We have to *try* to realize because for brains thus organized, enormous effort is required. Hellenic reasonableness, with its passion for conceptualizing—at least in its 17th-century incarnation—not only insisted on thinking by intellectual constructions but also sought to measure every human experience by their terms. Hence anything it could not contain—ambiguity, for example—was both dangerous as thought and faulty as expression; in our case, beyond the pale. Paradox or not, this heritage—vividly apparent in our automatic concern for causality—succeeded by the splendid force of its logic in arriving at its own dethronement. And if it survives, it does so only by acknowledging itself now as being nothing greater than one element of *inclusive* understanding—of the mode of thinking that naturally arises when confronted with a work of art.

The classic example of science is the theory of light, with its two mutually exclusive explanations—the "corpuscular" (light is a stream of particles flying at enormous speed from a source) and the "wave" (a beam of light is a wave traveling through a medium, the ether). By the end of the last century, the first theory has been completely superseded by the second. "Light consisted of waves and matter of atoms. Anyone who dared to question these foundations of the science of physics would have been regarded as a dilettante, or an eccentric" (in the words of Hans Reichenbach).[2] Suddenly, however, Max Planck's discovery of the quantum (1900) reopened the question, and thirteen years later Niels Bohr's theory which linked the atom model with the energy quantum led to a very strange consequence. Physicists were now compelled to treat light as a stream of particles in explaining some phenomena *and* as a wave in explaining others, despite the fact that one theory excluded the other by the standards of a logic which knows only yes-and-no. The seemingly impossible had thus been insured beyond doubt: light can no longer be identified as *either* a wave phenomenon *or* a stream of particles.

The theories that followed (fully and correctly understandable only in their mathematical form) reflect a totality far more rich and complex than the ordinary observer could have suspected—a totality which forces him to think in ways which the logic of dichotomy denies. Bohr's principle of "complementarity" reflects the fact that this "irreconcilability" gives the mind no choice but to revise fundamentally its ordinary ways of conceiving experience. By enlarging its ways, by accepting what it had recoiled from as contradictions, the mind can grasp and entertain what it could neither grasp nor entertain before. It could understand with the expanded range now "compelled" upon its processes.

Odd though it may seem, the universe of poetry requires a similar enlargment of the mind. Moreover, while assigning to its appropriate functions the limited ways of ordinary conceiving, complementarity itself holds in balance only two entities, whereas poetry's universe has room for all that is possible for the mind to think. Hence, in place of two reconciled contradictions, we may expect to find in a poem together with the one type of thought called common sense every other that may be called non-common (whether nameable or not). A kind of negative model can be offered in terms of color. It is one thing to distinguish black from white; quite another, green from non-green (from purple, red, yellow, blue, and all other non-green colors, nameable or not). In its positive sense, such a model would suggest the full range of the mind when it is able—as it is in creativity—to proceed upon what Valéry happily calls the "freedom of its processes."

In a word, pluralism in modes of thought, a number of which any poem might contain and the reader accept quite naturally. No less pluralistic in its response is the mind of an uncivilized person; and, as those who have studied it observe, also quite naturally so. People do better than they realize when they liken the response of civilized persons before a work of art to the "early" or "primary" mode of human thinking. They do worse, however, when they go on to infer in the uncivilized a lack of capacity and a negative naivete. Actually such conclusions were made untenable years ago by the discovered grammatical complexity of primitive languages; yet it has required great pains of scholars to convince the civilized that the mind of the primitive is neither incapable of logical thinking nor negatively simple. Very much to the contrary, as Claude

Lévi-Strauss declares with impressive conviction and evidence. The essential difference between civilized and primitive logic flows out of the materials used and the resulting contrasts: the former tending to deal in wholly abstract entities (e.g., mathematical equations); the latter, content with the sensory qualities it draws out of concrete objects (e.g., male-female, raw-cooked). Both mentalities are able to "structure" reality with logic ("The savage mind is logical in the same sense and same fashion as ours," says Lévi-Strauss) though not necessarily for practical purposes. Moreover, both also tend to utilize abstractions (primitive magic—civilized science; totemism—morality; myth—literature).

The other capacity shared by both mentalities has greater bearing on poetry's ways of speaking: wholeness of range, which in the primitive goes beyond even Terence, in refusing to be indifferent to anything human or even living. But it is less in area of interest than in operative process that the wholeness relates to poetry. Lucien Lévy-Bruhl called the primitive mind "pre-logical," by which he did not mean a type of reasoning antecedent to logical thought, or an illogical or even anti-logical type. The confusing term (which he later abandoned) meant only a process of thinking in which logic was inappropriate. No view could be more opposed to that of Lévi-Strauss, and yet *La Pensée sauvage* also makes it evident that primitive mentality cares little about the nature or logical level of what it structures, nor is able to see why inconsistency, when it arises, should matter. For all their acute disagreement, both writers point to the wholeness, the "totalizing" quality, of primitive thought. Lévi-Strauss is attracted by the movement it takes toward "a science of the concrete," Lévy-Bruhl by the different direction—toward "participation."[3]

To the extent that every person is a product of his native tongue and culture and of the attitudes embodied in both, the primitive sees the world through the collective representations of his group. These cause him to interpret and structure reality by the "primary processes" of thought at the center of Freudian man. Civilized restraining simply does not interest the primitive mind, even though in ordinary affairs of life it can be (by our standards) entirely logical. The contradiction as such has no real consequence for him. If in one situation he reasons by myth and ritual and in another by rational procedures, his approach always takes the form of participating in all that happens to engage him—in responding directly, losing himself in what he is thinking without stopping to question or to test. He surrenders himself; he is borne along much as a reader unselfconsciously joins himself to a poem and participates in its reality—which is to say, in the mode of discourse that distinguishes a poem from all other arrangements of language.

Metaphor: Narrow and Broad

It s easier to identify the presence of poetry than any force or quality responsible for bringing it about. Nothing is gained, for example, by referring to poetry as *emotive* discourse when "all mental phenomena are modes of feeling" (Suzanne Langer); or as *alogical* when rational utterances abound in poetry. Most identifications of this kind fall down because they rise from shaky dichotomies which turn out to be contrasts of degree, and of doubtful validity. In every case, they leave out of account the significant phenomenon I pointed to earlier in speaking of the pluralism of the modes of thought that typify creative imagining.[4]

At a certain point—upon having reached completion—a work of art automatically takes on attributes peculiar to any self-sustaining entity. Everything within its "closed system" intensifies for the perceiver—hue, shape, pattern in a picture; the mere fact of their being framed in for attention endows them with force and significance. Equally in a poem: whatever powers the words possessed unconfined are heightened by the concentrating pressure of the frame. Equally obvious is another enlarging effect. "A word in isolation," to use L. B. Salomon's phrasing, "has only the potential meanings codified in a dictionary, but it takes only a little context to start it vibrating with overtones no lexicographer would venture to divine." Mallarmé, thinking of the ideal movement of words within a poem, hoped that his own would "light up by mutual reflection." But all words in all poems reach out in all directions, influencing everything around them, both near and distant. Their order alone compels them to mean in a special way, their uniqueness acting selectively. The position that each word holds in relation to the others causes parts of its content to be magnified and other parts diminished. Some of the meanings recede as others come to the fore, stirring in the mind of the reader a commingling of overtones that no analyst could venture to divine with anything approaching comprehensiveness.

> Full fathom five thy father lies

begins the "Sea Dirge" from *The Tempest*. If it were humanly possible (as it is not) to deafen your ears to everything but the bare denotation, you might come away with a straightforward piece of fact. True, the overtones vibrate incessantly, every word "acts up," yet the thought conveyed when abstracted from the line is very ordinary. What immediately follows, however:

> Of his bones are coral made

is part fact, part fancy. And line 3 makes anything but common sense:

> Those are pearls that were his eyes

Yet the three lines that follow are defensibly rational, including the bias of the last:

> Nothing of him that doth fade
> But doth suffer a sea-change
> Into something rich and strange

And then the closing lines swing off in yet another direction:

> Sea-nymphs hourly ring his knell:
> Hark! now I hear them—
> Ding, dong, bell.

Every line of the tiny poem is charged with overtones. Even the "rational" first and fifth vibrate with more than can be heard in the "purely" informative fragment from *Little Gidding* when read without context:

> There are three conditions which often look alike
> Yet differ completely . . .

But I have assumed the ears to have been theoretically deafened to everything but denotation; and Shakespeare's dirge exemplifies with simplicity some of the complex ways by which a poem quite naturally flows out of one kind of sense and into another and yet another, and the effortless ease with which a reader moves out of one mode of thought into another and so on. Advance preparation would be the last thing needed by a mind that can "participate," that can respond upon the freedom of all its processes. *La Pensée sauvage*—the mind in its untamed state—is at once the mind of the primitive and of the civilized. If it has evolved, it has been largely in learning habits for diminished response when the codes of the culture demand it. With a poem the fullness of the mind's capacities can come instantly into play because they are always there, and always ready.

Ordinary mixed with extraordinary, common with uncommon sense—Joseph Jastrow said years ago that "Some thinking and some dreaming enter into every mental procedure." He said nothing about tension created by opposites for the good reason that these two are not opposites but dissimilars. Mackenzie's point—that we think in a great variety of modes—bears repeating. Poetry's universe reflects this great variety: a poem is made of a number of things . . . which somehow hold together. What keeps them from tumbling apart? Obviously the question cannot be handled without knowing what the pieces consist of. Words? Clusters of words? The linguistic unit of a poem, the irreducible component, may be as small as "Palmes!" in Mallarmé's "Don du Poème" and larger than "The lights in the fishing boats at anchor" (Stevens) and "I will show you fear in a handful of dust" (Eliot). In each instance the essential effect is an indivisible image, regardless of origin as extraordinary or ordinary utterance. Such is at least their impact as isolated entities, in contrast to their miraculously magnified aliveness the instant they vibrate from within the poem. Once restored to their native context, they reach out in every direction, exerting on one another a force whose effect is to intimate complexities of resemblance. As certain parts of each recede and others come forward, new entities begin to emerge very much as new relationships emerge in a metaphor.

Hence when I now use the last term for describing the basic force or quality that holds a poem together, I ask that it be taken in its broadest possible conception. Which is to say, without regard for technical terminologies. Thus both "My luve is like a red, red rose" and "My luve is a red rose" are metaphors though the first is defined as a simile. For my purposes it makes no difference that Traherne's metaphor "Boys and girls tumbling in the street, and playing, were moving jewels" becomes a simile when "like" is inserted before the last verb. Whether a metaphor be called a simile-compressed, or a simile a metaphor-with-a-preface, every such figure of speech results in an image, a verbal copy, a likeness, a picture which stimulates more than the "organs" or sight:

> And many a rose-carnation feeds
> With summer spice the humming air [Tennyson]
> The unplumb'd salt, estranging sea [Arnold]
> The slow smokeless burning of decay [Frost]
> His helmet now shall make a hive for bees [Peele]

or the last two lines of Ungaretti's elegy which (in English) evoke the "Wild, dogged, buzzing/Roar of a naked sun." A single verb can at times have the force of a file of adjectives: Robinson's Richard Cory "Glittered when he walked," Yeats's rough beast "Slouches toward Bethlehem to be born." Also a single noun: Herrick indites the "liquefaction" of Julia's clothes.

Such images, with their unalterable rightness, exemplify Aristotle's observation that "a good metaphor implies an intuitive perception of the similarity in dissimilars." No better statement has ever been made despite all attempted improvements: that a metaphor (for example) is a comparison for presenting resemblances or differences; an analogy for stressing attributes or resemblances; a juxtaposition of hitherto separate elements; that it is tension; fusion; and so on. Some of these definitions include not only intuitive perceptions but commonplace comparisons and analogies of everyday discourse. A speaker joins two familiar elements so as to make one of them more emphatic or certain ("then you come to a hairpin curve"; "the next thing you will do will be something like this: . . ."). In general these comparisons or illustrations, with their practical purpose, add nothing that is striking or new. Essentially visual aids to understanding, once used they can promptly be forgotten—unlike an imaginative metaphor, which tends to cling on, whose fused elements sternly resist separation. Writers quite naturally emphasize the inexplicable, organic, the spontaneous aspects. The poetic metaphor is "a powerful image, new for the mind, [produced] by bringing together without comparison two distant realities whose relationships (*rapports*) have been grasped by the mind alone" (Pierre Reverdy). A poetic metaphor is "the use of material images to suggest immaterial relationships" (Ernest Fenellosa). It is "the expression of a complex idea, not by analysis, nor by direct statement, but by a sudden perception of an objective relation" (Herbert Read).

That some metaphors are poetic whereas others are not, no one questions. Function in itself, however, cannot make the distinction, relevant though it sometimes is—for example, to Augustan verse, with its abundance of low-keyed figures that clarify and compare; point up a moral or a satire; describe, contemplate, reason, embellish, explain. Dante also makes wide use of low-keyed figures which also clarify and compare. The 15th canto of *Inferno* has a well-known example:

Already we had got so far from the wood that I should not have seen where it was if I had turned backward, when we met a troop of souls who were coming alongside the bank, and each looked at us as men look at one another under a new moon at dusk, and they puckered their brows on us like an old tailor on the eye of his needle.

After experiencing this passage even through literal translation, a reader will find it difficult to visualize this crowd except as peering in the dim light, each member knitting his brows "like an old tailor on the eye of his needle." The metaphor (technically an extended simile) has disclosed a sudden perception of a strong objective relationship. The crowd has become transformed by the image. It is no longer a crowd but a particular crowd marked by and bearing the tailor's presence.

A different kind of extended comparison appears in Canto 5 (the frequently cited Paolo and Francesca passage) which introduces the shades of the carnal sinners whirled ceaselessly about in tormenting winds. Lines 46-50 tell what the speaker experienced when he beheld them:

And as the cranes go chanting their lays, making of themselves a long line in the air, so I saw approach with long-drawn wailings shades borne on these battling winds.

The picture of the shades wailing while being borne on the battling winds that torment them is so insistent as to push the image of the cranes to the background. The cranes have not transformed the shades as the peering tailor transformed the crowd. The cranes look out from the background, but they are there and they will not leave the mind of the reader who feels them as disturbing presences which are now no longer separable from the picture of suffering. The joyous sight of the birds singing as they curve through the serenity of the heavens has become part of the grief of the shades. The torment and terror magnify as the image of suffering bears down against the image of bliss. The one can longer be experienced apart from the other.

It is the relationship between the elements in a metaphor that overwhelms any fact of rhetoric or function. Both passages from Dante are comparisons in structure, but they do not act for the purpose of comparing or clarifying. Whether the elements within them press forward or remain in background, they have fused into a viable totality that no longer can be sundered.

The last quatrain of Shakespeare's sonnet 29 closes on a poetic metaphor of another structural kind:

> When in disgrace with fortune and men's eyes
> I all alone beweep my outcast state,
> And trouble deaf heaven with my bootless cries,
> And look upon myself, and curse my fate:
>
> Wishing me like to one more rich in hope,
> Featur'd like him, like him with friends possess'd,
> Desiring this man's art, and that man's scope,
> With what I most enjoy contented least:
>
> Yet in these thoughts myself almost despising,
> Haply I think on thee,—and then my state,
> Like to the lark at break of day arising
> From sullen earth, sings hymns at heaven's gate . . .

The final figure, a small poem in itself, sweeps up with suddenness all that preceded. The speaker's "state" is no longer compared with that of other people, as has been done up to this point; it *becomes* the lark singing hymns at the gate of heaven. "Like" loses its force in the actualization of the image of soaring. The elements blend together in the new con-fusion that names a feeling which cannot be named by other means.

Ordinary, unaffective discourse never calls for language of this kind. Low-keyed arrangements of words suffice. Hence the bald impropriety of imaginative figures of speech in practical situations, for example. Only certain specified modes are acceptable by agreement too clear to need stating, and if someone breaks the rules, communication wavers or halts. Each plane of discourse is its own pattern of expectation, many of which demand only rational utterance. Hence no one is prepared to hear in a commonplace conversation, a newspaper account, or a lecture on politics that the earth now lies "all Danaë to the stars" or anything remotely like it. A nonpoetic figure, however, can be taken in stride, even a farfetched comparison, explanation, or illustration. It will not "fly in the face of reason" as any poetic metaphor by its nature must:

For the elements in the newly perceived objective relation both retain and surrender their integrity. In Wordsworth's

The sea that bares her bosom to the moon

the primary term "sea" evokes the total variety of the meanings it can bring to the reader as does also the second term "that bares her bosom to the moon." At the same time, certain members of these varieties come forward while others recede. Those that come forword prevail to establish the fusion of resemblance; the others establish disparities and, though subordinate in effect on the mind, they also remain there. This amounts to saying that while the reader is affected by the likenesses embodied in the metaphor, the disparities also act within his response.

For I. A. Richards, the peculiar power of a poetic metaphor derives from both kinds of verbal content. Citing "What should such fellows as I do crawling between earth and heaven," he says

When Hamlet uses the word *crawling* its force comes not only from whatever resemblances to vermin it brings in but at least equally from the differences that resist and control influences of their resemblances. The implication there is that man should not so crawl.[5]

Difference of this kind is simply the obverse of the coin of resemblance: a negative asserting of likeness. It is not the kind that can make poetic metaphors fly in the face of reason. Wordsworth's line, to be sure, will not make a reader stop with questions of other meanings of sea—becalmed to a level flatness, tossing with breakers that shoot up in angular waves, and so on. Nor will Eliot's fusion of an abstraction with a concrete object—

> I will show you fear in a handful of dust

—make him ask which dust is referred to—pollen? house dust? a pile sweeping over a road? But, as Richards adds, "In general, there are very few metaphors in which disparities between tenor and vehicle [primary and secondary terms] are not as much operative as the similarities." Quantitive questions aside, in a great many poetic metaphors, disparity exerts a powerful counterpull away from resemblance.

I have cited one instance in passing without looking at this aspect: Tennyson's remarkable line with the figure of Danaë, the beautiful daughter of a king of Argos who had been told by the oracle that she would bear him a son who would kill him. The king imprisoned her in an underground bronze chamber watched over by guards. Its roof remained open to provide her with light and air. Zeus visited her in a shower of gold, embraced her, and in time she gave birth to a son. I have never heard of anyone familiar with the myth who failed to be moved by

> Now lies the earth all Danaë to the stars

and yet there is something incongruous in the womanly figure of earth as a virginal young girl, not to mention the conflict between the image of the underground enclosure in the myth and the infinite expanse of earth under the sky. The reader's mind, however, draws out of a metaphor as little or as much of the disparity as the objective relation demands, and without any straining. For the mind when free to respond cannot help doing two things to whatever confronts it: it connects and it animates. It joins to the object or event or idea, other objects or events or ideas out of all it possesses. It projects on whatever it beholds traits of aliveness analogous to its own and to the organism it is part of.[6] These natural drives do not operate in a void but at a particular time, in a particular place, and under the influence of a particular context of beholding. The courses they take are thus directed by the force of their surroundings into identifications of likeness, unification. The verbal contents of the metaphor that might logically destroy the objective relation simply fall into place.

If this did not happen quite naturally and without strain on the mind, any number of the mixed metaphors found in poetry would fail. What could analytic reason alone make of Milton's

> blind mouths
> That scarce themselves know how to hold a sheep-hook.

How could it, by its widest standards, accept the figure, even when furnished with the plain meanings of the references—to the clergy, corruption, the cleric as pastor-shepherd, and so on? Or the couplet from Hamlet's soliloquy:

> I bridle in my struggling muse with pain
> That longs to launch into a nobler strain.

"Bridle" will not easily combine with "launch," even after logic adduces the necessary creature implied by the second word. Or another kind of figure from Shakespeare which occurs very often, especially in the later plays:

> Was the hope drunk
> Wherein you dress'd yourself? hath it slept since
> And wakes it now, to look so green and pale
> At what it did so freely?

If the mind that responds to a poetic metaphor had to go through the logical steps of visualizing the terms, Shakespeare's

> O how can summer's honey breath hold out
> Against the wreckful siege of battering days

would be rejected as hopelessly mixed. No amount of analytic gymnastics can put it in order. When, as Wellek and Warren admit, "one tries to fit together neatly in one image the battering siege and the breath, one gets jammed up. The figurative movement is rapid and hence elliptical."[7] Perhaps; yet this misses the question. For if the pieces actually are there, it should be possible to fit them together—as of course the mind of the reader, acting upon not logic but the freedom of all its processes, can do. Acting upon a restriction —and with a process that does not think in the mode of thought that thinks in this figure—it fails. As Marlowe's

> Was this the face that launch'd a thousand ships?

would also have to fail—if ordinary logic prevailed in the response to poetry.

Ellipsis pertains not to the mixed but to the telescoped metaphor. Here the tenor and vehicle together do not offer the reader's mind the process of objective relating that took place in the writer's. And when the reader is unable to imagine the intervening omissions, someone else will have to do it for him. So Hart Crane, in response to the questions of the editor of *Poetry*, filled in the ellipses that had mystified her in his lyric "At Melville's Tomb":

> "The dice of drowned men's bones he saw bequeath
> An embassy"

in the first place, by being ground (in this connection only, of course) in little cubes from the bones of drowned men by the action of the sea, and are finally thrown up on the sand, having "numbers" but no identification. These being the bones of dead men who never completed their voyage, it seems legitimate to refer to them as the only surviving evidence of certain messages undelivered, mute evidence of certain things, experiences that the dead mariners might have had to deliver. Dice as a symbol of chance and circumstance is also implied [etc.]

A good many totally untelescoped metaphors, however, can also contain ellipses, but of another kind, which reader (and writer) may forever remain unaware of. In the opening of Shakespeare's 77th sonnet:

> That time of year thou mayst in me behold
> When yellow leaves, or none, or few, do hang
> Upon those boughs which shake against the cold,
> Bare ruin'd choirs where late the sweet birds sang.

The quatrain, one of the finest in the language, has been praised as much for its imagery and sound as for the way by which the "season" is named by three different images of leaves and boughs, which enlarge into the memorable fourth line. Explanation would seem preposterous. Nevertheless, as Press points out:

"Bare ruin'd choirs where late the sweet birds sang" takes on a richer poignancy when we reflect that the England of [Shakespeare's] day was strewn with the wrecks of abbeys and monasteries, their inhabitants martyred, or comfortably ensconced in fat livings, their altars desolated, their music silenced.

All that a reader possesses in his mind is, of course, unknowable; hence a poet cannot tell what will happen there when the lines as he has to write them are given unglossed. For example in a recent poem on the imagined life of Mallarmé:

> Even flesh can be burned
> To the whitenesses of a song.

One of the terms, "whitenesses," calls up an entire aspect of Mallarmé's writings which are themselves metaphors. The lines will bring something to a reader unaware of all that is condensed in the "whitenesses" here combined with "burned" and "song," but he will not experience what a reader familiar with these referents in the career of Mallarmé will be able to hear or see.

Nevertheless, it is everything that a word can call up in a reader that finally determines for him the meanings of individual words in themselves and in relation to the others. I say "can" call up because the meanings he possesses before entering into the poem are fated to undergo some changes and enlargement developed by the suggestions of context. As he participates in the poem, he can respond with all his capacities: to what the words evoke and express as both rational and emotive utterances, since they can never be wholly one or the other in a discourse which arises from and draws upon the freedom of the mind's processes. Changed and enlarged signification results inevitably from the ways by which the presences bodied forth become known. But not exclusively in a poem and not exclusively to a reader of poetry. A person who reads none at all participates in a related way whenever he dreams.

Condensation (*Verdichtung*)

Frederick Clarke Prescott, a literary scholar, first published his thought on this subject in 1912 in the *Journal of Abnormal Psychology*, to expand it ten years later as part of his comprehensive work on *The Poetic Mind*. Basing his study on Freud's description of "dream work," he pointed to similarities in the ways by which the language in poetry and the pictures in dream condense. Both are "overdetermined," that is, overloaded with meanings, with a variety of references which embody meanings too elusive to identify and ultimately impossible to talk about clearly. If dreams tend to condense into a single picture a multiplicity of references *ignoring the limitations imposed by the demands of logic,* poetry tends to do the same thing. (The astonishing extent to which it can do so is apparent in the sources J. L. Lowes tracked down in *The Road to Xanadu*.) The italicized phrase of Freud's is the ground of the relation: both poem and dream condense by processes wholly alien to analytic thought.

Freud's (German) word for condensation, Prescott carefully remarked, "encloses" the word for poetry. The French psychoanalyst Jacques Lacan, however, goes further:

The *Verdichtung*, or condensation, is the structure of the superimposition of signifiers, which is the field of metaphor, and its very name, condensing in itself the word *Dichtung* [poetry], shows how the process is connatural with the mechanism of poetry to the point that it actually envelops its traditional function.[8]

Prescott illustrates the principle of condensation with a line from the "Eve of St. Agnes." The figure is technically ordinary enough (neither telescoped nor mixed), yet, as he says, it has probably given critics as much trouble as any other in the work of Keats. It represents Madeline, in "her soft and chilly nest," as

Clasp'd like a missal where swart paynims pray.

Leigh Hunt explains it as "Clasp'd like a missal in a land of pagans, —that is to say, where Christian prayer books must not be seen, and are, therefore, doubly cherished for the danger." Another critic, calling it wrong to make "clasp'd" mean "clasp'd to the bosom," claims the true meaning to be "fastened with a clasp." Another: "Clasp'd missal may be allowed to suggest holiness which the prayers of swart paynims neglect." Still another: "Missal, a prayer book bearing upon its margin pictures of converted heathen in the act of prayer." Finally: Jules Jusserand: "A string of beautiful words, suggesting, at most, a meaning rather than having any."

I should think [writes Prescott] most if not all of the puzzled annotators were right, including the last. At least the line has all the meanings that an intelligent and imaginative reader, if not a puzzled annotator, will attach to it. The precise critic will of course note that in this line Keats first wrote "shut like a missal," and that this is final as to the meaning of "clasp'd." But the matter is not quite so simple. The fact that Keats tried this line in three different ways before he settled on the text in question shows that he wrote it, as indeed he did this whole passage, with thought and care. Why, then, did he change the original "shut" to "clasp'd"? Partly perhaps because he wanted "shut" for the last line of the stanza but partly also because "shut" is here a prosaic rather than a poetic word. "Clasp'd" not only says all that "shut" would say; but secondly it goes better with "missal," to fit the mediaeval character of the piece and to "suggest holiness"; and thirdly it admits the very meaning of "held closely and tenderly," which Leigh Hunt was too much of a poet to miss. "Clasp'd" was adopted by Keats, in other words, precisely because it meant two or three things instead of one, and was accordingly more suggestive and poetical.[9]

Note the last sentence: precisely because it has condensed two or three meanings into one and is accordingly more poetically evocative. As Prescott points out in prescriptive fashion, "Whereas in true prose words should have one meaning and one meaning only, in true poetry they should have as many meanings as possible, and the more the better, as long as these are true to the images in the poet's mind."

There is more to be said of condensation, and not only in a poetic metaphor but equally in the irreducible units of a poem:

Each image seen by the poet's imagination is a *complex of many images* and tends to involve the associations—thoughts and feelings—of each of these constituents, so that the language of any poem recording this imagination has many roots in the poet's mind; and therefore this language and *even each word* of it has not single, but manifold meaning and implication. [my italics]

For these meanings "run on into the manifold meanings which are beyond analysis, and," he is careful to add, "the latter are the commonest." Taking the apparently simple

> We are such stuff
> As dreams are made on; and our little life
> Is rounded with a sleep.

he considers it

useless to analyze the meaning of such lines. Dreams are surrounded by sleep; and likewise our brief life is surrounded by the greater sleep, which is constantly compared by poets to the lesser one. But is life also *rounded out* and fulfilled by this sleep? And does life go on in this seeming oblivion, as dreams may go on in what seems dreamless slumber? The expression is beyond the understanding, but it goes on sounding in the imagination. . . . The principle applies to all expressions of the imagination—to every word of poetic value in every imaginative poem.

Which is to say, to every working unit in every authentic poem.

Condensation, however, accounts for more than the dream-like reasoning-reasonableness of these units within their context. It points to their emotional power. It explains why analytic thought cannot go far in tracking down their meanings—"one has only to listen to poetry to hear a true polyphony emerge," says Lacan. Condensation does still more. It denotes the nature and the burden of a poem as an appeal to the mind, hence also the imaginativeness in which it asks to be experienced. For the poem as a whole is a metaphor of an all-enclosing kind, condensing all the elements, large and small, that existed apart, to identify a newly enclosing relationship, one which is memorable and meaningful in the same way that individual metaphors are meaningful and, ultimately, every unit of expression within the poem: through manifold meaning, reference, and implication.

The statement is cumbersome, attempting as it does a comprehensive view of how condensation applies to all poems. For if Lacan is right, if *Verdichtung* is connatural with the processes of poetry, then it provides the master key. But each poem is a door and each door has a different lock.

Simpler statements tend to generalize at arm's length, all figurative language being metaphor in essence. There are, moreover, pithy sentences about the "purposes" served. One of the best was minted by Frost: "Poetry provides the one permissible way of saying one thing and meaning another." (As it stands it is large enough to apply to allegory and fable also.) I shall return to this sentence with a question, for at this point some other refining is in order, since I have been using "metaphor" and "image" and similar terms interchangeably and all as imaginative figures.

A comprehensive view of metaphor takes in its extra-literary range: "All nature," says Emerson, "is a metaphor of the human mind." If the maxim is valid, we should find metaphor in all expressions of the mind—and of course we do, for language is ultimately traceable to metaphor, as writers since Vico and Shelley keep discovering. One has only to break up such a word as "symbol" (*syn*: together + *ballein*: to throw) to know the physical relationship out of which they arose. For most people most words are metaphorically dead, not only etymology's transferred abstractions (often a marvel to behold) but the everyday pictures they talk with —"mouth of a river," "arm of a chair," and so on. Such metaphors are as invisible to their users as the strikingly imaginative creations of unknown Miltons. But however vibrant "going off half-cocked," "Dry up!," or "Get lost!" may reappear to an innocent eye, they do not perform as metaphors do in a poem. Tossed back and forth and never seen, they are lifeless coins.[10]

The domain of images, though appropriated by psychology, spreads wider than any science could contain, even one that takes in man's entirety. As for its native extent within poetry, it is enough to nod at the "types" into which they supposedly divide, adding to the proverbial five all sorts of refinement, such as pressure, color, temperature, and reminding ourselves that synesthesia is a given within a biological universe which thinks and feels by likenesses. For a likeness is all that an image can be; it is never exact. Edith Sitwell's "The morning light creaks" implies and demands no more than does "a sweet voice" (that a reader can taste a sound).[11]

"Every spontaneous image," a psychologist informs us, "is to some extent symbolical."[12] By blurring distinctions, the statement clarifies, for metaphor, symbol, and image run into one another. "One cannot long discuss imagery without sliding into symbolism," says

Kenneth Burke; "We shift from the image of an object to its symbolism as soon as we consider it." Why, then, separate them? The reason may seem arbitrary since "symbol" has simply come to denote something more significant than the other two because of the frequency with which it appears in a writer's work. "Strange fire," says Tate, is Poe's "leading visual symbol." "Caves," says Yeats, is a "ruling symbol" in Shelley's. To some readers, however, great recurrence may seem mainly an obsession which the poet was unable to resolve (the clock for Vigny, for example); to others, his fascination by a specific significance he could never seize yet continued to reach for. Thus a symbol may rule in dissimilar ways. For Baudelaire, the word "vast" often stands for the "infinity of infinite space," says Bachelard, at other times for "the highest degree of synthesis." Some writers make a great point of their symbols (Mallarmé, Bridges, Yeats). Others show no such need: the largeness is there in the presence of Moby-Dick, in the settings of Poe's stories, in the characters of the later Henry James.

Of the assertive force of a symbol, I know no plainer example than "The Idea of Order at Key West." The reader soon realizes that Stevens' girl singing by the sea is more that a metaphor, and the singing as well. The girl and the song and the sea rise up as symbols—the girl as singer-poet, the song as verse, the sea as the source, the life from which song rises.[13]

Phases of Totality

If poetry by its metaphorical character says one thing and means another, what composes its "body"? Luckily we can see all we need of the poem's anatomy without murdering to dissect. Its body, as we never tire of disclosing, is made of words, and each word speaks with incomparably more than the unambiguous denotation that science seeks in its terminology. But the words are not the linguistic units and a poem may contain propositions, questions, statements, exclamations, and other expressive groups which when read outside or in isolation prove very like prose. It goes without stressing that a poem may also—and commonly does—contain images, similes, metaphors, symbols, and other figurative expressions *as well as* propositions, questions, statements, exclamations, which in or out of context are unmistakably imaginative.

Not all expressions of this order appear in every poem. Not even figures are needed. Not a single figure can be found in all 69 lines of Wordsworth's "We Are Seven." The only passage that might be called heightened occurs in the opening stanza:

> Her hair was thick with many a curl
> That clustered round her head.

But the heightening, if such it be, is followed by a dialogue so plainly textured as to exemplify what Mark Van Doren in another connection calls a "poetry of statement." Figurative language is absent from Bridges' "I love all beauteous things." Not a single metaphor can be found in a great many excellent Chinese poems; in the following, by Emperor Wu-ti, for example:

> The sound of her silk skirt has stopped.
> On the marble pavement dust grows.
> Her empty room is cold and still.
> Fallen leaves are piled against the doors.
>
> Longing for that lovely lady
> How can I bring my aching heart to rest?

The ubiquitousness of metaphors and similes in Western verse makes them seem indispensable, yet they seldom appear in the great body of Scottish ballads. They do not appear at all in a number of recent admired poems—such as W. C. Williams' "The Red Wheelbarrow" or H. D.'s "Lethe"—or in the masterpiece of Cavafy, "Waiting for the Barbarians." In Wu-ti's poem, each "picture" acts as a term of a multiple fusion, and much the same can be said of non-figurative verse in general. Each such poem is a total unification formed of smaller unifications. Through its fusions of resemblance, it identifies a relational unity, producing the effect of figures but without their presence.

Turning now from a poem's materials to their sequence, we note at once that they move in the "more than usual order" that Coleridge proclaimed and everyone echoes. And how could such arrangement of words appear otherwise alongside the predictable, step-by-step manner by which common sense logic tries to order its ideas. Even in poems that develop propositions, dis-order bristles. One might suppose, then, that some analogous principle had been found to encompass the multiplicity of alogical ways in which poetry arranges words. Nothing that has been proposed tells us more than what poems do *not* do—which we have known all along. And the only other offered truth invokes "unalterableness"!

Any hope of discovering an all-inclusive "order" evaporates in analyzing a handful of varied poems, such as Marvell's "To His Coy Mistress," Wordsworth's *Prelude*, Shelley's "Ode to the West Wind," *Hamlet*, *Paradise Lost*. The internal arrangement of each is as unique as the word-materials with which it emerges. The order is there, but only as an attribute projected by looking at a poem with order in mind. It is there, to be sure, but as an outcome.

Of what? Of an over-all logic that controls all elements in all poems? If so, what type of elements? Such things as, for example, in *The Ancient Mariner:* subject matter (a specific ocean voyage), theme (call it crime), sonal pattern (of recurrent meter and rime), and further meaning (implied rather than stated)? These are elements we elect to draw out of the totality embodied by the language. Does some all-inclusive logic hold it together? Do the words hold themselves together? When we look at a number of poems, we find as many subject matters, themes, sonal patterns, further meanings, and orders, as there are poems—and as many logics. To see *how* differently each poem does *what* it does, one has only to look closely at a random few—one expressing a state of mind that moves from despairing confusion toward clarity and hope (Shelley's "Ode to the West Wind"), another from distress or despair to an emotional resolution (*Lycidas*), a third that proceeds by argument (Marvell's "To His Coy Mistress"), a fourth by narration (*The Ancient Mariner*), a fifth by exposition (Pope's *Essay on Man*), and so on and on . . .[14]

Despite, if not because of, such manifest dissimilarity, writers, critics, and readers have maintained that one all-subsuming law or logic must exist. Coleridge learned from his headmaster that "Poetry, even of the loftiest, and, seemingly, that of the wildest odes, had a logic of its own, as severe as that of science. . . ." Kant, in his study of art, had already proposed an analogy to "an organised product of nature in which every part is reciprocally purpose (end) and means." But, as Meyer H. Abrams points out, Kant's immensely influential contribution was qualified by the author himself as "merely a philosophy of as-if." It is a compelling fact that none of the assertions of the existence of an all-subsuming logic defines what it is. Its failure to be born is at least suggestive. The nearest we come to a definition is in Coleridge's remarkable description of varied characteristics:

This power . . . reveals itself in the balance or reconciliation of opposite or discordant qualities: of sameness, with difference; of the general, with the concrete; the idea, with the image; the individual, with the representative; the sense of novelty and freshness, with old and familiar objects; a more than usual state of emotion, with more than usual order. . . .

Readers to whom Hegel is more than a name may not instantly think of the German philosopher despite the associations (which Abrams also points out) between the "reconciliation of opposite or discordant qualities" and the Hegelian triad of thesis-antithesis-synthesis. If any association arises in the poetry-reader's mind, it will no doubt be with metaphor, "opposite or discordant" recalling Aristotle's "dissimilars."

To follow the results of this passage from Coleridge is to be taken far from the logic that Coleridge affirmed. To follow Elizabeth Sewell, for example, is to learn that the organization of language in poetry is dual in a different way. Sounds are affected in one manner, meanings in another. To be more precise, the organization of what she calls the "sound-look" of words is in the direction of order, the organization of their "reference" in the direction of disorder. These are the discordant opposites that the language of poetry expresses simultaneously. "The aim of poetry is to create from Language a closed relation system by resolution of the two forces of order and disorder . . . by utilizing each so that each may cancel the other out and a momentary equilibrium be formed." We are deep in the woods of structure, whose infinitely varied growths invite us to gaze and gaze, forgetting what brought us there. . . . And we have yet to locate *the* logic. Can it be found somewhere in a composite of all the ways in which good poems think? Perhaps. In any event, we shall never know, because all the possible "ways" cannot be flushed out of the too many good poems in the world.

We can, however, add to "condensation," discussed earlier, three other unignorable ways. Like condensation, they are familiars of the world of dream and just as alien to practical thought.

A poem can establish the significance of something merely by presenting it, and the reader, without an instant's doubting, will respond to its presence as both knowledge and feeling though nothing is argued to prove the twofold import. Presence in itself is enough, in poem as in dream. Perhaps, as Whitehead believes, "the sheer statement of what things are, may contain elements explanatory of why things are." Whatever the explanation, such assertion in the poem amounts to proof.

This happens even when accompanying words deny the presence, as in Keats's

> The sedge is withered from the lake,
> And no birds sing.

The reader experiences a presence not only in the first of these lines but also in the second, for the "no" cannot stop him from feeling and knowing what the negation tries to remove. "No birds sing," however, is not the same presence as that embodied by "And birds sing." The "no" casts a darkening veil which, as it were, causes the presence to recede—to recede in brightness, not to disappear; for it remains there, fully visible, its veiled significance bodied forth by the negative naming. Such strangely affecting presence cannot be evoked except in a poem and by the poem's power to place it there while saying it is not there.

A poem can present even polar-opposite embodiments—of love-with-hate, of joy-with-sadness—and the watcher will take from them meanings not otherwise understood. As the world knows, the nightly occurrence of such presences led Freud in his study of dreams to a thesis of ambivalence. But the "inseparableness" of opposites is no recent discovery as a principle. "In the seasons of the year, in the life of plants, in the human body, and above all in civil society," Plato had remarked, "excessive action results in a violent transformation into its opposite." Shelley said somewhere that love is the reverse side of hate. At times roughly analogous terms are used by scientists for phenomena in the physical world. But uniquely for the world of the poem, in the reader's response some degree of ambivalence colors every feeling; for in that world a feeling comes forward in freedom as *whole*. One of its selves bodies forth some sense of its opposite—much as "And no birds sing" comes forth as a whole, its self with its opposing self, though not always strangely veiled.

Other characteristic ways of the imagination might perhaps be added, but this composite is inclusive enough—condensation; asserting by merely presenting; evoking while negating; ambivalence. With discursive ingenuity, one might draw out of it some definition of Poetic Logic. But what purpose could it serve? Would it add to what we know? That *the* logic is metaphorical? As much demands to be declared of everything else, however present, in any authentic poem; even of those words which if spoken outside or alone could affect us as prose. Hence a poem is not only a grand, all-encompassing image "composed" by individual images but a self-containing field of reciprocal forces in which each element is suffused with and suffuses metaphoric influence. This condition bears witness to the transformation that occurs within what is seen from outside as a framed-in universe of an extraordinary sort. It explains why the relation there among words changes as they quicken one another, and why they pulsate with interresponding, intensifying life. Only when we keep steadily in mind such simultaneously quickening forces can we be willing to characterize a poem with our inevitably static term "metaphoric totality"—and to speak again of an all-enclosing metaphor that produces a new relationship out of elements hitherto existing apart, one that is memorable and meaningful in the way that individual poetic metaphors are meaningful: by "saying one thing and meaning another." (The foregoing sentences, like our earlier ones on condensation [p. 97], are cumbersome, finical; but to write down even the comprehensive little that may surely be said of a poem and to convey its indispensable at-onceness would require a book-long sentence.)

The words quoted earlier from Frost—"Poetry provides the one permissible way of saying one thing and meaning another"—has been something of a refrain in the last pages, crying out that the poem is a symbol, not more. Yet for the reader, both during and after it has said one thing while meaning another, the poem-as-a-presence remains. It has not been lost or submerged or destroyed in the meaning of the symbol. It is steadfastly there as a structure for contemplation, knowledge, pleasure, surprise: an artifact of words that stand before the eyes and sound within the ear. If one wishes to think of the two as the presence "within" that is meaning and the presence "without" that is saying, the Frost refrain enlarges into symbol-and-more. In any event, every poem will be saying one thing while meaning another thing and also *itself*.[15]

Or, brushing aside these remarks and thinking of the presences as feeling-knowledge, we can take one kind from the meanings of the sayings and another from those of the artifact. Two inseparable presences, then, and reciprocally alive. But not forever, surely not in a reader's forever. The words of even a profoundly affecting poem may with time diminish into memory, whereas some part of their meaning will remain in the reader as an embodiment into which they change. Poetry, says MacLeish, "gives knowledge of the chaos and confusion of the world by imposing order upon it which leaves it still the chaos and confusion which it really is," yet some sense of that order may have entered the reader, leaving upon him a trace or a wound. With poems of slight emotional meaning for him, the trace may diminish and lose force. Poems of profound emotional impact, on the other hand, may so "wound" him as to make him thereafter perceive related experiences of the chaos and confusion with altered sight. The experiences evoked by the poem, thus incorporated, will if sustained as embodiment alter his living response. And the words that gave birth to this event for his mind may recede as the change they fostered emerges as the "real" poem. I can best document these statements by my own "Poetry: The Art," subtitled "In the form of an Apostrophe to Whitman." At the time of its writing I was unaware that Whitman had said: "The words of my book nothing, the drift of it every thing."

The "Incompatible" Forces

Of the various actions that a poem is said to resemble, the closest is a mode of dramatized-speaking-to-some-other, involving an object, an event; a time, a place, a condition. Neither speaker nor listener plays a role. Rather the poem's presences form the characters created for self-enactment within the reader. There they spring to life as an interior drama of human feelings and values, and there the meanness or richness of the coming alive but partly depends on the poem. I mention this evident limitation not only because of the differences among what each reader possesses and is, but equally because of those within the same reader, varying as they do with mood, place, and with time as it ceaselessly widens or narrows his capacities for response. So it is no tricking up of Heraclitus to say that the same person can never step into the same poem twice. The poem is unchanged, the person is not. Yet while the poem itself remains identical, in the reader it relives as innumerably varied experiences. " 'Cap and Bells,' " Yeats said, "has always meant a great deal to me though . . . it has not always meant quite the same thing."

Though the powers inhering in an authentic poem assault and compel the well-attuned reader with manifold meanings, when you ask him to say all that they are he throws up his hands. If pressed, he may start telling how the poem makes him feel, even why; but his description soon bumbles, as it must. The facilities of discursive language can take him to a point, not beyond. The subject flies out of hand; this hand lacks the organs to contain it. Yet something remains in its grasp which suggests what has fled. The poem "still seems to be trying to express something beyond itself," as A. C. Bradley observed long ago. Its meaning seems "to expand into something boundless which is only focused in it,"[16] nor can its creator explain what it is. Goethe could not tell Eckermann what the "idea" of *Faust* was: "As if I knew, as if I myself could tell! From Heaven, through Earth, down to Hell,—there's an explanation, if you want one; but that is not the idea, that's the development of the action." So Blake might have replied about the "idea" of his four-line "Auguries of Innocence," much also as the Greek poets whom Plato had addressed in vain. For every authentic poem, as Jacques Maritain aptly remarks, "will make present to our eyes, together with itself, something else, and still something else indefinitely, in the infinite mirrors of analogy." I take this final word in its widest implication, recalling Bacon's great remark on "the footsteps of nature" and Anaxagoras' (as quoted by Lucretius): "everything is latently involved in everything else." I take it also in the sense of Eliot's reflection on "the song of one bird" and other humble subjects, where he says that "such memories may have symbolic value, but of what we cannot tell, for they come to represent depths of feeling into which we cannot peer." We are urged to magnify our widest conception of the subtleties and ranges of the human organism's response and to accept our limitations as we search them.

From the foregoing pages and the examples we have followed, a number of observations emerge as virtual axioms. Poetry, far from being a field of discourse governed by a single aspect of the mind— far from being "emotive" or "alogical," for example—is an open area, the human mind unbounded, the only field of discourse in which thought can participate in its entirety. Poetry draws thus on the fullness of man, enveloping all partial capacities of his thought. It is as though its modes when waking and when dreaming are present with all their potentialities ready to participate in the object, the event, the ideas embodied in the words.[17] As in the miniscule "Full Fathom Five," the mind of the reader shifts effortlessly back and forth from the most commonplace to the most exalted, from the most palpable to the most fantastic, and at intermediate levels. My analogy here to polarity is, as always, inadequate. More faithful is a picture of breadth, fullness, and not with contrasting extremes but, as I have taken pains to emphasize, a plurality of possible modes of thought existing together in harmonious, unimpeded participation. It is the miracle of the mind that when it thinks as it does in poetry —whether in creating or responding—it operates upon the freedom of all these processes, moving easefully, naturally, from one to another as it discovers the presences that mark its voyages.

We have come full circle back to the fragments of verse with which we began. But the linguist's term may now be replaced as we ask the question implicit in the last few pages. Do "rational" and "emotive" utterances retain any degree of "ordinariness" and "extraordinariness" when they are read *within* their contexts? To say that they do—to insist that every line within a poem is at one and the same time filled with both ordinary and extraordinary meanings— might seem to deprive poetry of its claims as "imaginative discourse."

It is the narrow conception of such a term that creates the confusion; for even the most imaginative figure of speech retains, in addition to its utterly unparaphraseable meanings, many traces of ordinary signification. "Ripeness is all," "Mine, O thou lord of life, send my roots rain!", "How can we know the dancer from the dance?"—you cannot read such imaginative passages, which send out endless subtleties of evocation, without also having a sense of what they mean on the most ordinary plane of understanding. For the human creature when confronted with anything strange—and these passages are supremely strange—instantly, almost by a reflex of the organism, begins to assimilate it to the known, to his world of the familiar; to make ordinary meanings from the messages. Humankind, unable to bear much uncertainty, must relate them to what it knows.

This is not to say anything more than that both ordinary and extraordinary meanings are present in poetry simultaneously and in the same passages. If you prefer, you may say that "ordinariness" is tied to the "actual,"[18] and the "extraordinariness" to everything else. But whatever the terms for these two significations, their presence accounts for the difficulty of saying what poetry is. For if it can be said to be anything at all, poetry is a complex of seemingly incompatible forces of meaning that are nevertheless quite compatible—forces to which we respond without any concern for the fact that the poem is simultaneously both actual and non-actual, real and imaginary, that *it makes both common and uncommon sense together*. This is not to say that in the poem the two can exist on a parity. Ordinary meanings are limitable whereas we cannot even begin to define the ranges of shape, substance, suggestion, and evocation that arise from passages which evoke the worlds of the extraordinary.[19] Moreover, I am not suggesting that the two modes of meaning in poetry can in any sense exist separately. As A. C. Bradley might have put it, any such separable aspects of a poem lie only in our analytic heads—which is equally the only place where "form" and "content," for example, might be said to exist. But just as you cannot talk of how a poem or any other work of art is formed without also talking of what is being formed, ordinary and extraordinary meaning exist as a seamless phenomenon. Finally, there is no possibility of seeing any modes of meaning as acting on the reader in any ratios of their forces. They are simply both there together forming part of the sum of the meanings experienced in any authentic poem, along with meanings of sound, of the bodily mimicry, and others, which depend on the time and the nature of the reader. One can never go far in enumerating all the forces of meaning that a good poem is. Nor need anyone try.

Complex and multiple though they are, all the types of meaning touched on in the foregoing pages nevertheless constitute only one order of human experience: the one that a human being lives as a part of the culture he has evolved, seeing himself and his experiences within the terms of this culture. All such meanings, therefore, arise out of the relationships and resemblances of feelings, ideas, objects, events embodied in the poem to those he encounters and knows in this world he has made in which he moves. There is, however, another order of meaning mediated by every authentic poem. It derives, not from the relationship between the embodiments of the words and his ongoing human existence, but from the way in which the poem structures language. This action draws us into areas of man's existence as a creature inhabiting the earth. It forms the subject of Part II, which follows.

NOTES AND COMMENTS

1. I do not think that language possesses such sharply distinct types of meaning or function; on the contrary. But for my purposes here, the two categories are more manageable than any other. ("[T]here is no ground for assurance that the most rational-sounding utterance is without emotive content, or vice versa."—L. B. Salomon, *Semantics and Common Sense*, Holt, 1966, p. 103.) My division reflects the so-called linguistic dualism which, though an improvement on the too cognitive, too intellectual traditional view of language, has itself been rejected by those favoring a quite untraditional linguistic monism and by others who move toward a linguistic dualism. See *Language, Thought, Culture*, Paul Henle, Ann Arbor, University of Michigan Press, 1965, p. 122 and Ch. 6. • Almost all the fragments are from well-known poems. Others: 6, Stickney; 12, Hardy; 13, Rilke; 17, Hopkins; 21, Stevens; 23, Browning; 28, 32, 37, Eliot; 41, Pound.

2. See Hans Reichenbach, *The Rise of Scientific Philosophy*, California, 1953, Chap. 11, especially pp. 168-176. Speaking of the myths of

the gods of Egypt in the great age of the Pyramids (2700-2250 B.C.), J. A. Wilson says: "From our modern point of view they might also seem to be self-contradictory. . . . For example, the creation story was told in several different ways. . . . These varying explanations of the same act were not felt to be inconsistent; rather, they strengthened the concept. . . . Osiris became the dying god and the god of the dead because (a) he was drowned in the Nile and thus was identified with its annual renewal in the flood period, or (b) because he was cut into pieces and strewn around the land by his wicked brother Seth and thus shared in the annual revivification of every part of Egypt, or (c) because he was smothered in a wooden chest by Seth and this was caught in a tree, so that he thus became identified with plant life and its annual rebirth. If you are not arbitrary, these different myths converge and are the same."—*At the Dawn of Civilization*, E. A. Speiser, ed., New Brunswick, N. J., Rutgers University Press, 1964, pp. 285-286.

3. See Claude Lévi-Strauss, *The Savage Mind* (a misleading translation of *La Pensée sauvage*), Chicago, 1966; Yale French Studies Nos. 36-37, pp. 41-65 and *passim;* "Structuralism," by Peter Caws, *Partisan Review*, Winter 1968. Sentence quoted from Lévi-Strauss's book: p. 268. See also p. 269: "The physical world is approached from opposite ends [etc.]" • Lucien Lévy-Bruhl, *How Natives Think* (*Les Fonctions mentales dans les sociétés inférieures*, 1910), introd. by Ruth L. Bunzel, pp. xi ff. • "The complete freedom and independence of vision of primeval art has never since been attained. It was its distinguishing characteristic. In our sense, there was no up and no down, no above and no below. Whether an animal appeared in a vertical position or in any other position was irrelevant to the eye of prehistoric man. Nor was there a clear distinction or separation of one object from another. . . . Violent juxtaposition in size as well as in time were accepted as a matter of course."—Siegfried Giedion, *The Eternal Present*, Washington, D.C., Mellon Lectures, 1957.

4. Suzanne K. Langer, *Mind: An Essay on Human Feeling*, Johns Hopkins, 1967, vol. 1. • ". . . our thoughts . . . are indeed the representatives of all our past feelings."—Wordsworth. • Croce remarks that the *Divine Comedy* is made up of not only poetry but also theology, pseudoscience, etc.; Mark Van Doren discusses a "poetry of statement," in his *John Dryden*, Bloomington, Indiana University Press, 1960, pp. 82 ff.

5. Richards continues: ". . . similarities. Some similarity will commonly be the ostensive ground of the shift, but the peculiar modification of the tenor which the vehicle brings about is even more the work of their unlikenesses than of their likenesses." *The Philosophy of Rhetoric*, Oxford, 1936. Norman Friedman defines Richards' tenor as "the purpose or general drift of thought regarding the subject of the metaphor" and vehicle as that "which serves to embody the tenor as the analogy brought to the subject."

6. See pp. 267 f.

7. References here and on the next pages: René Wellek and Austin Warren, *Theory of Literature*, Baltimore, Penguin Books, Inc., 1963, p. 202; Hart Crane, *Poetry*, Oct. 1926; John Press, *The Fire and the Fountain*, p. 172; "Even flesh . . .": Stanley Burnshaw, "The Hero of Silence," *Lugano Review*, Summer 1965.

8. "What in the dream appears as compromise and is explained in terms of overdetermination appears in the work of art as multiplicity of meaning, which stimulates differentiated types of response in the audience."—Kris, *op. cit.*, p. 25. Jacques Lacan in *Yale French Studies*, Sept. 1966, p. 129.

9. F. C. Prescott, *The Poetic Mind*, Macmillan, 1922, pp. 169 ff. I disagree with Prescott's statement that this is "final" as to the meaning of "clasp'd": nothing is "final" for the reader, as Prescott himself emphasizes.

10. Chesterton: "All slang is metaphor, and all metaphor is poetry."

11. Compare: Milton's "con-fusion" of senses in:

a soft and solemn-breathing sound
Rose like a steam of rich-distilled perfumes,
And stole upon the air.

12. Charles Baudoin, *Psychoanalysis and Aesthetics*, Dodd, Mead & Company, 1924, p. 28; Kenneth Burke, *Attitudes Toward History*, *New Republic*, 1937, vol. 2, pp. 154-5. Tate: "Poe's strange fire. . . . You will see it in the eye of the Raven; in 'an eye large, liquid, and luminous beyond comparison' of Roderick Usher; . . . in 'Those eyes! those large, those shining, those divine orbs,' of the Lady Ligeia." • Jean-Paul Weber, noting the frequent occurrence of a clock in Vigny's writing, "for confirmation, turns to biography and uncovers its source in an early traumatic event. . . . Weber finds in eight authors similar key themes, and adds to this number in his second [book]."—Laurent Le-Sage, *The French New Criticism*, University Park, Penna., State University Press, 1967, p. 18; see also pp. 149 ff. Gaston Bachelard, *The Poetics of Space*, The Orion Press, 1964, p. 191.

13. But according to Harvey Gross, "The singer represents the mind which creates the reality it contemplates—the imagination which orders the world into being, knowledge, and, ultimately, value."—*Sound and Form in Modern Poetry*, Michigan, 1964, pp. 239-240.

14. Personal communication from M. H. Abrams to me. Coleridge quotations from *Biographia Literaria*, Oxford, vol. II. References are to M. H. Abrams, *The Mirror and the Lamp*, Oxford, 1953; Elizabeth Sewell, *The Structure of Poetry*, Scribner, 1952, p. 85.

15. ". . . the poetic symbol is not merely employed but enjoyed; its value is not entirely instrumental but largely aesthetic, intrinsic."—Philip Wheelwright, *Kenyon Review*, 1940, pp. 263 ff.

16. See A. C. Bradley, "Poetry for Poetry's Sake" in his *Oxford Lectures on Poetry*, Oxford, 1909.

17. Poetry draws on the fullness of man because poetry is made of speech whereas the other arts are not. And it is into poetry's mode of discourse—into "the open area, the human mind unbounded" that we must bring the classic questions: "mind vs. body," "free will vs. determinism." Dualisms of this order arise out of a conception of the human mind as consisting of only one "part" of all that it actually is. The questions need to be re-situated to accord with the nature of the human organism and in the light of its all-encompassing function: maintaining itself in relation to the world in which it exists. "Mind," as I have said earlier, must be regarded as the totality of processes utilized by the organism for this function which is the prerequisite of all its other functions. Within such a view of mind, free will and determinism cease to be either-ors; they become terms for conceiving certain aspects of human behavior.

18. Marianne Moore's references to the "actual" go so far as to include footnote sources. For Hardy's "In Time of 'The Breaking of Nations,'" the title serves the same purpose. For Yeats's "The Second Coming," the date of its writing.

19. So-called "pure poetry," however conceived, is no exception, for no arrangement of words can deprive them of their ordinary meanings for the mind—whether the poem be pure according to George Moore's or to Henri Bremond's definition; or according to one modern practice which tries to expunge the poem of everything except figures; or another which justifies a poem-as-a-series-of-images-without-links by pointing to the technique of the cinema (forgetting something present in Shakespeare: a train of images that "communicates" mainly by the intervening associations). The drive toward poetic "purity-by-images-only" is the polar opposite of the scientist's passion for purifying terms by stripping each of them of all but a single denotation.

II

Creature-Knowledge

4 · Poetry versus the Culture

Unlike the colors in a painting, the shapes in a sculpture, and the sounds in a musical composition, the words that comprise literature cannot leap the barriers of language. A poem in French offers one kind of poetic experience for a Frenchman and other kinds for people who think in other languages. Nobody seriously disputes this if for no deeper reason than the absence of one-to-one correspondence between the totalities of each word in translation. The barrier does not, of course, affect only creative literature. Necessarily, as Cocteau remarks, "Baudelaire's prose, like Montaigne's, is unfortunately untranslatable because like all beautiful prose, it depends on inner rhythms, syncopations, soundwaves, and verbal clusters indigenous to the language in which the sentences are written." Even commonplace expressions which one might assume to be interchangeable present difficulties; of some 500 of the words most frequently used in English, each has an average of 28 meanings. There is, however, vastly more to be said about the nature of thinking in one's mother tongue, and nobody has been more zealous than Benjamin Lee Whorf in suggesting why.

Native Language and the Conditioning of Thought

According to his theory of "metalinguistics," since all higher levels of thinking depend upon language, the language a person habitually uses conditions his perception and understanding of the world. As a consequence the picture of the universe shifts from tongue to tongue. It could not be otherwise because the language in which a person speaks and thinks exerts a paramount influence on his behavior, his outlook, and his culture. As for the underlying assumptions on which many actions of individuals are founded:

> We dissect nature along lines laid down by our native languages. The categories and types that we isolate from the world of phenomena we do not find there because they stare every observer in the face; on the contrary, the world is presented in a kaleidoscopic flux of impression which has to be organized by our minds—and this means largely by the linguistic systems in our minds. We cut nature up, organize it into concepts, and ascribe significances as we do, largely because we are parties to an agreement to organize it in this way—an agreement that holds throughout our speech community and is codified in the patterns of our language. The agreement is, of course, an implicit and unstated one, *but its terms are absolutely obligatory;* we cannot talk at all except by subscribing to the organization and classification of data which the agreement decrees.
>
> This fact is very significant for modern science, for it means that no individual *is free to describe nature with absolute impartiality* but is constrained to certain modes of interpretation even while he thinks himself most free.[1]

Even in ordinary conversation the structure of the language exerts a controlling power. "We all hold an illusion about talking," says Whorf:

> an illusion that talking is quite untrammeled and spontaneous and merely "expresses" whatever we wish to have it express. This illusory appearance results from the fact that the obligatory phenomena within apparently free flow of talk are so completely autocratic that the speaker and listener are bound unconsciously as though in the grip of a law of nature.

Whorf's demonstrations together with examples cited by anthropological linguists make illuminating reading for people unaware of the ways in which different languages presumably compel their speakers into taking different views of reality. Since the Hopi language, for example, does not treat time as a flow, a Hopi Indian has less difficulty than an Englishman or a Spaniard in conceiving the Einsteinian view of relativity. As Clyde Kluckhohn observes, you cannot say in Chinese "Answer me yes or no," because Chinese gives priority to "how?" and nonexclusive categories; it has no words for "yes and no." As for the fundamental categories of the verb, in French they are before and after (tense) and potentiality vs. actuality (mood), whereas in one American Indian language (Wintu) they are subjectivity vs. objectivity, knowledge vs. belief, freedom vs. actual necessity. Much smaller peculiarities of linguistic usage are no less revealing; as Kluckhohn remarks:

A whole monograph could well be written on differences in the social structure of European nations as exposed by linguistic habits relating to the second personal pronoun. In France one comes to *tutoyer* few people after adolescence. The familiarity is restricted to immediate relatives and to a few intimate friends. In the German-speaking world, however, a student who did not soon come to use the familiar *Du* with those whom he saw frequently would be regarded as stuffy. In the army of imperial Austria all officers in the same regiment called each other *Du* regardless of rank. Failure to use the familiar form was equivalent to a challenge to a duel. . . . In Spain and Italy the introduction of the *tu* relationship in later life is considerably easier than in France but less frequent than in southern Germany and Austria. In Italy there is the further complication of a special form of respectful address (*Lei*). Choice of *Lei* or the more common formal pronoun became a political issue. The Fascist Party forbade the use of *Lei*. In Sweden also, passions have been aroused over the pronoun *ni* which is used toward those of lower social status. . . .

For anthropologists, linguistic behavior is inseparable from the total behavior of a cultural group. Thus, the lack of "true equivalences between any two languages is merely the outward expression of inward differences between two peoples in premises, in basic categories, in the training of fundamental sensitivities, and in general view of the world." It is not, as Harry Hoijer remarks, "that linguistic patterns limit sensory patterns but that they direct perception and thinking into certain habitual channels." They condition each speaker's ways of constructing the world.

Many linguists, quite expectedly, object to the sweep of Whorf's conclusions. Mario Pei, for example. While agreeing that the structure of language exerts "a compulsive force on the speakers, bending their outlook and activities in one or another direction," Pei emphasizes the question "of degree, which still remains to be proved." Yet he never questions the central fact that "once firmly established, language patterns our thoughts, since they have to be expressed in terms of the available language."

In the light of Young's picture of brain organization, this must be so. Each brain sets up its own characteristic ways of dealing with new situations: these become the rules or laws of its particular behavior. The cortex of every new-born human baby is in this respect a blank sheet of possibilities which becomes organized minute by minute, day by day, in the world that surrounds it. Having discussed the process at length (Chapter 1), I mention it now as confirmation of what Whorf deduced from a different analysis. The language a person learns conditions his ways of thinking because of its magisterial influence in building their rules. One can hardly exaggerate its impact, since "The chief intellectual classifications that constitute the working capital of thought have been built up for us by our mother tongue" (John Dewey). Linguists may object to technicalities in Whorf's demonstrations or to absolutes in his conclusions, but the biology of the brain (as we now know it) rules out any possible alternative. That the vocabulary, structure, and other elements of the language each person has learned to think with are inseparable from his way of perceiving and of acting upon the world is the inevitable outcome of the processes by which his brain creates its own ways of thinking out of the functional remnant of its original endowment and the mothering culture in which it was taught.

Barrier of tongue = barrier of thought? Babel? An endless diversity among languages—yet also the persisting possibility of a single original source: an original genetic relationship followed by long, infinitely complicated mutations. Some 3,000 languages, each of them a unique universe of sounds and structures, are spoken by people who entered the world with virtually the same biological structures for vocalizing, hearing, and associating. And each of these languages is contained not only in a logic of its own but in one that is highly systematized. By no possible stretch of the imagination could any of them be classified as primitive. "The crudest savage," Whorf discovered, "may unconsciously manipulate with effortless ease a linguistic system so intricate, manifoldly systematized, and intellectually difficult, that it requires the lifetime study of our greatest scholars to describe its workings." No wonder Jespersen exclaimed that "learning to speak is the greatest feat in one's life," however civilized or uncivilized the society. For part of man's gift for creating tongues is a gift for complicating them. Moreover, as they evolve, all of them seem to change in similar ways.

Is some unitary principle at work in language behavior? For a number of years the sinologist Erwin Reifler has been noting many semantic parallels with the Chinese.[2] For example, the identical sound in Chinese means both "child" and "pupil of the eye," and exactly the same phenomenon occurs in a large number of unrelated languages. Among the examples:

1. *English* "pupil" is derived from Latin "pupilla", meaning "little girl" as well as also "pupil of the eye". "Pupillus" means a little boy. English "pupil" in the sense of "pupil in the eye" and "pupil" in the sense of "school-child" are not mere homophones, but one and the same word.

2. *Greek* "kore" means "girl" and "pupil of the eye". "Koros" means "boy".

3. *Hebrew* "'iyshōn", primarily meaning "little man", is used in the sense of "pupil of the eye".

4. *Japanese* has two words for "pupil of the eye", namely:
    a) "ma-na-ko" which literally means "child of the eye", and
    b) "hito-mi" which literally means "a human being's appearance".

To be sure, whenever we look into another person's eyes, we can see our own reduced reflection there. But what of the Mandarin word that means both "to flow with water (etc.)" and "sheep, goats," and of such semantic parallels as the following?

1. *Greek* "aiges" means "goats" and "strong waves", "Aigaios" means the "Aegean",

2. *French* "mouton" means "sheep" and "foamy waves", and "moutonner" means "to cover oneself with small foamy waves",

3. *Spanish* "cordero" means "sheep" and "foamy waves",

4. *Russian* "barashki" means "sheep" and "foamy waves".

5. *Haussa* "rak'umi" meaning "camel" and "waves".

6. *English* "horses" in "white horses" meaning "horses" as well as the white caps on the surf,

7. *Russian* "volna", though with a difference in the position of the stress accent, means "wool" as well as "wave".

Waves or the white caps of the surf, as Reifler says, "reminded" all these speakers—not only modern Frenchmen, Spaniards, Russians, Haussa, and English but also ancient Chinese and ancient Greeks— of a herd of moving sheep, goats, camels, horses, or of the wool of sheep. There is no other accounting for the "coincidence." A comparable explanation must be given for the relationship between the Chinese character that signifies both "sun" and "one," and its six semantic parallels that Reifler uncovered in Latin, Greek, Kiowa, Cree, Japanese, and Korean. And what are we to make of a purely grammatical Chinese example—the semantic affinity between the concept of a demonstrative pronoun and of a verb meaning "to be" —that exists in six groups of languages at least fourteen of which are not related to Chinese?

If such findings are not objective evidence of a common human logic, what are they? They appear in unrelated parts of the globe, at unrelated epochs, and in unrelated languages. Every such parallel testifies to the continuing presence within the organism of common structures or tendencies for interpreting reality. It suggests that beneath the diversity of languages, the same human intelligence is at work tracing through the chaos and confusions of the surrounding environments an order in accordance with its nature. An order no different in kind from the one that reveals itself also in those metaphors that are larger than single words or phrases: poems. Hence beneath the overwhelming drive toward cultural diversity that has led to a Babel of languages, a contrary force—of human sameness— survives. It would seem that despite the difference found by anthropologists among all languages "in premises, in basic categories, in the training of fundamental sensitivities, and in general view of the world," despite the fact that "each language is a special way of looking at the world and of interpreting experience," a universal definition—a "creature definition"—of poetry is at least a possibility.

Partial and Conflicting Definitions

To begin with the plainest of facts, all authentic poems are manmade objects having the power to evoke in a properly prepared reader or listener a recognizable kind of experience. And being objects added to the phenomenal world, they may justly be regarded as creations. These definitions, however, say nothing about the expectations of the generic experience in its relations to the epoch or to the culture.

At the time of the earliest human efforts to maintain existence, all the arts—it is variously supposed—must have served different purposes, from utilitarian propitiation for fertility to spiritual exultation in prayer. Moreover, all implied true belief in their own magic, which is to say that representing invisible god-powers or visible animal-powers through an act of singing, naming, dancing, or picturing provides a means for bringing them under control. You will not dance for rain unless you have faith that your imitation may somehow draw the longed-for water from the sky. You will not plot out with pictures the strategy for hunting a quarry without believing that your symbols will compel it to obey your wishes. Although all explanations of early human behavior rest on the shakiest of projections, the utilitarian in art—in one metamorphosis or another—seems to have continued down the centuries along with something referable to as religious awareness, and more often than not, in combination. So the mentality of the West must reconstruct the traditions of purpose, though it would rather have lighted, as always, on a single neat cause. Nevertheless, it comforts itself with assuming that in any case all poems have been the outcome of some clear objective of which the poet was quite aware.

The last conclusion cannot possibly be reconciled with the organism's cycle of accumulation and release, the biological processes that begin and end in the creating of a poem. As emphasized in Chapter 1, the poet is driven by a physical need to "ex-press" the discomfort that takes possession of him: it is this condition that makes composing a physical necessity. And as the propelling force in the genesis of poems, the drive to unburden subsumes all other possible drives. But, it may be objected, the motivating impulse is not the whole of the creative process; once the poet discovers what it is that he is saying—or being used for saying—he collaborates voluntarily with all his powers of awareness. Certainly the emphasis upon discovery is crucial in defining the emergence of the poem's referential purport, which the author recognizes at some moment in the course of composing or at its close. Nevertheless, the poet's initial innocence of aim and destination need not prevent anyone who feels so inclined from attributing a purpose that may have been latent somewhere within the poet's organism. He would then have to face the problem of locating the time and the place, a task of supernal difficulty (and, to my mind, one that could bring little point). We are, of course, dealing with the much-argued attribution to the writer of "intention"—something which becomes nonsensical when denoting a total creative act of deliberateness but harmless enough when rationalizing that the writer's organism must have intended such and such things even while its creative self remained ignorant until they laid themselves bare.

We are back with reflexivity, from which no one can ever get far in any treatise on art. And we are also pressed from maker to object made: to considering only the outcome, for only there are we likely to discover what it is that poems embody which accounts for the generic experience that we assume they always evoke. Such concentration on object to the exclusion of subject can serve as an approach toward the view that must eventually comprehend both. In the light of the ever-elusive aspects of creativity, we have no manageable way for arriving there other than by looking first at the poem itself, for which the maker at some stage—if you like, after learning its intention—assumed responsibility by releasing it to the world as his own.

Considered as an object only, what is its nature? Freud's statement that "Art constitutes an immediate territory between the wish-denying reality and the wish-fulfilling world of phantasy," for all its interest, does not take us very far. An uninterpreted fact has more use: that a poem is a self-containing structure of words whose elements and whose totality refer beyond themselves to possible human experiences. And though the ways by which they refer are varied and uncountable, the response evoked in the reader or listener is always the same in kind. Call it, for the moment, "indirect" or even "virtual" experience, which is to say that feeling the sun on one's body differs from feeling the sun when this feeling is evoked by the words of a poem. The terms at least distinguish esthetic encountering from the first-hand mode in the physical reality. Moreover, as remarked at the end of the preceding chapter, a poem evokes two different fields of "indirect" response: one which derives from the relationship between the embodiments of the words and the reader's ongoing human existence within his culture; the other, from the way in which the poem structures its words and the relationship between this way and his existence as a creature.

Some of the most attractive definitions consider but one of these fields; for example, the insistence that poetry is inseparable from play. Not only is all poetry born of play, says Johan Huizinga, but the affinity between them is "also apparent in the structure of the creative imagination." "Underlying all creative writing is some human or emotional situation potent enough to convey . . . a tension that will 'enchant' the reader and hold him spellbound." And "the common denominator" is the means for achieving enchantment: "The rhythmical or symmetrical arrangement of language, the hitting of the mark by rhyme or assonance, the deliberate disguising of the sense, the artificial and artful construction of phrases—all might be so many utterances of the play spirit." In fact, says Huizinga, the "definition of play might serve as a definition of poetry." But the difficulty is that play (as he makes clear at the beginning of his analysis) "is not susceptible to exact definition, either logically, biologically, or aesthetically." Moreover, *Homo Ludens*, from which I have been quoting, lays no claim to inclusiveness; as its subtitle makes explicit, it is a study of "the play element" in culture. Like so many other attempts to get to the essence of poetry, Huizinga's definitions turn out to be no more than a compelling emphasis upon a single characteristic quality or type of effect that can be traced to a poem.[3]

The same limitation will be found in all other cultural definitions of poetry. Consider, for example, the unimaginably varied definition as "moral instruction" and as "knowledge" in the broadest conceivable meanings of these words. The attitude derives historically from the ancient Greek view of art, for the value of any man-made re-presentation must be judged as an effort to project the true, the beautiful, and the good; and thus mimesis becomes involved with both instruction and truth as part of the tradition that justifies art as having use. In the course of its ingenious development in the hands of theorists, it has led, in one extreme direction (of philosophi-cal idealism), to knowledge of a transcendent kind, one that goes beyond even the Romantic view (familiar in Blake) to assertions of the all-inclusive knowing that issues from man's collective uncon-scious into poems that re-present archetypes. As it evolves in the contrary direction, the meanings of imitation-knowledge-truth stick closer to the earth. Stendhal, in fact, will never leave it: "A novel is a mirror riding along the highway." Certain other variants of the same general conception describe the knowledge conveyed by art as "truth to nature," "images of reality," and with comparably re-alistic phrases.

Apparently there will be no limit to the range of beliefs that "knowledge and instruction" can subsume, regardless of intra-disparity. Under the same rubric, poetry is a re-presentation of the spirit, of the inner world (Novalis), and it is also a weapon for per-suading readers to take up arms and fight the war of the classes (Marxist propagandists), for both assertions are based on conceiving poems as re-presenting knowledge and instruction. The same con-ception underlies Arnold's view of poetry as "a criticism of life" as well as Brecht's behavioral theory of inducing action (*Lehrstücke*). It also makes possible another utilitarian definition (of I. A. Richards), that poetry is composed of pseudo-statements which organize our emotional attitudes and thus lead us into proper modes of action—and to the Marxist Bukharin's related insistence that whereas "science classifies and arranges men's knowledge, art sys-tematizes their feelings." Equally obvious is its position as the founda-tion for current critical emphases on the "moral quality expressed by the poem itself" (W. K. Wimsatt, Jr.) and for the various charac-terizations of the kinds of knowledge that poetry makes available, among them the "special, unique, and complete knowledge" (Allen Tate) which differs from that of science. Some of these conceptions presuppose analogical modes of mimesis, which were commonplace enough in medieval Western belief long before Swedenborg sys-tematized them and Baudelaire brought them into poetry with his keystone sonnet of the Symbolist movement, "Correspondances." Still other related definitions of knowledge issue from analyses of man's processes of perception—for example, the assertion that art is "a way of exploring the nature of experience, not just of sense-experience, and of reaching conclusions" about its character, quality, and value (Ralph Ross).[4]

None of the foregoing conceptions has proved so appealing to contemporary America and Britain as the one that Coleridge, drawing generously on his German mentors, proposed a century ago. Poetry is produced by a "synthetic and magical power," the creative imagination, whose self-organizing process and laws of growth correspond to the self-organizing process and laws of growth in the world of nature. It is a wonderfully attractive paradigm, especially in its famous passage on the lawfulness reflected in "the balance or reconciliation of opposite and discordant qualities. . . ." Although Coleridge does not speak of knowledge as such, its presence is implicit in his analogy between the creativity of the human imagination and the transcendent creativity of God. Moreover, the principle of organicism at the base of his assertions is pure correspondence, analogy, and as such falls into the capacious tradition of mimesis. Yet in terms of what a poem *does*, of bringing knowledge or instruction or moral guidance, what Coleridge offers does not define. Like a number of other proposals as to the nature of the poem, it contents itself with describing. Moreover, this description is said to hold true of supreme expressions only, and regardless of whether they are formed in verse or in prose.

By contrast, the definition of poetry as pleasure applies to all successful poems, regardless of degree of loftiness; and though little if anything has been recorded before the time of the Greeks, the tradition must surely have been ancient. Even Plato, who as everyone knows feared poetry because it feeds and waters the passions, hesitated before deciding to admit into his ideal State only hymns to the gods and praises of famous men. He suggested that the advocates of poetry be allowed to argue in its behalf:

Let them show not only that she is pleasant but also useful to States and to human life, and we will gladly listen, for if this can be proven we shall surely be the gainers, that is to say if there is a use in poetry as well as a delight.

Soon enough Aristotle's demonstrations—that poetry teaches general truths by means of specific images, that it also serves to purge the listener through pity and terror—supplied irresistible proofs of poetry's utility. Indeed throughout the ensuing centuries down to the modern period, pleasure was not considered to be sufficient in itself. Poetry teaches while it delights, Horace had said. And even though delighting might be its ultimate virtue, instruction could not be excluded. Nevertheless in time the obbligato of morality became steadily fainter. Toward the close of the eighteenth century, Beattie declared that "The end of poetry is to please," and a few decades later Wordsworth, in his Preface to the *Lyrical Ballads*, explained why "The Poet writes under one restriction only, namely, that of the necessity of giving pleasure."

But what is pleasure? Wordsworth refers to the poet's necessity of producing immediate pleasure as

an acknowledgment of the beauty of the universe; . . . it is a task light and easy for him who looks to the world in the spirit of love: further, it is a homage paid to the native and naked dignity of man, to the grand elementary principle of pleasure, by which he knows, and feels, and lives, and moves.

Lionel Trilling, while remarking that Wordsworth's "pleasure always tended toward joy, a purer and more nearly transcendent state," sees this grand elementary principle "not as a mere charm or amenity but as the object of an instinct, of what Freud . . . was later to call a drive." As such it comprehends vastly more than had ever before been hinted, for it is by this principle that man "knows, and feels, and lives, and moves."[5] Yet even when so richly conceived, pleasure does not define the effect of such poems as *Oedipus Rex*, Baudelaire's "La Charogne," Yeats's "Purgatory," or the individual's expectation before confronting them again. Keats, "On Sitting Down to Read King Lear Once Again," not only prepares himself for pain:

> . . . Once again, the fierce dispute
> Betwixt damnation and impassion'd clay
> Must I burn through; once more humbly assay
> The bitter-sweet of this Shakespearian fruit.

As Trilling points out, "He is by no means certain that [what he calls] the disagreeables really will evaporate, and that he will emerge whole and sound from the experience" of the tragic drama.

But the characteristic function of tragedy, as Aristotle made clear, is catharsis: in the presence of the excitation it creates, pity and fear will bring relief. Relief from pain and disturbance, a transformation of feeling—but into pleasure? Wordsworth, writing elsewhere in the same celebrated Preface of "pathetic situations and sentiments . . . which have a greater proportion of pain connected with them," maintains that

Shakespeare's writings, in the most pathetic scenes, never act upon us, as pathetic, beyond the bounds of pleasure—an effect which, in a much greater degree than might at first be imagined, is to be ascribed to small, but continual and regular impulses of pleasurable surprise from the metrical arrangement.

In a later passage he warns the poet "especially to take care that, whatever passions he communicates to his Readers, those passions . . . should always be accompanied with an overbalance of pleasure." This can be produced by "harmonious metrical language, the sense of difficulty overcome," and other resources of poetic expression: "all these imperceptibly make up a complex feeling of delight, which is of the most important use in *tempering the painful feeling* always found intermingled with powerful descriptions of the deeper passions" (my italics). Such reliance upon meter "to divest language, in a certain degree of its reality, and thus to throw a sort of half-consciousness of unsubstantial existence over the whole poetic composition" recalls Aristotle's "pleasurable accessories," "the several kind of embellishments," as well as the "esthetic distance" between the beholder and the tragic enactment which detaches him from the immediacy of the passions evoked. Even Wordsworth's observation that "wherever we sympathize with pain, it will be found that the sympathy is produced and carried on by subtle combinations with pleasure" adds virtually nothing to what has been said to dissolve the dilemma.[6]

The stubborn fact that nobody has succeeded in explaining "the pleasantness of the unpleasant in art" casts doubt on the phrase itself. Surely "pleasure," no matter how we stretch its meaning—and Wordsworth has justly stretched it to encompass life itself—is a questionable name for whatever it is that draws us to the painful in art, to *King Lear*, for example, and fixes us there. It is not even the adequate term for the strange, partly terrifying emotions evoked by such poems as Unamuno's "En un cementario de lugar castellano," Rilke's "Leichen-Wäsche," Ungaretti's "Tu ti spezzasti," or Frost's "The Most of It."[7] All these poems attract and hold us motionless; they exert a fascination—but of what? Must we call it "truth to life" and stop there, with merely one more variant of mimesis? That all such poems are "true" tells nothing of why we can be enthralled by the elements of pain in their representations. Nor is anything explained by adding that even pain may at times be desired. For every desire does not necessarily fulfill itself in pleasure, unless cessation of desire be equated with a negative pleasure—which is close to what recent psychologists have said of biological drives: that their aim is an end to discomfort and little else. Is this what can be meant by this curious type of pleasure—relief from pain?

The "pleasantness of the unpleasant" is by no means found only in art. As Freud demonstrated in *Beyond the Pleasure Principle*, "unpleasure" is a fact of the life of the human psyche; it can bring gratifications which are often deeper than those of "pleasure" itself. The German word that he uses, *Unlust*, does not denote—as its Englished equivalent "unpleasure" suggests—a lack of something; rather it stands for a positive feeling of pain, discomfort, disagreeable malaise. Moreover, this *Unlust* is connected with a perpetually compelling aspiration to gratify a need: with tendencies independent of and more primitive than the pleasure principle—with "a compulsion to repeat which overrides it." How else understand, for example, the recurrent dreams of men who have suffered traumatic war experiences: dreams in which the original trauma is reenacted again and again? Are they driven by the hope of enjoying the pain or by the possibility of somehow binding or mastering it through reliving the terror until it has at last been neutralized of its menaces, accepted as an enemy overcome, and put to rest?

Although the same process appears in the recurring pattern of self-injuring behavior in the lives of certain people and in the tendency of patients to act out again and again even painful experiences of their childhood, this "repetition compulsion" is not limited to the couch or the clinic. In Conrad's *Heart of Darkness*, as Trilling points out, one of the persons speaks of the primitive life of the jungle as "base and sordid—and for *that* reason compelling: he himself feels quite overtly its dreadful attraction." Indeed, the "painful and scornful conclusions" of *Notes from the Underground*, as Mann remarked, "have long become parts of our moral culture."[8] By this time we are so accustomed to unpleasure in contemporary art that we can be surprised when it does not appear. And not only do we expect to experience it often; we ignore the distinction established by Freud: we roll the pleasure with its opposite into one ball. Yet the two can never make one, even if we define the pleasure of poetry to mean both what it is and is not. Nothing could be gained by such gymnastics; on the contrary, a significant human profundity would be ignored. In the world of the poem, pleasure attracts by its promise of delight; unpleasure, by inviting us as empathizing participants to overcome discomfort, disturbance, even pain and horror, and not because of the consolation of the "several kinds of embellishments" or "pleasurable accessories" of its art. In the grim arena evoked by the poem, imaginative re-presentation affirms man's capacity to endure the most awesome of trials. The *Unlust* of art bears the intimation of our ultimate creature victoriousness.

If "pleasure" has proved to be less than an inclusive definition of poetry, what can be found of religion? Mention of only a few celebrated poems such as "Venus and Adonis," "To His Coy Mistress," and "My Last Duchess" should be enough to dispose of the notion that poetry might be consubstantial with religion— with "expressions of belief in a divine or superhuman power or powers to be obeyed and worshipped as the creator(s) and ruler(s) of the universe." You can of course improve on the dictionary's definition to include whatever you please, yet even the wildest proposal could never encompass the boundless range of existing poems. Viewed objectively in terms of expression, however, the religious mode is separated from the poetic by only a shadowy borderline. The fact in itself is compelling, even if it does not necessitate such conclusions as Henri Bremond's (that all the arts "aspirent . . . à rejoindre la prière") or that of some Romantics (that poetry expresses Nature, which is divine).

Such ways of looking at poetry-and-religion, for all their

charms, are arbitrary, partial—as resistible as any of the private or social functions assigned to poetry by philosophers, critics, clerics, and sometimes writers themselves. Can poetry, for example, become an adequate substitute for religion? Apparently it can for a number of people dissatisfied with conventional religious procedures who require very special means for worshipping and believing. The phenomenon, whether widespread or not, can hardly astonish anyone familiar with archaic cultures, where poetry was inextricably part of prophecy and ritual of all kinds. The poet was possessed, God-smitten, a seer, filled with extraordinary knowledge. Gradually this personage split up into the specialized figures of the prophet, the priest, the soothsayer, the mystagogue, and the poet as we know him. Even among the early Greeks, the poet shows traces of his archaic progenitor and continues to be inspired by divine power. Thereafter the conception evolves and alters; yet throughout Western history as late as the 18th century, inspiration was widely believed to be drawn from outside the poet. (By now, as every English major can tell you, it is securely located in the "Unconscious.") As for prophecy, few people today give it serious thought despite the fact that only a century ago, for Shelley, Wordsworth, and Emerson, it was central to the poet's vocation.

No wonder that the affinity between religion and poetry has come to depend on language and the feelings it evokes. However, the dividing line between the religious mode of expression and the poetic has never changed. It is as shadowy as before for the plain reason that poetry always and religion at times must resort to imaginative-symbolic configurations. No other means exist for expressing what each would convey: a knowledge-and-feeling of exaltation. But the borderline, though shadowy, can be seen. Whereas poetry at all times speaks an extraordinary-ordinary language of its own, religion speaks poetically only in its "highest" moments. In its equally necessary moments of explaining and guiding, it uses practical discourse. Moreover, as Shakespeare remarked centuries ago and linguists repeat today, religion is not the only user of poetic language:

> The lunatic, the lover, and the poet
> Are of imagination all compact . . .

Only in such works as the *Oresteia, Divine Comedy, Paradise Lost, Ash Wednesday,* and the devotional lyrics of Donne, George Herbert, Vaughan, Crashaw—to take celebrated examples —do poetry and religion coincide. As for their consubstantiality, though religion must at times speak poetically, the converse is spectacularly untrue.

There are more things to be said of the relationship and many of them take on confusion. Matthew Arnold, writing in the last decades of the nineteenth century, when religion had already "materialized itself in the fact, in the supposed fact [that now was] failing it," found the strongest part of the religion of his day to be "its unconscious poetry." Nowadays, when as Emile Capouya puts it,

the altars have been deserted even by the priests, poetry and the novel have taken on the duty of celebrating, castigating, denying the absent God. The nay-sayers themselves of modern letters—Joyce, Céline, Kafka, Beckett—are so many modern Ezekiels, eating dung in the marketplace. . . . The sermons in *Moby-Dick* and *Go Tell It on the Mountain* are professions of faith in a creed that the authors have consciously discarded but to which they half-consciously adhere.[9]

One says yes or no to such statements, depending on whether one demands that "religion" stand for all its traditional components or only one. For some who maintain that poetry and religion are consubstantial, it may be enough to consider "the breath and finer spirit of all knowledge" that Wordsworth attributed to poetry, which for Arnold a century ago as for Tate today is quite literally an all-subsuming all. For others to whom religion amounts to an ethical imperative, there is an abundance of literature to point to, and not only among the writings of Existentialists and Marxists. However, when one raises the crucial issue of divinity—of "a belief in spiritual beings"—the reasoning becomes harder to credit. For the question of the existence of a supernatural Power is blandly tucked away under the covering of awe-and-exultation—an action is replaced by a response— without so much as acknowledging that awe-and-exultation are also often evoked by other stimuli. On balance it would seem that with the acknowledged disappearance of God, the relation of poetry and religion has broken down into arbitrary questions of terms and disputation. And yet an inclusive definition of poetry must finally recognize why each must at times appear to serve the purpose of both.

Meanwhile we face the quite contrary conviction that art serves no purpose other than itself. A poem, being a self-developing organism governed by its own principles, "needs no end, no purpose for its presence outside itself, but has its entire value, and the end of its existence in itself." So declared Karl Philipp Moritz in 1788, to be echoed forever after in elaborations of every sort—most impressively by Immanuel Kant and most self-consciously and contagiously by Gautier in his preface to *Mademoiselle de Maupin*. For Kant, esthetic experience is neither possessive not utilitarian: it is wholly autonomous, to be distinguished from all interests, such as pleasure, emotion, and knowledge—in short, "purposiveness without purpose." It cannot in any way be associated with use (Gautier). It is *l'art pour l'art:* art for the sake of art—or, as Poe was to phrase it later, "the poem written solely for the poem's sake." Poetry is to be defined as "art"—but what is art? Only a dictionary can avoid never-ending dispute—"creativeness, and the products of creativeness." The definition takes us back to the question Boswell asked of Johnson.

But if it has proved easier also for many modern critics to say not what poetry is but what it is not, others among them have taken the opposite stand: they define poetry with the totality of principles that can be used to illuminate the poem. This is inclusiveness with a vengeance and yet it fails, for the sum of this everything-said does not equal the whole. Not that I argue by the side of the "metacritical" followers of the later Wittgenstein— that all such definitions are arbitrary because unverifiable by scientific logic—but that every definition we have reviewed is a *cultural* explanation and as such ignores the sources of the poem's birth. To anyone personally acquainted with creative artists, the picture of poets busying themselves for the high purpose of producing objects to give other people pleasure or instruction or knowledge or moral guidance is simply too ludicrous to be borne. At least as self-interested as other creatures on the crust of the earth, poets when they seek to make a gift, like the rest of humanity, usually direct it to themselves. And as I have stressed more than once, the desire that results in their creating of a poem was driven by the need to free the organism itself of a burden that would not let it rest.

All our definitions have come from looking only at the poem and, as I tried to make clear at the outset, such concentration on object to the exclusion of subject can serve only as an approach toward the view that might comprehend both. In itself it can bring only partial understanding. And as we now can see, it has brought only partial definitions—of effects in terms of instruction, ethics, morality, religion, human pleasure and unpleasure, all of which are rooted in the culture. And all of which assume that poetry and culture are at one; which is to say that poetry issues from capacities which are the product of social evolution exclusively. But the bearer of these capacities is here on earth because he evolved from simple chemical compounds by a process of natural selection; and although from time to time he was able to create societies, another form of evolution has also been taking place: much in his nature has evolved under the pressure of natural selection alone—and *these pressures continue to exist today*.[10] To ignore their operating presences is to fragment and to diminish man; therefore to misconstrue his behavior and his works, especially his expressions in art.

The Culture as Fate

"Once one has become adjusted to the idea that we have evolved by a process of natural selection," writes the British biochemist Sir Francis Crick, "it is remarkable how many of the problems of the modern world take on a completely new light." For "modern world" read contemporary culture, for "the problems," certain outcomes of the clash between natural selection and social evolution. In the last hundred years we have gathered some information about each of these mystifying forces that have shaped and continue to shape us, but we are far from understanding how they interact within us or the effect of their interrelationship upon our behavior. Not that we have never been aware of collisions. Chapter 1 cited some examples of what occurs when certain responses that were useful during man's animal ancestry act as a handicap under the conditions of civilized existence. But such phenomena as the aberrations of mob psychology and of verbal conflicts in a business office do not suggest an even remote connection with the relationship between poetry and the culture. For poetry is unthinkable apart from the culture—indeed everything suggested by the very mention of the word "art" brings thoughts of civilized arrangements.

Some 150,000 years ago, man had already obtained his biological foundation, but during the period in which that foundation was being laid a new type of development arose: cultural evolution. Its building blocks, to quote Hermann J. Muller, are not mutations or genes "but innovations arising in people's minds, and they do not become disseminated by biological reproduction but by imitation and communication." Cultural evolution is thus incomparably swifter than biological evolution. As it advanced,

it fed the processes of natural selection which led to further biological evolution. And then, in consequence, as the genetic basis continued to advance, it allowed a faster, firmer cultural progression. However, with the pressure of the environment effectively held back for a considerable period by cultural means, the operation of natural selection has been faltering to a halt and, as Darwin pointed out, it may even have become reversed.

Worse, as Muller maintains. Genetic retrogression, even more evident today than in Darwin's time, actually threatens the future of mankind.[11] And if it is the unmistakable outcome of cultural evolution, the means for remedying it will have to be devised by the very forces that brought it about: science and technology.

It would be quixotic to deny that, at least in Western experience, they are the end-results of the social evolution of the last 150,000 years. The enormous extent to which science and technology dominate and control practical aspects of contemporary life is all too manifest. As for their effect upon thought and action, one need not be a Marxist to recognize the impact of "modes of economic production" upon mental processes and behavior. One has only to recall the relationship in the earliest of recorded cultures between livelihood and survival, on the one hand, and magic, fertility rites, propitiation dancing, and painting, on the other. As communal life became specialized, its monolithic character necessarily altered, but not to displace religion from its ruling position. Long after the decline of the ancient Middle Eastern civilizations, when science and technology had already gained importance, God and His Works still continued to dominate "the culture"—by which I mean the concepts, habits, skills, arts, instruments, institutions, attitudes and similar phenomena that constitute what we mean by "civilization."[12] Only with the dethronement of religion, as science and man-centered faiths grew steadily more controlling, could the greatest upheavals in social evolution begin. Yet even the Industrial Revolution paid its (curious) tribute to religion; and if, as Crick and other scientists now assure us, the "old, or literary culture, which was based originally on Christian values, is clearly dying," its ties with its successor have not been severed. Indeed, certain values still defined as "humane" are now being sought *from* science, and scientists—even those intoxicated by "value-free" dreams—are not entirely willing to scorn them.

For the ties are as old as civilization, and they have continued in paradoxical interdependence as they split from the original entity into opposing directions: into the "ideal" and the "practical"—religion-philosophy-literature-art on the one hand, and science-technology on the other. As the first evolved and broadened, it goaded and freed the second, until the attitudes that culminated in what we call the Renaissance had licensed human thought to follow wherever untrammeled inquiry might lead. Needless to insist, consequences that never could have been imagined surround us now. For example, systems of philosophy, which had always been (as Whitehead remarked) a footnote to Plato, must today be blessed by science in order to survive. Conversely, "value-free" studies of psychopathology and related organic dysfunctions end by challenging the very sanity of the kind of existence that civilization now imposes on the people it serves and who must serve.

Paradox does not stop there. Social evolution leads from the biological "completion" of man to effects upon his biology, to revelations of what these effects have produced. It civilizes and then holds up to accusation the very outcomes it caused. As Muller and others now warn, the medical sciences, dedicated only to biological welfare, have reached the point of endangering the physical survival of the race, by saving the unfit, prolonging the life span, fostering overpopulation, perpetuating "weakness genes." Similar perils are also being publicly mourned, involving the oxygen we breathe, the water we drink, the nourishment we shall have to produce for the multiplying number of human mouths—the list goes on and on, to include the very safety of the biosphere . . .[13]

A kind of terrifying logic seems to inhere in social evolution, transforming its objectives into their opposites. What was once much desired, in time brings on evils seemingly beyond remedy. It is not that the contradictory end-result is inevitable but that no forces come forward to counteract the processes in time. After all, "who" would act as the protecting agent for the culture? Things happen and take their course, and only when situations become acutely perilous is anything even suggested about remedying them. Any solution is almost certain to create new problems, and when these are managed, still others may undermine the erstwhile success. Whatever the laws of growth, ontogeny does not repeat phylogeny in the world of the culture. The difficulties are doubtless aggravated by the vastly greater speed of social evolution as compared with that of natural selection. Often enough changes in the culture do not allow men time to assess their new situation. Though the tempo has been uneven, technology in the last century, and especially in the last decades, has moved with ungaugeable swiftness and pervasiveness. One can no longer say, even with a smile, that the sky is the limit.

So much as suggesting a limit would be heinous heresy. Men no longer adjust; they remake their environment to suit their wishes, even when "wishes" is a euphemism for desperation. Thus, to cope with the astronomical number of stomachs precounted by demographers, food is to be manufactured from petroleum or, better still, sea life, ecological balances permitting, not to mention cities in the ocean and countries in the sky. Or sea water made into fresh. Or electronic brains into factual storage plants, since vastly more information is now being gathered than any group of human brains could contain. The generalist was long ago replaced by the specialist, but the latter seems clearly deficient compared with machines. No one will pretend any more to know "all about his subject"; the only all-knowing sages are hardware sages and in time they may come to breed. But even if they prove childless, their indispensability will steadily magnify, for more and more of the products of technology can no longer be entrusted to human beings, whose brain is too slow, too narrow, and much too fallible. So the diagnostic physician holds consultations with a machine. And his opposite number, at the controls of a jet fighter-plane, has to ask his computer to tell him where to fly and aim. It is time to start revising the great ode of *Antigone*.

Jacques Ellul, among others, would call instead for an elegy.[14] A hundred years ago man began to disengage the human muscle from the productive process and now the human brain is being disengaged. Despite this final liberation, according to the French sociologist, man is no longer technology's master but its victim. Throughout the Industrial Revolution no one could have doubted that human beings were in charge. Today they have lost their control: technology has gradually been acquiring a kind of autonomy. Not that material power has suddenly shed its inherent neutrality but that their technology to a great extent determines the alternatives from which men can choose. And if, as Ellul maintains, a technical "take-over" has already taken place, it is because men have not intervened. Ellul indicts neither the machine nor specific technologies but "technique," which is "the totality of methods rationally arrived at and having absolute efficiency (for a given stage of development) in every field of human activity." Because technique tends to "transform everything it touches into a machine," people are driven to look only for the "one best means" for dealing with whatever confronts them. Efficiency becomes not only the touchstone but an end-in-itself to which men must adapt themselves despite its effect on their moral values. For technique conditions the ways by which values are perceived. This phenomenon has been remarked before, but the headlong speed of evolving technique is today greater than can be encompassed by human minds—and so are the consequences, whether for government and ideology or for mass idleness and existential meaninglessness.

I have cited Ellul at some length not out of personal affection for doom. I could as well have paraphrased Marshall McLuhan's paean to the paradise already in our midst, with its theme of tribal return by the grace of electronics. Whether men are moving back to primitive wholeness or forward to dehumanization, the processes seem quite beyond their reach. Even those who disbelieve the jeremiad recognize that the direction of technique is irreversible— that "our present society is organized in such a way that those making the decisions find themselves *forced* to advance technique" (Robert Theobald, his italics). Each of our evolutions has a life and a power of its own. Men and women can at best stand by and reflect while biology and the culture bear them into their future —unless somehow as a species they attempt to act. So Hermann Muller, for one, proposes a global program for genetics which, if implemented, would also have crucial outcomes for the culture. As for the environment, the ability to alter it by no means brings the power to control it also. "The rate of change increases at an accelerating speed, without a corresponding acceleration in the rate at which further responses can be made," says the British social scientist, Sir Geoffrey Vickers; "and this brings ever nearer the threshold beyond which control is lost."

But is control in fact desirable? Does it accord with "nature"? Nobody asks if it was natural for human beings to have developed ways for improving their chances of survival by food cultivation, settlement, domestication, and ensuing techniques. The implication is that anything is natural if it flourishes man's creature-will to keep alive and perpetuate his kind in a world of mystery and danger. But is there a point in social evolution at which cultural change might be found unnatural—when, for example, the body, removed from its native environment, begins to break down? Regardless of what occurred in past periods, continuous living in large and congested cities no longer necessarily harms human health. When fortified by medical science, the organism seems capable of getting along even when completely alienated from the natural world. And men and women in such hostile environments as the African, Australian, and Arctic deserts or the Congo and Amazon rainforests can do the same even without technology. If environment provides no criterion for "what is natural," perhaps we must seek it in the unique and subtly changing equation between a people's way of life, however primitive or advanced, and the creature-values it cherishes.

Western civilizations, for example, have made a steady withdrawal from nature. Rather than regarding themselves as borne on its processes—rather than acting with nature and as part of it—they have sought to conquer both the external world and the "nature" within each individual. To picture these civilizations as a landscape of restraint is to see mountain peaks rising with the Hebrew prophets, Plato, the Church, with numerous lower ranges of ethical and moral systems. Emblazoned upon each is a motto directing its denizens to allow their innate impulses and desires no possible anarchy. And the imprecation is followed by descriptions of values as far greater than the cost, in a system that exalts rewards-to-come above all immediate deprivations. Yet not only the West but every human society has been founded on some kind of contract whose terms none of its children has ever a chance to choose or to refuse. It is his birthright, his sentence, his hope. And it does not matter that every human infant is born wild. By the time he has begun to organize his own thinking, his ways of responding have been conditioned far past recall. How otherwise could the rules of his brain arrange themselves except by imitating and incorporating those of the world that shapes him into its image by instructing, correcting, and explaining with steadfast denials and lofty promises?[15]

If the culture is thus man's fate, what are his poems? Paradox, whose presence has shadowed each step of our way, makes doubtful the truth of a simple answer. Yet poetry has appeared in every human society we know. Is it therefore also man's fate? And can the two fates be identical? The very life-breath of a culture hangs on its power to restrain, whereas art bursts forth with opposing power to express all that men know-and-feel with "the fervent emotions of the mind."

The words are John Keble's, written a century ago, and none are more apt in suggesting why poetry opposes the culture or how it can sustain rebellion; for poetry reveals the fervent emotions of the mind "under certain veils and disguises." The "strong and deep feelings" "cannot endure publicity" in civilization's landscape of restraint. "Direct indulgence" must be "somehow repressed"; hence their "indirect expression in words."[16] It need hardly be argued that implicit in this conflict between poetry and the culture are clashes within man that Western philosophy has been steadily trying to cope with and put to rest. Presumably for his own good, "reason," from at least the time of Plato, has been holding back man's creature-drives toward gratification. Whether the rationalization be embodied in Aristotelian or, finally, in Hegelian terms, repression is ever exalted. Only with Nietzsche does the direction shift toward an affirmation of the will to gratify the "life instincts." Yet even here, in the concept of the "eternal return" that crowns the Nietzschean vision, we find celebrations of suffering and of domination. They serve different ends, to be sure, but they are still the pain and the power flown high in traditional moralities.

Naturally the justification advanced by Western philosophers has not in the least affected man's innermost tendencies to fight whatever threatens to stifle his spontaneous responses. They show no interest in the alleged fact that systematic inhibiting of the "destructive" aspects of his drives has enabled man to master both himself and external nature, to the higher glory of the individual and of social morality. These innermost tendencies of the human organism, freely directed toward pleasure, toward desire and gratification unconstrained, express themselves in a great many forms, and most memorably in the imaginative projections of art. It should not be surprising, given the circumstances of restraint, that every such imaginative expression must be at least in part a denial of civilization, a self-assuring cry of the organism that freedom and wholeness and joy have not been lost.

Nor should it be surprising that the language it uses is not the language proper to the culture. Although nobody knows how speech evolved, nobody can question the functional fitness of practical discourse to the practical demands of society. Like civilization itself, it is a later, secondary development. But out of what primary mode? All that a metaphysician has at his disposal, says Anatole France, for constructing a philosophic system of the universe is the perfected cry of monkeys and dogs. According to one of Jespersen's remarks, human speech originated in some form of play. Most scholars, however, lean toward his larger statement that "Men sang out their feelings long before they were able to speak their thought." Democritus had said the same thing, so had Vico and Rousseau; but the thesis remained speculative until Darwin supplied its biological basis in *The Expression of the Emotions in Man and Animals.*

If the behavior of children even but dimly mirrors the evolving behavior of the species, there can be no doubting the spontaneous, emotional, playful, imaginative character of speech at its beginnings or the secondary process by which "communicativeness" takes precedence over "exclamativeness." As the symbolic character of human language becomes part of his existence, the child "passes from a more subjective state to an objective state," says Cassirer, "from a merely emotional attitude to a theoretical attitude." Moreover, "eagerness and enthusiasm to talk . . . mark the desire for the detection and *conquest* of an objective world" (my italics).[17] It is this gradual transformation from responsive expressiveness to deliberate manipulation that marks the two stages of human language. Through specialization and adaption with the growth of civilization, practical—"secondary"—discourse came to evolve and to replace the associative and imaginative—"primary"—mode of thinking and speaking.

Primary language is of course the language of poetry, having the power and purpose of "restoring," as Valéry said, the significance, value, and integrity of "sensuality and of the emotional power of things." Hence its potential danger. Plato believed that a man could be transformed by the things he imagined; Goethe and Baudelaire were no less convinced of imagination's enormous powers. Moreover, as Edgar Wind observes, if the release of these forces is a threat to the artist and must be controlled by him with care, the same threat, in some less degree, is transferred to the reader when he participates in the poet's imaginative experience.[18] Nevertheless, and despite the fact that imaginative creations flow out of the depths of the organism untrammeled by controls, society does not seem in the least worried. If poetry has become a socially acceptable way of flouting the culture, it is because it speaks in a language that society knows to be outmoded, undependable, unfit for the important business of practical living. Civilization has no fear of what this primary mode of speech can arouse not only because of its ubiquitous countercontrols; it "knows" that men are much too realistic to risk all they have achieved. Doctors of psychoanalysis, reflecting the attitude of the world they serve, have a word for this turning back to the self outgrown: regression. Though employed mainly in discussing immature behavior, it may even play a part in explaining the enchantment of art. So, for example, much of the language of *King Lear*, we may suddenly learn, is—like the language of other affecting poems—basically regressive. As indeed it is, in comparison with the type of discourse perfected over the centuries for transacting commerce, delivering an ultimatum, and framing an armistice.

And not only language. The very direction of art is similarly regressive, whether it be a backward turning toward an earlier natural state of supposed freedom or a turning away from the Noes of an everpresent reality. The organism's innermost tendencies, unable to accept the conditions in which they are caught, thrust out in all directions to find such escape as imagination can project. If these fulfilments, when viewed all together, show great contradictions in values, it is not merely because each of them carries the marks of the world it fled; there is no limit to the kinds of desires that can project their imagined gratification. Hence it makes not the least difference whether the setting be wholly natural or even partly technological so long as it assures the organism the kind of refuge it would have. To flee, to escape—this is the inherent direction of the creative imagination; all other considerations are secondary: the specific world it breaks from or the specific newfoundland it chooses. Forest primeval—even airconditioned pleasure-dome, *if* its winds are not winds that stifle.

Heavily italicized *if*, for the direction of civilization, wholly unlike that of the creative imagination. thrusts irreversibly forward toward ever intensifying control as it consolidates all its components. As it must. Not only because society is so organized that those making the decisions find themselves forced to advance technique but equally because social evolution has risen to the point where human survival now depends on a pooling of global arrangements. What the resulting planning and control of monolithic existence holds out for the organism's innermost tendencies need hardly be discussed. Even at present, in the greater part of their experiences, men are blocked from immediate confrontations with reality. As Ernst Cassirer makes clear, they "cannot see it, as it were, face to face," for "physical reality seems to recede in proportion as man's symbolic activity advances." One-world technological consequences not only must intensify this recession; it may have to subordinate individuality to a point of its virtual extinction. Perhaps ways will be evolved for promising the continuity of the race without placing all hope on its capacity for adapting to automata or to becoming their caretakers.

Meanwhile the culture moves forward inexorably, and poetry moves against it inexorably. And even though the creative imagination—borne into existence by social evolution, inconceivable apart from civilization—is in essence a striving against the culture's restraint, the definitions of poetry maintain a fancied assumption of concord. Yet underneath all the seeming quiet of the surface, poets have always risen in violent defiance, calling for excess, exuberance, audacity, wildness, rage . . . Whatever the terms of the battlecry, they celebrate acts of defence. They proclaim what poetry must oppose, what it saves itself from. The more important, the crucial, question remains untouched: what does poetry declare itself for, in affirmation?

NOTES AND COMMENTS

1. "Science and Linguistics," in *Four Articles on Metalinguistics*, Foreign Service Institute, Washington, D.C., Department of State, 1949. Second long quotation from "Linguistics as an Exact Science," in *Language, Thought and Reality*, M.I.T. Press, 1956. See also Clyde Kluckhohn, *Mirror for Man*, McGraw-Hill, 1949, pp. 39, 51 (his chapter on "The Gift of Tongues" includes many varied examples). Mario Pei, *Modern Language Journal*, Feb. 1957. • According to Ortega y Gasset, each language has a normal and unique physical or physiological posture, *Diogenes*, Winter 1959, p. 11. • A century before Whorf, the German philologist Wilhelm von Humboldt had remarked on the psychological

difference between the Greek and Latin words for "moon." The former (*mēn*) reflects an interest in the moon's function in measuring time, the latter (*luna*, from *luc-na*) in the moon as a light-giving body. • No discussion of metalinguistics may omit mention of Edward Sapir and his article "Language," *Encyclopedia of the Social Sciences*, Vol. ix, Macmillan, 1933 ("The fact of the matter is that the 'real world' is to a large extent unconsciously built up on the language habits of the group"). • Every language is constantly subject to the influence of the world in which it is used and the social conditions and evolving thought of its speakers. A metalinguistic "effect" has been evident in the impact of American culture on both the French and German languages in the late 1960's. • For a critical view of the Whorf-Sapir thesis, see Francis P. Dinneen, S. J., *An Introduction to General Linguistics*, Holt, 1966, p. 236, and J. P. De Cecco, *The Psychology of Language, Thought, and Instruction*, Holt, 1967, pp. 62 f. • Harry Hoijer goes so far as to adduce cultural correlations between cultural norms and linguistic patterns, "Cultural Implications of Some Navaho Linguistic Categories," in *Language*, 1951, 111-20.

2. "Linguistic Analysis, Meaning, and Comparative Semantics," paper read before the Conference on General Semantics, Chicago, June 22-23, 1951; published in Holland, *Lingua*, vol. III, 4, August 1953. Much of what I say here repeats or paraphrases Reifler. The grammatical example was offered at the Eighth International Congress of Linguistics, August 1958, at the University of Oslo; published in the *Proceedings*, 1958. • Common human logic: In 1945 the French linguist Joseph Vendryes had appealed for a general linguistic approach in unrelated languages: "From such a comparison, one should be able to derive valuable indications for the thinking processes of different people." Reifler had discovered and announced several semantic parallels before hearing of this article. • "There must necessarily exist, as part of the very nature of created things, a common essential language capable of universally describing the substance of things."—G. B. Vico, *Scienza Nuova Seconda*, 1744, Book I, p. 161. • Noam Chomsky maintains that the different languages of man arise out of a unity lying at the depths of the species (see *Psychology Today*, No. 1, 1968, pp. 48-51, 66-69). • To go one leap farther: as *Signals in the Animal World* makes evident, "many of our era's so-called inventions were anticipated, in the course of evolution, by millions of years" (D. Burckhardt, W. Schleidt, H. Altner, eds., McGraw-Hill, 1968). • The quoted phrases at the end of this section are from Kluckhohn, *op. cit.*, pp. 51, 45. For obvious reasons, the principles of metalinguistics do not apply to the "international" languages employed in a number of sciences.

3. *Homo Ludens*, Roy Publishers, 1950, p. 132; see Chap. VII.

4. Bukharin, cited in Max Eastman, *The Enjoyment of Poetry*, Scribner, 1951, p. 222. Ross, "Art as Knowledge," *Sewanee Review*, Autumn 1961, p. 597.

5. Lionel Trilling, *Beyond Culture*, Viking, 1966, p. 61. • Representative definitions of poetry's function, from the British tradition, following the typical medieval defence as allegory (the tales of the poets were made symbols of moral and spiritual truths), are for the most part variations on Horace's dictum, with changing emphasis ("to profit or to please, or to blend in one the delightful and the useful"). Thus, Sir Philip Sidney: chiefly for moral effect, secondarily for delight. Bacon: magnanimity, morality, and delectation. Johnson: "to instruct by pleasing." Wordsworth: "to please and instruct." Coleridge: "for its immediate object pleasure, not truth." But—Mill: "to cultivate feelings and help in the formation of character"; and Shelley: "The instrument of moral good is the imagination." Note, in this very general connection, Yeats's remark: "I think, too, that no fine poet, no matter how disordered his life, has ever, even in his mere life, had pleasure for his end," "Anima Hominis" in *Per Amica Silentia Lunae*, Macmillan, 1918, p. 658.

6. See below, p. 33, John Keble, who also speaks of the veil, in the *British Critic*, 1838, vol. xxiv, p. 435. Goethe rewrote tragic scenes of *Faust* in rime "for there the idea is seen as if under a veil, and the immediate effect of the tremendous material is softened." Nietzsche: "Rhythm casts a veil over reality"; "Art makes the aspect of life endurable by throwing over it a veil of obscure thought"; etc.

7. The "pleasantness of the unpleasant in art" is a phrase of Ernst Kris'. See Gregory Zilboorg's introduction to Freud's *Beyond the Pleasure Principle*, Bantam Books, 1959, pp. 12-13 for meaning of *Unlust*. The poems by Unamuno, Rilke, Ungaretti: see my *The Poem Itself*, Schocken, 1967.

8. Lionel Trilling, "On the Modern Element in Modern Literature," in my *Varieties of Literary Experience*; see also Trilling, *Beyond Culture*, p. 20.

9. Arnold, in the concluding paragraph of his introduction to The Hundred Greatest Books, London, 1879; also, "The Study of Poetry." Emile Capouya: *Saturday Review*, August 13, 1966. The minimal definition of religion—"a belief in spiritual beings"—is the British anthropologist Sir Edward Tylor's.

10. I am paraphrasing both René Dubos (see Chap. 1) and Sir Francis Crick (*Molecules and Men*).

11. Hermann J. Muller, "Mankind in Biological Perspective," *Centennial Review*, Spring 1962, pp. 183, 188. • [T]he biological characteristics of man have not changed much since Paleolithic times. . . ."—Dubos, *Man Adapting*, p. 10.

12. By "the culture" I am not, of course, referring to "receptiveness to beauty and humane feelings" (Whitehead) or manners of breeding, but to what Clyde Kluckhohn calls "all those historically created designs for living, explicit and implicit, rational, irrational and nonrational, which exist at any given time as potential guides for the behavior

of men," *Science of Man in the World Crises*, Ralph Linton, ed., Columbia University Press, 1945, p. 45. T. S. Eliot, taking a different route, views "the culture" as virtually the equivalent of "civilization," in *Notes Toward the Definition of Culture*, Faber, 1948, p. 23. • "In reality, any form of organized social life (and all human life is socialized) has its own brand of restrictions, conflicts, and frustrations. . . ." —Dubos, *So Human an Animal*, p. 161.

13. I know of one internationally esteemed benefactor of humanity who is often troubled by the thought that his contribution to medicine will create problems incomparably greater than the one it has solved. • Typical of the belated concern in the United States for the safety of the biosphere: P. R. Ehrlich, "The Coming Famine," *Natural History*, May 1968; "The Age of Effluence," *Time*, May 10, 1968; "To Save the Spaceship Earth," *N. Y. Times* (editorial), June 2, 1968; *The Subversive Science: Essays Toward an Ecology of Man*, P. Shephard and D. McKinley, eds., Houghton Mifflin, 1969; "Can Man Survive?" exhibit marking the centennial of the American Museum of Natural History, New York, 1969.

14. Jacques Ellul, *The Technological Society*, Knopf, 1964, presents only the first part of a two-part work, *La Technique*, written in 1952 and issued in 1954. For significant differences between the two publications, see Robert Theobald, "The House that Homo Sapiens Built," *The Nation*, Oct. 19, 1964. It has taken surprisingly long for Americans to grasp the implications Ellul made plain a dozen years earlier. Erich Fromm's statement typifies the delay: "We are moving toward an entirely new form of society in which man becomes a part of the machine and is programmed by these principles: (1) that one *ought* to do what is technically *possible* to do; (2) that the primary values are maximum efficiency in production, maximum consumption, with minimal human friction—and this is minimal individuality. Technical progress becomes the source of all values [etc.]."—(*N. Y. Times*, May 22, 1968). • Folk wisdom has long recognized the effect upon a person of his vocation and of the instruments he uses ("he has the mind of a bookkeeper," etc.). For observations on values, see James K. Feibleman, "The Philosophy of Tools," *Social Forces*, March 1967. • "By trying to conquer nature in a hostile spirit Western man (as well as his African and Asian imitators) . . . is not aware that the physical world is an integral part of his own body, and thus attempts to bulldoze it into submission instead of trying to act *with* it and *as* it, fully respecting those inseparable connections between all events which are studied in the science of ecology. Taoism is, in fact, mankind's first formulation of ecological principles, of the interdependence of all forms of biological and geological existence."—Alan Watts, *N. Y. Times Book Review*, April 17, 1966.

15. "The style in which we shall do our thinking, the framework of our reasonings, the matters of our subjective apprehension, the distinctions and relations to which we shall direct our chief attention,

are thus determined in the main for us, not by us . . . [E]ach generation feels always the leading hand, not only of the generation that immediately instructed it, but of all who have gone before. . . ."—W. D. Whitney, *Language and the Study of Language*, Scribner, 1867, pp. 445-446. See also Robert Bierstedt, *Emile Durkheim*, Dell Publishing Company, Inc., 1966, pp. 146, 166, 195, 213.

16. John Keble, *Lectures on Poetry*, Oxford, 1912, vol. 1, p. 47.

17. Ernst Cassirer, *An Essay on Man*, Anchor, 1956, pp. 170 ff., 152.

18. Edgar Wind, *Art and Anarchy*, Knopf, 1964, pp. 7, 107. • In a non-authoritarian society, everything is fair game to the communication media, including the most contemptuous indictment from would-be destroyers, provided it can be used. Anything newsworthy is data to be appropriated, processed, incorporated—some years ago, Surrealist art techniques into advertising; more recently, anti-establishment philosophic statements into feature articles; fashions, argot; etc. • Doctors of psychoanalysis: I am, of course, referring to the stereotype only: not to the psychoanalytic approach of R. D. Laing, for example (*The Politics of Experience*, Pantheon, 1967). • According to Lewis S. Feuer, "No society altogether succeeds in molding the various psychological types which comprise it to conform to its material, economic requirements. If there were a genuine correspondence between the material economic base and the psychological superstructures, then societies would be static, and basic social change would not take place."—*Saturday Review*, Jan. 18, 1969, p. 53.

5·Divisiveness

It is impossible to gain an inclusive understanding of the phenomena we call poetry without basing it on the relation of *Homo sapiens* to the rest of creation. All extant views bear the limitations of an intra-societal vantage point; even when they look upon poetry in terms of its function, they do so quite within the purview of the culture. To break from their narrowness, one must take the widest possible concept of function and ask what poetry—and by extension, all art—can do *for* the human creature. This question is dealt with in the chapter that follows. For the present, instead of discussing poetry, we seek the groundwork for an all-inclusive view of this phenomenon which only *Homo sapiens* has had to add to the earth.

Of the virtually numberless species of plants and animals that have inhabited our planet only a tiny percentage survives, and this remnant through recent millennia has been ruled by man. Such dominion we regard as only proper. With characteristic humility, we view ourselves as the loftiest achievement of evolution, even though we cannot be sure that long before our arrival superior creatures may not have come and gone without leaving traces. By pragmatic tests, they could hardly have been our peers, whatever powers they might have possessed, for survival is all. They are nowhere to be encountered and we are here. How much longer we shall remain is a starker question, yet even men who lack faith in human nature agree that doom is not inevitable. On the contrary, in the course of our tenancy of the earth we have gathered numerous bundles of information which by the terms of our own defining constitute knowledge. Theoretically, at least, we know enough to enable us to survive and to retain lordship of this planet "forever"— which is to say, so long as the sun allows. All that is required is to be intelligent; and though this is asking a great deal of a self-styled *homo sapiens*, it may not be asking too much.

Knowledge, we are certain, offers power, and no other living organism has any such storehouse of information to draw on for planning the survival of his kind. By piecing together great masses of data, we have been able to tell ourselves plausible stories about the earth's origin and the course of life on its surface. And despite disagreement over details, it is possible to put some faith in the current view of how our world began. Whether the original ball of solid rock dates back five or ten billion years interests us less than the approximate birth date and manner of living creation. It began almost three billion years ago, the inorganic (physiochemical) phase of the planet giving rise to the biological, as self-reproducing and self-varying living matter emerged from the warm primal seas. Since the self-reproductive potential always far exceeds the available food supply, there arose among the different variants a competition for existence marked by a process of natural selection. The best-adapted not only survive; they also in time make improvements on the genetic endowment with which they had begun. As a consequence, progressive changes enter into the biological organization of living things in relation to their respective environments; the organic world, at critical stages in its evolution, could give birth to new dominant creature-types. Thus, less than 400 million years ago, during the "Age of Fishes," ancestral forests made their appearance as well as the first amphibians.

Life had invaded the land, though birth itself continued to depend on the waters. Not until the arrival of a new type of animal which reproduced shelled eggs—"portable and [biologically] compendious oceans"—could exclusively terrestrial existence take hold and flourish. Yet in the course of its 150 million years, and despite the great range of its creations—including the birth of flowers— the "Age of Reptiles" finally gave way to a new biological type, one that was marked by still another departure in the reproductive process: the warm-blooded placental mammals. Like the dominant types that it succeeded, this new biological organization produced an enormous range of new creatures, among them rodents and bats, ungulates and carnivores, whales and primates. The "Age of Mammals" is still with us, as it has been for the last 70-odd million years; yet, as biologists are fond of remarking, about 100,000 years ago a new dominant type emerged from among the primates which has come to mark the third mode of evolution. Physiochemical . . . biological . . . and now cultural.

"With man," says Weston La Barre, "genetic evolution and organic experiments have come to an end. Without involving the animal body

and its slow, blind genetic mechanisms, man's hands make the tools and the machines which render his own further physical evolution unnecessary . . . Nothing like this has ever happened before in evolution. . . . Man, with tools as his projected body and machines the prosthetic creatures of his hands, is not merely a promising animal biologically: he makes every other animal wholly obsolete. . . . This new kind of human evolution is fully proved in the positive sense by man's conquest of reality. . . . In range and in variety of environmental adjustments, no other animal remotely rivals him. . . . [He is] unquestionably the cumulative triumph of animal striving. . . . The creation of culture is the technique, as the social organisms engendered are the means and unit, of survival in mankind. [Culture is] the adaptive mechanism. . . .[1]

Self-celebration of this kind is anything but rare; scientists are deeply in love with the biological production of time as it emerges in mankind. For example, Julian Huxley: "the individual human is the highest and most wonderful organization we know of . . . mankind is the highest type in the solar system"; moreover "A purpose has been revealed to us—to steer the evolution of our planet toward improvement." Loren Eiseley: man "has created an invisible world of ideas, beliefs, habits, and customs which buttress him about and replace for him the precise instincts of the lower creatures." Clifford Geertz: "By submitting himself to governance by symbolically mediated programs for producing artifacts, organizing social life, or expressing emotions, man determined, if unwittingly, the culminating stages of his own biological destiny. Quite literally, though quite inadvertently, he created himself." . . .

These are only four variations on the happy theme; one could keep quoting for days. The implication, if not actual assertion, is that *Homo sapiens* has somehow—unwittingly, inadvertently—risen to a supra-animal condition where, for all practical purposes, he is immune to the determining power of his own biological nature and of biological evolution. Such a conclusion falls short of reality. Though a certain amount of genetic selection is brought about by social, economic, and political forces, there is "no evidence," as René Dubos observes, "that the operation of natural selection has been entirely suspended or bypassed." On the contrary, "man is still slowly evolving anatomically and physiologically." Indeed, "almost every aspect of the biological and physio-chemical environment can alter his body and his mind, even more rapidly and profoundly than do cultural influences"; and in the subsequent chapters of *Man Adapting*, Dubos takes care to show why.[2]

We are suddenly back on earth, once again a member of the animal world. What is more, with sociocultural forces now more powerful than biological ones, man—Dubos reminds us—has "entered a phase of evolution in which many of his ancient biological attributes are no longer called into play and may atrophy through disuse. . . . [His organism] is geared for responding to challenges . . ."; it loses many of its "essential qualities in an environment that is so bland as to make life effortless. . . . The complete absence of challenge can thus be as deleterious as excessive intensity of environmental stimuli." Moreover, the possibility of genetic deterioration is not the only threat arising from biotechnical advances. Adjustments which seem to be successful—to polluted atmosphere, emotional stresses, disturbances of biological rhythms, for example—can in fact result in delayed organic and mental disease. Indeed, some of man's adaptive reactions "may be potentially dangerous and even fatal in the long run." It would seem that the farther we go from our sources as creatures, the more we encounter to remind us that "Above and beyond all, man is still of the earth, earthy, notwithstanding all the technological and medical advances that superficially seem to dissociate him from his evolutionary past."

Uniqueness

What, then, justifies our plangent self-celebrations? What leap of man set him apart from the rest of the animal world? Is technology, for example, an exclusively human invention? Long before the study of animal behavior had enlisted the interest of scientists, Charles Darwin had discovered on the Galapagos Islands a bird that was using a tool: the woodpecking finch, which made up for its lack of a bill by holding a cactus thorn lengthwise in its short beak for prying insects and grubs out of the bark of trees. By now, thanks to the documents of ethologists, we are quite accustomed to such "ingenuity." Jane Goodall has seen more than one chimpanzee in the forests of Tanganyika making chewed-up leaves into sponges for sopping up drinking water from a hollow log, or turning a leaf into a napkin for wiping their hands. Others have observed a small capuchin monkey as he selected a marrow bone and proceeded to employ it as his tool for cracking walnuts. Considerably more impressive is the behavior of the California sea otter, who makes a regular habit of diving to the bottom and coming up to the surface carrying a stone under one arm and a shellfish under the other—mollusc, sea urchin, crab. Then, floating on its back, the otter places the stone on its chest and bangs the prey against the stone till the shell breaks open. After eating the meat, he again dives to the bottom and returns to the surface carrying another shellfish and the same or another stone.[3]

Tool-using is by no means uncommon among mammals—it exists even among insects—but what of tool-making? A chimpanzee, Miss Goodall found, will "fish" for hours for termites by using a twig or a piece of vine which he sticks into a hole in an anthill.

In preparation, he breaks the twig or vine into a suitable length, trims away side branches, and strips off the leaves with his lips or fingers. If this is "tool modifying" rather than "tool fabricating," the distinction dwindles before the more significant fact that a chimpanzee may also prepare his twig in advance of setting out to discover a promising anthill. This adds a new dimension to non-human technology: the seeking and obtaining of an instrument for a future contingency. It takes us squarely into the controversy that exploded in the wake of Raymond Dart's article in *Nature* (February 7, 1925) which not only announced his discovery of *Australopithecus africanus* but also named it an extinct race of apes intermediate between living anthropoids and man. He suggested that a new family be added to the taxonomy of primates and, in addition, he made a few inspired guesses.

The polemical fury with which his upsetting discovery was resisted made a travesty of the proverbial open-mindedness of the scientific brotherhood. Yet in time even experts may come to their senses, and forty-two years later one of them, Sir Wilfred Le Gros Clark, published a gracious account of the whole episode.[4] As it turns out, *Australopithecus africanus* was not an ape at all but the earliest ancestor of man, dating back almost two million years. He was a small, lightly built, erect, and bipedal creature living on animal flesh as well as vegetation, and though his brain was quantitatively small, his hand had already developed sufficiently to make not only crude "pebble tools" but the advanced type of hand ax as well. According to Dart, he assembled an entire arsenal of instruments and weapons made of bone, teeth, and horns, some of which he used for dressing animal hides. That this physically unpowerful creature inhabited open grasslands where food was scarce and where he had to defend himself against dangerous larger animals is evident enough; but how would he be able to succeed? Something in addition to weapons was required. As Le Gros Clark points out, hunting animals in open country implies a social organization: "the coordination and cohesion of their group activities must have depended on a subtle system of communication (whether by vocalization or gesture) between members of each group." They had no choice but to make "conscious efforts to overcome the difficulties of their environment by sheer ingenuity and improvisation." One of the most telling events in the entire *Australopithecine* story was the discovery, on a "living floor" strewn with crude stone implements, of many tools fabricated of material not indigenous to the site which had doubtless been transported there for processing.

If, then, the roots of human technology (to say nothing of the foresight and teamwork) were already flourishing in a small-brained ape-like creature who had emerged well over a million years before our later ancestors, we ought not be surprised to find evidence among contemporary animals of other traits long regarded as strictly human. Though interpreting here is often self-deceiving, the chance is exceedingly small when dealing with sex. Human types have quite obvious animal counterparts, and not only in *femmes fatales* and *ménages à trois*. Permanent adult homosexual partnership exists among porpoises, monkeys, giraffes, elephants; marital fidelity among wolves, beavers, gibbons, foxes, chinchillas, swans, penguins, and so on, and also among a few fish. Obviously when Haldane declared summarily that "many animals are more monogamous than most human beings" he was risking nothing. One seldom does with statistically based pronouncements whereas one has only to speak out of other-than-replicable data for eyebrows to lift.

Is it romantic to talk of animal "grief," "hate," "jealousy"? Is "friendship" too rich a word for defining so remarkable a non-sexual attachment as Konrad Lorenz observed for nine years between two of his ganders? How explain the behavior of two male baboons hurling themselves to their death as they dropped from a cliff onto a leopard which was preparing to attack their troop? The witness, Eugène Marais, offers only "what happened" in the African dusk—a series of pictures perceived by his brain. But every reader of his report is also a mind which strives to make human sense of whatever confronts him. He does not need to be told what it means: the elements spontaneously relate themselves to other patterns guiding his thought. And though each human brain organizes itself uniquely, pervasive similarities in experience and in mental process often make agreement inevitable.[5] Moreover, the frames of perceiving that limit the thought of a human being have the virtue of judging not only others but also himself. So C. R. Carpenter could remark on the present subject, in an address to the New York Academy of Sciences:

Those activities which are ethically accepted—such as altruism, strong emotional affection, and co-operation—are attributed to man's higher intellectual processes if not to superhuman origins. The naturalistic approach to the study of human behavior, competitive and co-operative, egoistic and antagonistic, recognizes roots at a pre-human level.

In defensive actions involving, as he puts it, the close co-ordination of all group members, individuals will be killed but the group survives, the species is perpetuated. So Haldane could declare as plain fact that many animals "display a greater degree of altruism" than their human betters and "devote more of their time to securing the welfare of future generations."

But this is all instinctive, it will be argued. No other creature can think as we do—just look at the puniness of their brains! According to Le Gros Clark, the mere mass is not so important as "the organization of the intrinsic structure. Even in *Homo sapiens* the extremes of cranial capacity in individuals range from 900 cc, or even less, to almost 2000 cc, without in every case any evident difference in intelligence." At least one of our ancestors far outstripped us in size of brain: the extinct Boskop people, forerunners of Africa's Bushmen, who lived at the threshold of the Ice Age. Some of them attained a cranial capacity of almost a third more than the modern average, outrivaling in brain volume any people of Europe, ancient or modern.[6] Though *Australopithecus africanus* of the small brain would not be in the running, indirect evidence of his endocranial casts suggests that the gray matter of his cerebral cortex was convoluted complexly. What counts more than mere mass is indicated here—perhaps in the implications of structural complexity, some of which have been suggested in foregoing paragraphs. But indications of this kind do not offer any specificities. What, for example, of one astonishing capacity of the human mind without which man's world could never have become what it is?

W. H. Thorpe maintains that although no animal language "involves the learnt realisation of completely general abstractions . . . animals can evidently go a very long way toward this," and he refers to some of Otto Koehler's studies which show that animals, and especially birds, are able to "think unnamed numbers."

A raven confronted with a series of boxes with a varying number of spots on the lids, was taught to open only that box which had the same number of spots as there were objects on a key card placed in front of it. This bird eventually learnt to distinguish between five groups indicated by 2, 3, 4, 5 and 6 black spots. . . .

The experimenters took care to eliminate all extraneous clues, changing the number of units, positions, and situations, yet the raven solved the problem by choosing the only item that had not been altered: the number characteristic of the pattern. A gray parrot, observed by P. Lögler, could do something even more impressive:

having been shown, say, 4 or 6 or 7 light flashes, [it] was then able to take 4 or 6 or 7 (as the case might be) of irregularly distributed baits from a row of food trays. Not even numerous random changes in the temporal sequence of signal stimuli impaired the percentage of correct solutions. Having learned this task, a signal of successive light flashes was replaced by successive notes of a flute. . . . [T]he change had no effect on the number of correct solutions. Nor was the accomplishment hindered by the completely a-rhythmic presentation of stimuli or by a change of pitch.

The parrot could not solve the problem of "transfer" (which would mean recognizing, for example, four blasts of a whistle after training to respond to four dots on a paper as standing for four grains to be eaten). Yet the very least to be conceded, says Thorpe, is "that we have here extremely strong evidence that animals can perform the mental abstraction of the quality of number which in human children can only be accomplished by conscious cerebration." Bernard Rensch goes considerably further. Attributing concepts, judgment, and reasoning to creatures other than man, he maintains that all animals capable of learning are also capable of abstraction. Such a conclusion, rather than standing as extraordinary, reflects the currently prevailing view. C. Judson Herrick, for example, in the light of recent experimental work, reverses the position he held thirty years earlier: symbolic thinking can no longer be regarded as a new kind of function peculiar to human beings, for insight, conceptual learning, reasoning, and abstraction are also found in animals.[7] When we move toward the pole opposite to such thinking—to dream—there is little comparable to the data that support such a statement. Many owners of dogs and cats simply "knew" all along that their animals sometimes dream. The barking, growling, twitching, and leg movements in sleeping dogs were compelling enough. They had all they needed of "proof" long before scientific investigators looked for—and finally found—experimental evidence involving changes in the electrical pattern of animal as well as human brains.

It will now be objected, and justifiably, that none of these conclusions takes account of human language. But to do so leads us far afield, for human language includes very much more than articulate sounds. As R. G. Collingwood makes clear, an infant's cry

deliberately uttered in order to call attention to its needs . . . is not yet speech; but it is language. . . . Every kind or order of language (speech, gesture, and so forth) was an offshoot from an original language of total bodily gesture. . . . Speech is after all only a system of gesture, having the peculiarity that each gesture produces a characteristic sound. . . . "Language" [signifies] any controlled and expressive bodily activity. . . . Different civilizations have developed for their own use different languages. . . . Buddha expressed a philosophic idea in a gesture, . . . the Italian peasant uses his fingers hardly less expressively than his tongue.[8]

Language in the fullness of its meaning as communicative expression is not, of course, limited to sound or to sight but can draw on other capacities of the organism. For every language consists ultimately of signs perceptible to a receiver which influence him by having conveyed information of some kind. As known to us at present in their range of operation, the signs may address themselves to hearing, sight, touch, or smell (to list them in descending order of familiarity). The earth is alive with sounds (thanks to the syrinx of birds, the larynx of mammals) and so is the sea (thanks to percussion and other noise-making organs of fish). Since sound, sight, and touch can serve them only for immediate reception, many mammals (badger, marten, brown bear, hippopotamus, Indian antelope, rat, porcupine, beaver) and even some insects resort to odors for conveying messages delayed in time. These markings—which define, for example, territorial boundaries or group membership—constitute communication of the very baldest type. At the opposite extreme, at least from a human point of view, are the facial signs of primates and wolves among animals. One has only to glance at diagrammatic sketches to appreciate the subtlety and variety of the meanings expressed by this purely visual mode of bodily language.

Yet, as Adolf Portmann pointedly observes in his discussion of "Form as an Expression of Inwardness," among the higher animals it is not merely the face but the entire posture that nearly always expresses the mood of the moment—rest, tension, or fear; threat or readiness to attack; and so on. But some will insist that mood does not equal thought. Granted even that animal language may express something in addition to feeling, there is nothing in animal communication that even remotely resembles a proposition. Such a statement might have sounded valid two decades ago, before Karl von Frisch had issued his *Bees, Their Vision, Chemical Senses, and Language,* an astonishing work which shows in detail how the "nectar dance" of the honeybee communicates precise information about a food source, including its distance and direction from the hive. "If we were to employ the terminology of the logic of Peano and Russell," writes Haldane, "we should say that the 'dance' was a propositional function with four variables, translated as follows: 'There is a source of food smelling of A, requiring an effort B to reach it, in direction C, of economic value D.' "[9]

Working with a transparent hive, von Frisch studied the behavior of the scouting bee upon her return home after having discovered a source of food. Other bees immediately surround her, stretching out their antennae to collect the pollen or to drink the nectar she disgorges. Then, followed by the other bees, she performs either of two dances, depending on the information to be conveyed. When the source is nearby (up to, say, 100 meters), she puts on a "round dance," running on the vertical honeycomb in small circles from right to left, then from left to right, in succession. When the source is farther away, she does a "wagging dance" in a pattern resembling a figure eight, moving in semicircular loops interrupted by straight runs during which her abdomen wags continually. The farther the source, the slower the dance, distance being precisely indicated by the number of figures traced in a given time (9-10 wag-

ging runs per 15 seconds = 100 meters, 7 = 200 meters, 4½ = 1 kilo-
meter, 2 = 6 kilometers, etc.). Von Frisch was able to show the graph
which made it possible to calculate the distance up to 11 kilometers.
As for the direction to be followed to the site of the source, this is
indicated by the axis (straight runs) of the figure eight in its relation
to the sun. According to its inclination to the right or to the left, the
axis gives the angle that the site forms with the sun. By their particular sensitivity to polarized light, bees can find their bearings
even when the sky is overcast, just as their highly developed sense
of time enables them to calculate distance with astonishing accuracy.

"We are faced here," says Emile Benveniste, "with a language in
the strict sense of the term, considering not only the way it functions
but also the medium in which it takes place: the system is operative
within a given community, and each member is capable of using and
of understanding it." Indeed, one cannot begin to say much about
language without also opening up the crucial question of culture.
Was culture, as so many people imply, an exclusively human evolutionary leap or does it—like the other capacities I have touched on—
have roots in nonhuman behavior? That the animal world is social is
an old and celebrated story, whether it describe the most primitive
type, the anonymous swarm, or the most advanced, interpersonal
society (to say nothing of the sociality that makes possible the
construction by termites of airconditioned mounds or by beavers of
houses and dams). Fish join together into schools, birds into flocks,
mammals into packs, troops, hordes, and herds. And within these
communities individuals proceed to compete—for available food,
shelter, and mate—being as capable of aggression as of self-defence.
Inevitable analogies to the human species appear in the scholars'
reports, typically in the bond between newborn offspring and
parents and its sudden rupture when the young attain maturity.

As for the practical benefits that derive from living in groups,
they are by no means limited to collective defence or location of
food, being sometimes evident also in self-nourishment and in
physical development. Moreover, some of the social techniques
evolved are too interesting not to mention—such as the sparrows'
defence against a sparrow-hawk by forming themselves into a mob
to drive it away; the American antelope's raising of its white rump
patch as an alarm against danger detected and the spreading of the

signal across the plains from one antelope to another. Such co-ordinated actions depend on the language of bodily gesture, the precision of which often exceeds our ability to perceive. Scientists, moreover, have at times been able to establish the existence of a repertoire of communicative signals—among baboons and macaques, for example, it is impressively large. Finally, as more than one animal behaviorist reminds us, in order to form and to maintain closely knit social groups with coordinated social behavior, the members have to be familiar with one another's traits and capacities and also be able to communicate their moods, needs, or intentions.

In brief, they must *know* one another. And such knowing also involves each member's position within the group. Whereas status in the insect communities is determined by birth, among vertebrates it must be won through competition and rather early in life. So each individual comes to realize where he stands, what he can and cannot attempt. Dedicated to unequal opportunity, the social hierarchy can, however, diminish conflict and promote coexistence within the species. Not that the decisions must always be made by the oligarch. Leaders may at times be observed in what might conceivably be interpreted as consultation with their colleagues.[10] In any case, Martin Lindauer's observations on the choice of a new home by a bee swarm add a quite unexpected dimension to the picture we have been given of intraspecific dominance:

Bees which have found possible sites return to the swarm and indicate their directions and distances by the same symbolism as is used for food sources, save that the dance, being a call to the whole swarm, usually lasts for over five minutes, and may continue for an hour. [I am quoting Haldane's summary.] Other bees follow their direction, explore the sites indicated, and may dance on returning to the swarm. At first a dozen different sites may be indicated. Lindauer gives the history of a "debate" in which bees, to use Lenin's phrase, voted with their feet during five summer days. A site which had at first received only two out of twelve "votes" gradually gained support. During the penultimate day, the dances favouring it rose from seven out of the twenty-two to sixty-one out of sixty-three. On the next day unanimity was reached, and the swarm set off.

Culture cannot, of course, exist without social organization but the converse does not hold; hence none of the foregoing animal behaviors can settle the question of cultural leap. If, however, as Miss

Goodall reminds us, culture consists of "behaviour patterns transmitted by imitation or tuition," then the termite fishing of the wild chimpanzee is a social tradition that represents the emergence of a primitive culture. No less can be said of other acquired habits which have become accepted parts of the life of the group. For example, the characteristic pattern of the European chaffinch's song in a given locality where it has been handed down from generation to generation. These local variations, equivalent to a dialect, are by now an established tradition. Perhaps in time as much will have to be said of a very recently developed animal custom—washing sweet potatoes before eating—which was invented by a young female monkey and soon adopted by all other members of her group and even by some others outside. Meanwhile, we have compelling information about a fellow mammal, the brown rat, which by mood-transmission is able to communicate the knowledge of the danger of a certain bait. Not only is this knowledge passed on from generation to generation but it long outlives its original discoverers. The difficulty, says Lorenz, of combating effectively "our most successful biological opponent" "lies chiefly in the fact that the rat operates basically with the same methods as those of man, by traditional transmission of experience and its dissemination within the close community."[11]

Reasonableness

When even culture, our *sine qua non*, has counterparts in the nonhuman world, can we yet hope to find anything that is man's and man's only? One by one the supposed distinctions collapse under contrary evidence. Whereas it was once thought that play was uniquely human, we now know that animals not only behave differently when in earnest and when making believe but that among some of them, playing takes on the aspect of elaborate, even of organized, games. As for curiosity—or, if you prefer, the "exploratory drive"—it appears not only, as proverbially, in cats but elsewhere also—indeed impressively among the primates. And not surprisingly, interest drops to the vanishing point when novelty wears off. As one would expect, scientists maintain that animal behavior is primarily accounted for by visceral or somatic drives, yet they possess published evidence that it may also be motivated by apparently "psychic" needs. Naturally they do not imply that such drives differ basically from other "biogenic" or "neurogenic" processes. It is their business to discover organic bases for everything that happens in the life of an animal; hence they identify as "nonspecific arousal" something that precedes exploratory activity and they can point to visceral and somatic changes as its accompaniment. Yet they are at a loss to identify any organic basis when they refer, as some of them do, to "animal awareness" and "conscious effort." Neurophysicists have no test for consciousness or unconsciousness. Such evidence as exists derives from other data. So Thorpe, for one, out of his long experience as a researcher in animal behavior and psychology, insists on the "powerful reasons for concluding that consciousness at one grade or another is a widespread feature of animal life." And Wooldridge, whose *Mechanical Man* reduces biology to physics, from a wholly different vantage point entirely agrees.[12]

At this stage it would be pointless to re-argue the pros and cons of "consciousness," for if Thorpe and Wooldridge are correct, the pertinent question is whether we ought to give up the search for an attribute unique to man. From one point of view, further inquiring is needless: that which sees difference in degree as equivalent to difference in quality—no other language is so complex as man's, no other technology, no other culture, and so on. But we can do better, for where is the counterpart in the nonhuman world to the way in which we organize our brains? Possibly we have not found one because we cannot get inside any other creature. On the other hand, from all evidence we can gather, it seems more than merely improbable that such a counterpart exists. Moreover, mentality in man has had an impressively unique genesis. "An animal *way of life* fomented brains in the first instance," says La Barre; "Early Pleistocene limbs of human *type* preceded brains of human *size*." And both the elaboration and expansion of the brain, according to Le Gros Clark, "followed, and was perhaps conditioned by, the perfection of the limbs for an erect mode of progression." Another fact, stressed by Kenneth P. Oakley, that "in most individuals, language associations are built up in part of the cortex which controls the right hand, is probably connected with their being right-handed—another indication of the close connection between manual activity and speech." Thus language, like tools, says La Barre, may derive in part from bipedal man's handedness, as it may derive, also in part, from the societality inherent in his food ecology. As for human culture, K. J. Hayes and C. Hayes maintain that "the 'higher mental functions' observed in man are more nearly results of the culture than causes of it" and that "the most important step in the evolution of modern man from an anthropoid ancestor was an increase in the experience-producing drives relevant to the skills of communication."[13]

For La Barre, whose "organismic thinking" I have been following closely here, the last remark holds an important clue. The carnivorous life in the open, among the Australopithecine hominids, he reasons, "surely put a premium on societality and semantic communication (hence symbol-using, and hence culture). . . . Truly human experiments with the environment are impossible without *hypotheses,* and hypotheses are impossible without *language* (linguistic structure *is* built-in hypotheses about the world). . . ."

Built-in hypotheses about the world! Is there an apter phrase for epitomizing both the processes by which we organize our brains and the consequences? We must teach ourselves what we learn from confronting the vast unknown outside and within us, and not only at first when as protoplasm we encounter society. So long as we live we have to keep hypothesizing or risk being overwhelmed. Thus each of us steers his life by his own shifting patterns of expectation— of order, reasonableness, even of justice—and counts on reality to conform. And when some part of it violates the model we have made of it, we balance the equation with a handy unknown, such as accident, perversity, luck, probability, deity. Yet to scarcely any of us does the possibility even occur that other models might be made for which no need of correction would arise.

Naturally such a notion does not rise in the very young. All that a human infant can learn is what the creatures who form his reality show him and tell him, their yesses and noes—the particular strength, weakness, wisdom, folly, customs, beliefs, superstitions of the group that by chance composes his fate. Choiceless at the start, he in time outgrows their yesses and noes, only to submit to others', then yet others'. And if his successive tuitions have been normative for his culture, he will finally have learned how to take its realities in his stride. That is to say, he will assume that the world and his view of it coincide. A bit roughly at some times, at other times not at all; but misfittings are also part of the normative outcome. One must count on cohabiting with bafflement, absurdity—history most certainly ought to exhibit a meaning! The palace of pleasure might better have been located farther from the precinct of excrement! Clearly the world's design could have used some improvement, yet the scheme of things, by and large, makes sense, always excepting those unforeseeable visitations of what our brains have no choice but to call insane caprice. The expectations we have built for steering our lives cannot bear with events that would smash them to bits, or with their trailing clouds of grief. So we make a truce, declaring that the ways of the world at times surpasseth understanding; which is all we can do if our brain is to resume the condition toward which it strives: isochronous, rhythmical beating freed from disturbances.

This grossly simplified recital takes no account of at least one crucial aspect: the tendency of the human brain to question its ways, and the consequences. Needless to elaborate, it ranges from mild to drastic—even in societies which quite proscribe challenge, alterations occur over large blocks of time as revised versions of the past, hence of the present and the future. Yet only the overwhelming event with its undermining realization can force the brain to alter its ways of making constructs—the new world of atoms and electrons, for example, which now compels it to give up its orthodox concepts of ordinary experience. Nothing of the kind results from discoveries which do not directly threaten our entrenched process of thought, whatever their surprise or mysteriousness. From earliest times *Homo sapiens* developed the habit of gathering in great assemblies; "he tends to come together," says Young, "at intervals in huge swarms." We are not able to say why, or (to take another random example) how it is that certain animals know how to control their populations in accordance with available food supply.[14]

Such unexplainables appear to demand only widening in our patterns of expectation. And if in some instances they give rise to sharp straining, we can always hide our impotence under an expedient tautology. We have much more negative capability than meets the eye, bandying about, as we do, many crucial terms which we cannot define—"fatigue," for example, and "life" itself. Biologists no longer even try: what they do about the latter is to recognize it. Comparable impotence holds true of our knowledge of the simplest cell: to grasp in detail its physiochemical organization is admittedly beyond our power. But we are able to go on discussing fatigue and life and the simplest cell quite without anxiety. Not so when we stare at such a thought as "eternity," or when we search for "purpose" in all phenomena, as we feel we must, on planes commensurate with understanding. One has only to follow the career of "teleology" to appreciate the insistence of the brain's demands and the way the brain meets them: with ever new arrangements of words to reconcile conflict. "Reason" readily supplies them. Involved only in the choice of means—not at all in the choice of ends—reason (in Bertrand Russell's phrase) consists in a just adaptation of the first to the second. What, then, determines the ends? They can hardly be regarded as chosen, since they are the natural outcomes of the ways in which we taught ourselves to think. And unless these ways undergo profound alteration, human beings must continue to ask questions which imply answers outside the range of their "organs" of thought.

Such paradox hovers above every advance. Whatever the rhetoric used—"challenge" or "problem"—we have long been aware that each answer bequeaths new questions. But of course we shall solve them all, even those detailed in Rattray Taylor's *The Biological Time Bomb*. If our science has spawned the dilemma, it can also dispose of it. We minions need only be intelligent, heed its demands, bear with it. But not—heaven forbid!—in all that we do. Or in most, if life remain livable. Not only, says Bridgman, the scientists' philosopher, must we "disregard determinism when dealing with ourselves; we have to disregard it also, within reason, in our everyday contacts with our fellows." Science has become another Sunday religion to be mocked the other six days. The world it gives us is alien to our world of experiences. Whence the bleakest paradox of all, emblazoned in programs which show why nature's conquerors must sue for peace or perish. The brain that replaced our native creature environment now searches for ways to salvage the essential-lost. The circle has come full round. Meanwhile, for all of Western philosophy and its footnotes, reason still remains what Hume had called it, "the slave of the passions," the desires, emotions, feelings. Wherefore we now force one of its cleverest incarnations to undo much that we had asked it to do throughout thousands of years. While we ask ourselves if this urgent act also is the natural outcome of a culture which began, however dimly, back in the Ice Age.[15]

Eden

Or is it rather the fate of a creature which had been somehow impelled to teach its brain to regard its owner as an other-than-itself? At a certain time, says Eiseley, ancestral man entered his own head. All that our kind has become goes back to this crucial moment, for to see oneself, to feel, to know oneself as an other is to do as much with the world. To break through the seamless web—no longer to be part of all that one senses and knows—is to enter a strangeness from which there is no return. Paradigms of the fate can be found in ancient myths which compress to a single moment long ages during which men slowly came to realize what they had "done" and lost. If the drama of Eden is much more explicit about disobedience-punishment-pain than about sin, no one can doubt that the latter stands for the sense of loss, uneasiness, and fear that accuses a creature outside the paradise-web. Nothing is so much as hinted of the wonders he may find there, the marvels he might achieve. The tales of the race's childhood are songs of paradise lost, of homelessness, helplessness: the lament of a creature aware of his alienation from the whole of living creation.

Though the fate of Eden is also the fate of every child, countless generations would pass before men and women could perceive this fact and their helplessness before it. As Trigant Burrow makes clear in "The Strifeless Phase of Awareness," the rudiments of human mental life

lie in the organic reactions of the unborn child. At first merely vegetative, later physiological, there develops within the embryo a synthesis of function which we may call primary, organic life. Here, in this preconscious mode, is embodied a phase of development in which the organism is at one with its surrounding medium. Here primitive consciousness is in a state of perfect poise, of stable equilibrium. Here, at its biological source within the maternal envelope, this organic consciousness is so harmoniously adapted to its environment as to constitute a perfect continuum with it.[16]

With birth, everything changes, though in the infant's earliest stirrings of consciousness, its sensation and awareness still remain subjectively identified with the mother organism. Nevertheless, with his "forcible expulsion from the paradise of peace and plenty,

he enters a totally different world of experience. Into the original, simple, unitary, homogeneous matrix of organic consciousness there now enter those gradual deposits of extraneous experiences caused by the organism's enforced adaptation to the external world, and these experiences constitute the nuclei of adult consciousness. The child has now entered a world of stubborn solidarity and can maintain life in consistent comfort and security only on a basis of relative adaptation to outer circumstances.

It is quite needless to add to what has already been said earlier on the subject of "outer circumstance" as it acts upon the child, beginning with the group of surrounding creatures who form his first reality. "Relative adaptation," on the other hand, demands some attention in view of Burrow's remark that the process of adaptation is "essentially outward-tending," that it is inherently a process of "objectivation":

With increasing objectivation, this outer rapport [between the organism and the external world] is later established in respect to the organism itself. Objectivation returns upon the very self from which it set out. The self becomes its own object, and consciousness is, as it were, infolded. Being thus turned in on itself, the organism has attained a state of mental development which distinguishes the human species from the rest of the animal world—the stage, namely, of self-consciousness.

The development proceeds by slow, irreversible stages, for consciousness of the "I" is not inborn. It grows very gradually within the human mind; it is something the child has to "do"—the "I" is not a fact but an act, said Fichte; it is something he has to learn. He has to learn it if he is to survive in the world that has brought him to birth. And the more civilized this world, the greater its demand that he think of himself as "subject" and all other creatures and things as "object." That this subjective-objective dichotomy of his experience is in fact illusory—that, in Sir John Eccles' words, "every observation of the so-called objective world depends in the first instance on an experience which is just as private as the so-called subjective experiences"—cannot matter to him or to his world. For both "know" where the boundaries lie: where *continuity with* ends and *looking at* begins. In the unreflective view of our own culture, the self is a discrete unit, something we can name and define. Such naming covers more than agency; it also includes possession. Each of us *owns* a self, an "I," about whom we sometimes think, with whom we converse, for whom we plan, and so on. More often than we realize, each of us watches this self as it behaves, observer and observed. Phrases of this sort do more than describe our thinking. They testify to the concomitant divisiveness within each individual that arose as the species gradually divided itself from the environment, rupturing the seamless web.

One cannot grasp the significance of any development in man's mind without also considering linguistic development, ignorant though we are of how language emerged and the forces that propelled its direction. We know only that something unprecedented occurred long eons ago, during man's phyletic infancy, when he lived in a natural continuum with everything around him. As Burrow writes, the entire experience of his common perception of the surrounding objects and creatures was a sensation—a physiological aspect—of man himself. And just as sensations and impressions were experienced by all men, so were their instinctual drives, their interests, their motivations. All their actions and responses were physiological in nature: organic behavior, arising from their needs, and common to all members of the species. Hence man's "compactness" at this time: compactness of man and environment, of individual and kind. It is here, in this bond between man and man, in this continuity between "objective" sensations and "subjective" feelings—between man's own physiological processes and the earth—that we see the primary pattern of human awareness and consciousness: the unitary condition of the species—man in a seamless web of relationships. What set in motion the forces that brought about change is as huge a mystery as any that can be conceived. All we may hope to gain are rudimentary notions of the process that developed within the organism. So, with our present modes of thought that reflect its altered course, we construct a model which at least does not hinder belief. It allows us to imagine that

Through the modification of a segment of the forebrain, man was enabled to produce (at first unconsciously and later consciously) symbols or signs in substitution for actual objects or situations. In other words, there developed the faculty of language, through which men not only responded to the same thing with the same symbol, but through which they ultimately came to *know* that they responded in a like manner to the same thing. Through an unprecedented miracle of nature, our organism contrived to take the universe of its surroundings into itself, as it were, to incorporate it in its own neural tissues. A tree or a stream became a vocal sound. It became a spoken or a written word, and a mechanism emerged that related us to our universe of external matter and energy through an entirely new system of receptivity and response. We now became related to the world of external objects and to one another through an entirely different system of neural reactions.

This step in biological evolution, this miracle of nature, opened up unimagined spheres to human behavior. One need consider only one of its numerous gifts—the economic gain in communication—to appreciate the enormities of power it brought for man to deploy. They were and still are unforeseeable, hence almost beyond any strength of restraining.

From the very outset, danger inhered in the emerging part-function. By its sheer range, efficiency, and momentum, the capacity for forming symbols tended to overwhelm other part-functions of the organism and to take control. As a result of its ever-increasing emphasis and dependence on word-sign-symbol, human behavior began to lose contact with the medium of actuality, "the good earth." In this physiological transition from action to symbols of action, says Burrow, "the human species, unaware of what was happening, gradually lost touch also with the organic origin of the word and therefore with the organic source of its own behavior. . . . Our feeling-medium of contact with the environment and with one another was transferred to a segment of the organism—the symbolic segment, or forebrain. . . . What had been the organism's whole feeling was transformed into the *symbol* of feeling." Moreover, "with the increase of symbol usage and the coincident transfer of the organism's total motivation to this linguistic system, man developed a self-reflective type of consciousness."

Viewed from where we now stand, the series of events-and-consequences seems to have driven forward with the inexorable logic of organic power. What begins as a highly advantageous part-function gradually attains over-all domination. And because of the intermediate position it holds between effectors and receptors in the bodily system, between stimuli and responses, the new symbolic-linguistic capacity finally remakes the organism's entire mode of relationship. *Continuity breaks up into divisiveness in the three crucial areas simultaneously. Man becomes alienated from the rest of living creation, from his fellow human beings, and from himself.*

Ideally all the discrete paragraphs of this chapter I have called "Divisiveness" should compose a single sentence to suggest how man's new acquisition has transformed his life. As compared with other creatures, says Cassirer,

man lives not merely in a broader reality; he lives, so to speak, in a new *dimension* of reality. There is an unmistakable difference between organic reactions and human responses. . . . No longer in a merely physical universe, man lives in a symbolic universe. . . . No longer can man confront reality immediately; he cannot see it, as it were, face to face. Physical reality seems to recede in proportion as man's symbolic activity advances. Instead of dealing with the things themselves, man is in a sense constantly conversing with himself. He has so enveloped himself in linguistic forms, in artistic images, in mythical symbols or religious rites that he cannot see or know anything except by the interposition of this artificial medium.[17]

Which is to say that more and more of the time, he lives in indirectness. No longer part of the seamless web of the natural order, he stands outside, thanks to what has been at least in part his own achievement—an achievement from which he cannot escape: his divisiveness.

Can he ever recapture the sense of creature at-oneness, the organic tradition in which he lived for millions of years?

NOTES AND COMMENTS

1. Julian Huxley, "The Crisis in Man's Destiny," *Playboy*, Spring 1967, p. 217. Loren Eiseley, *The Immense Journey*, Vintage Books, 1957, p. 92. Clifford Geertz in *New Views of the Nature of Man*, p. 111. Weston La Barre, *The Human Animal*, pp. 89-92, 162, 211.

2. Dubos, *Man Adapting*, pp. 11-21, 260, 13, 260-277, 279.

3. Jane Goodall, "Chimpanzees of the Gombe Stream Reserve," in *Primate Behavior*, Irvin DeVore, ed., Holt, 1965, and in *National Geographic*, December 1965. • Some examples of construction as a form of animal technology: the interior architecture of termite mounds, beaver houses (some more than 18 feet in diameter); beaver dams (one of them, 642 meters long, found in the Jefferson River, Montana); nest-building: of the weaver-bird (with perfectly tied knots); the tailor-bird (enclosed in broad leaves which the female sews together); the European long-tailed tit (the interior is lined with a thick insulating layer of feathers; one nest used 2,000 feathers). See Jacques Lecomte, *Animals in Our World*, Holt, 1967, Chap. 7; author also attributes the invention of the counterweight to the spider, p. 96.

4. I draw freely on Sir Wilfred E. Le Gros Clark, *Man-Apes or Ape-Men?* Holt, 1967, esp. pp. 113-124. Dart's term, combining a Latin prefix with a Greek suffix, is confusing (*Australo*=southern) and inappropriate (*pithecus*=ape).

5. Here I draw freely on Konrad Lorenz, *On Aggression*, Harcourt, 1966, pp. 199-204; W. H. Thorpe, *Science, Man and Morals*, Ithaca, Cornell University Press, 1966, pp. 127, and "Ethology and Consciousness," in *Brain and Conscious Experience*, J. C. Eccles, ed., pp. 491-493; and Robert Ardrey, *African Genesis*, Dell, 1963, pp. 59, 78, 172. I have said nothing of invertebrates because lasting unions are unusual among them. Note, however: dung-beetles do not separate after mating but work together in rearing their young. Termite marriages, which call for complex ceremonials—including a self-mutilation, a "nuptial promenade" which may last for hours and even days, and amputation of their antennae—continue for life, in some species, for at least eighty years.

6. Concerning brain size and convolutions: Le Gros Clark, *op. cit.*, p. 115; Eiseley, *op. cit.*, pp. 134-139 (Boskop people).

7. W. H. Thorpe, in *Brain and Conscious Experience*, pp. 478-479. Bernard Rensch, *Evolution above the Species Level*, Columbia, 1960, pp. 340-341, 344-345. C. Judson Herrick, *The Evolution of Human Nature*, Harper, 1961.

8. In their respective discussions, Thorpe, Rensch, and Herrick do indeed take account of human language. • R. G. Collingwood, *The Principles of Art*, Oxford, 1958, pp. 236, 246, 243, 241. See also D. Burckhardt et al., *Signals in the Animal World*, especially Part III; Altman, *Organic Foundations of Animal Behavior*, p. 456. Adolf Portman, *Animal Forms and Patterns*, Faber, 1952, p. 187; see drawings (after R. Schenkel), pp. 212, 213; also in Thorpe, *Science, Man and Morals*, pp. 94-95.

9. Frisch's volume was published by Cornell, 1950. • Haldane, *Diogenes*, Autumn 1953, p. 62: "The many-valued logic of Tarski and

Lukasiewic would be more appropriate than any of the systems which derive from Aristotle in which the principle of the excluded middle holds." Emile Benveniste, "Animal Communication and Human Language," *Diogenes*, I, 1953.

10. Sociality: for an account of "the division of labor which characterizes a social unit" among penguins (a group in which both sexes make genuine marriages), see D. Burckhardt et al., *op. cit.*, p. 135. Practical benefits that derive from living in groups: W. C. Allee, *Cooperation among Animals*, 2nd ed., Beacon, 1951. See also Altman, *op. cit.*, pp. 455, 459. Pecking order: T. Schjeldreup-Ebbe, "Social Behavior in Birds" in *Handbook of Social Psychology*, C. Murchison, ed., Worcester, Mass., Clark University Press, 1935. "Line Dominance" is the simplest type of organization (see Allee, *op. cit.*): A dominates B, who dominates C, and so on. However, sometimes A dominates B, who dominates G, who dominates A. Sometimes E dominates F, who dominates G, who dominates H, who dominates E. • The summary of Martin Lindauer's observation appears in Haldane, *Diogenes*, pp. 68 f. The local variations in the European chaffinch's song are discussed by Thorpe, *op. cit.*, pp. 71 f., the washing of sweet potatoes, by S. Kawamura, "The process of subculture propagation among Japanese macaques," in *Primate Social Behavior*, C. H. Southwick, ed., Princeton, N. J., D. Van Nostrand Company, Inc., 1963, pp. 82-90.

11. Lorenz, *op. cit.*, p. 161. "[R]ats appear to be the only mammals that have increased in numbers during the past century as much as men."—Dubos, *So Human an Animal*, p. 188. "The Norway rat . . . has successfully eluded over the ages man's most ingenious attempts to eradicate its species, yet it is an almost unbelievably naive prey to a kingsnake."—W. J. H. Nauta, *op. cit.*, p. 42.

12. ". . . the play of some mammals, where it may take the form of relatively elaborate or even 'organized' games, seems to be on a par with children's games such as 'touch' and 'hide and seek.'"—Thorpe, in Eccles, *Brain and Conscious Experience*, p. 725. For interesting details on the subject of "exploring play" in the nonhuman world, see Sally Carrighar, *Wild Heritage*, Houghton, Mifflin, 1965, pp. 208-210. See also Altman, *op. cit.*, pp. 463, 465-469 *passim*. Dean E. Wooldridge, *Mechanical Man*, p. 161. • For problem-solving in relation to conscious thought, see Wolfgang Koehler, *The Mentality of Apes*, 2nd rev. ed., Routledge & Kegan Paul, 1927; W. H. Thorpe, *Learning and Instinct in Animals*, Harvard, 1963, p. 259; Jacques Lecomte, *op. cit.*, p. 118.

13. La Barre, *op. cit.*, pp. 346-348.

14. "A stone weighing 9 tons was found hollowed on 6 sides by mortises 10 feet high which architects have been unable to explain, as if their function had been forgotten ever since by all the builders in history. Gateways 10 feet high and 12 feet wide have been cut out of a single stone, with doors, false windows and sculptures carved with a chisel, the whole weighing 10 tons. Sections of walls, still standing,

weigh 60 tons, and are supported by blocks of sandstone weighing 100 tons embedded in the ground. Among these fabulous ruins there are some gigantic statues, only one of which has been brought down and placed in the garden of the museum at La Paz. It is 25 feet high and weighs 20 tons."—Louis Pawels and Jacques Bergier, *The Morning of the Magicians*, Stein & Day, 1964, p. 164. • Keats could not have been more explicit when he wrote: "I mean *Negative Capability*, that is, when a man is capable of being in uncertainties, mysteries, doubts, without any irritable reaching after fact and reason" (Dec. 22, 1817).

15. Gordon Rattray Taylor, *The Biological Time Bomb*, London, Thames and Hudson, 1968. To the non-specialist, refinements in the number of years assigned to ancient periods do not matter very much. (It is enough to realize that a billion-odd years separate the origin of the earliest single-cell organisms from the advent of man.)

16. Throughout this section I draw heavily on Trigant Burrow, *Preconscious Foundations of Human Experience*, Basic, 1964, pp. 32 ff., 13-15, 28, 107-113, rephrasing statements or citing them. But because this is a posthumous work which has been "edited by William E. Galt," it is not always possible to know whether one is quoting Burrow or not. (I say this with appreciation of Galt's own qualifications, his career, and his own book on *Phyloanalysis*. Unfortunately Galt died before completing his task and additional editorial aid had to be obtained.) • It may seem contradictory for me to draw heavily on the writings of a man who had trained with Adolf Meyer and Carl Jung, who had for years followed Freud, and who had been a founder and one-time president of the American Psychoanalytic Association. Some of the reasons will be found in Dr. N. W. Ackerman's Foreword to Burrow's volume (especially pp. vii ff.). Dismissed from his university post and excommunicated from the A.P.A., Burrow continued from the mid-1920's to his death (1950) to work out his "phylobiological" vision of humanity. Although (possibly to some degree because) D. H. Lawrence had reviewed enthusiastically Burrow's *The Social Basis of Consciousness*, I could never get any social scientist to discuss its ideas. Meanwhile Burrow had been studying the social implications of neurosis and the biological causes of conflict and, from 1932 on, conducting group-analytic research which anticipated contemporary group-therapy procedures. • Herbert J. Muller, writing in 1943 (*Science and Criticism*, Yale, p. 126), remarked concerning organismic concepts by which biology approaches sociology, that "they supplied the basis for at least one revolutionary social-theory—the theory detonated by Trigant Burrow in *The Biology of Human Conflict*. Few thinkers appear to have noticed the explosion; but if Dr. Burrow is right, he has shattered the foundations of almost all the world's thought."

17. Ernst Cassirer, *An Essay on Man*, p. 43.

6 · The Seamless Web

Un homme n'est qu'un poste
d'observation perdu dans l'é-
trangeté.

—Valéry

Although everyone knows that humanity is only one strand in the web of creation, one can rarely speak about man's condition as a creature without eliciting defensiveness and confusion. Part of the problem grows out of language. "At-oneness," for all its plainness of statement, carries a portentous ring. "Seamlessness" is a wholly negative abstraction. Still more difficult to envisage is the "mixedness" of man's condition. Though physical reality recedes from him as his symbolic activities advance, man obviously does not live in indirectness all or even most of the time. Moreover, the innermost tendencies of his organism regularly insist on obtaining satisfaction: he is still very much a creature of earth despite all he knows of control. Indeed one of the largest mysteries in his behavior is the source of the balance he is able to maintain between his learned restraint and the needs that propel his organism.

Those needs, drives, instincts cause endless problems for the expert who would classify and define them and chart their courses. But whether they be presented as the "dominant" few (nourishment, reproduction, aggression, flight) or as more numerous "inborn behavior patterns" does not matter at all. For the experts totally ignore the organic tradition of man's biological evolution—of his drive to regain, to recover, his primary organic unity with the rest of creation: his "seamlessness," which endured through his millions of years, whose heritage is inscribed in his myths, his religions, his arts, his rituals. One is strongly tempted to explain the omission, but the reader can readily do this for himself, aware of the mind's self-protective way of "forgetting" things which might threaten its balance. Besides, at this point a more productive paradox beckons. The very capacities of the mind that were and are involved with man's divisiveness act toward fulfilling his drive toward unification. A part of the sickness itself must work toward the cure.

Drive, Desire, and Public Object

Readers of Malinowski's *Coral Gardens and Their Magic* may remember one of the incantations of the Trobriand Islanders as translated into commonplace English:

> It passes, it passes,
> The breaking pain in the thighbone passes,
> The ulceration of the skin passes,
> The big black evil of the abdomen passes,
> It passes, it passes.

The Trobriand Islanders did not need to be lectured on the evocative power of their words. Like the rest of humanity, they were acting as it were "on the knowledge" that something deeply desired can be imagined into believable existence. Their incantations imagine with words, words marked by rich phonetic, rhythmical, metaphorical, and alliterative effects, (according to Malinowski), by weird cadences and repetitions. But such language is only one variety of the several materials that the mind can use in attempting to fulfil the pressing demand for a much desired reality.

At this point a reader anxious to define imagination may try to choose from among the offerings of philosophers, critics, psychologists, writers, scientists. He may separate imagination from the fancy (as Hume, Dryden, Hunt, Wordsworth, Emerson, Croce, and many others have done in respectively different ways). Or he may break imagination itself into two or more modes, such as "productive and reproductive" (Kant), "primary and secondary" (Coleridge), "formal and material" (Bachelard), "penetrative, associative, contemplative" (Ruskin), and so on. This arbitrary list gives no idea of the modes of speculation, which often encoil metaphysics, philosophy, semantics. And on the whole the verbal arrangements tell more about the originators than the subject, since imagination can be made to include as little or as much as one chooses, issuing, as it does, from the mental power of forming images: "ideal" or "actual," spontaneously or with deliberateness. To be sure, in everyday affairs we draw on the publicly held store, whereas in visionary thought they arise on their own to lead a life of their own. Yet even this self-evident distinction does not hold; for whatever else it may be said to be—memory, invention, association, imitation, and so on —an image is always a symbolic representation responding to some need of a particular human organism.

This emphasis may seem too obvious until one realizes, with Suzanne Langer, that the image "which presents with something like the objectivity of a percept, still bears the stamp of the thing it really is—part of the cerebral process itself, a quintessence of the very act that produces it, *with its deeper reaches into the rest of the life in which it occurs*" (my italics).[1] Each person's images (whether they appear when he is awake, entranced, or asleep) are passages from the life of his own and particular brain. The quaternions came to Hamilton, a mathematician; the vision of dry bones to Ezekiel, a prophet. "Kubla Khan" was dreamed by Coleridge, a poet; the "Devil's Sonata" by Tartini, a composer.

One head of a state, "finding" an image to picture his social program, speaks of a "New Deal"; another, of a "New Frontier." A business-man, reaching out for words which others will be able to envisage, coins a phrase about "a product mix." By contrast, a mystic falters when he attempts to describe what he beheld. "The deliciousness of some of these states is too subtle and piercing a delight for ordinary words to connote," says St. Teresa of Avila, for whom union was not a vision but "rather some overmastering idea." And when the mystics proceed to represent it with any language, the imagery fails—as, moreover, they insist that it must. Wherefore Dr. Johnson reasoned, concerning Boehme, that "If Jacob had seen unutterable things, Jacob should not have attempted to utter them." Yet Jacob's fellows crowd line after line with imagery which evokes deep meaning only for themselves.[2] As do numberless non-mystics also. The inspiring sights and feelings fail to come alive on the page for others; they remain private possessions. Whereas the imagining that we call "creative" gives rise to public objects. Its touchstone is the power of the recorded enactment to be meaningfully "known" by others, to be a source of affecting, enlarging experience for others.

This power is of course the hallmark of the productions of creative artists and scientists, none of whom is primarily concerned with discovering what philosophers refer to as "knowledge": statements which are absolutely certain, irrevocably true. What Karl Popper observed of science—that it is cosmology, the problem of understanding the world, ourselves, and our knowledge as part of it— holds equally for all the arts. And the imagination is the only instrument available to a mind with this primary concern. In the arts obviously, but also in "the purest and driest parts of science, imagination is as necessary as in lyric poetry" (Russell). There is indeed no logical path leading to the universal laws which give a picture of the world, as Einstein stated three decades ago: "They can be reached only by intuition, and this intuition is based on an intellectual love of the objects of experience." One thinks of Rilke's earlier declaration about works of art: that "only love can grasp and hold them." By now, to be sure, the essential identity among all approaches to "cosmology, the problem of understanding the world and ourselves" is no longer questioned. "The pioneer scientist," says Planck, "must have a vivid intuitive imagination for new ideas, ideas not generated by deduction, but by *artistically* creative imagination." The dedication of a recent book on *Scientific Uncertainty and Information* affirms that "An artist's inspiration or a scientist's theory, reveal the unpredictable power of human imagination."

The statement might as easily have been made a half-century

ago, even earlier, for the involuntary nature of creative enactment had already been witnessed widely. In music and poetry the "unpredictable power of human imagination" had become an established tradition, pointed up with a number of cases of entire works composed at a single stroke, some of them during dream.[3] But quite as spectacular were some of the reports from science. Poincaré's theory of Fuchsian groups arrived one night when, contrary to his custom, he had drunk black coffee and could not sleep: "Ideas rose in crowds; I felt them collide until pairs interlocked, so to speak, making a stable combination." Kekulé von Stradonitz literally beheld one of his most important discoveries—of the benzine ring—one evening when he was trying to prepare some pages of a chemistry textbook. The writing did not go well:

. . . my spirit was with other things. I turned my chair to the fireplace and sank into a half-sleep. Again the atoms flitted before my eyes [taking the pattern of rings]. Long rows, variously, more closely united; all in movement, wriggling and turning like snakes. And see, what was that? One of the snakes seized its own tail and the image whirled scornfully before my eyes. As though from a flash of lightning I awoke; this time again I occupied the rest of the night in working out the consequences of the hypothesis.

("Let us learn to dream!" Kekulé urged his fellow-scientists.) Sir William Rowan Hamilton while walking with his wife to Dublin came up Brougham Bridge and "then and there felt the galvanic circuit of thought close; and the sparks which fell from it were the fundamental equations between i, j, k [quarternions]; exactly as I have used them ever since." Karl F. Gauss, having tried unsuccessfully for years to prove a certain arithmetical theorem, finally succeeded, but "not on account of my painful efforts. . . . Like a sudden flash of lightning, the riddle happened to be solved."

Suddenness, spontaneity—von Helmholtz had already discussed them in a pioneering speech to scientists in 1896. Today we take them for granted, together with the fact that creativity does not end with illumination in the arts or in the sciences. The flash, the dazzling intuition, the dawning recognition must be exposed to the common light and verified, perfected: moved toward "completion" —submitted to the inscrutably collaborative processes that in poetry are called, misleadingly, "conscious artistry." Poets consider words in the full range of their meanings; scientists, symbols of quantity and logical sequences. Each specific procedure takes a different direction, whereas the over-all processes take the same. Today it is usual to hear it remarked that in the testing of hypotheses as well as in their discovery, imagination is the indispensable factor.

Though we have come to learn something about the course of creative activity, we still remain mystified by its genesis. Whence— not to ask Wherefore—this imaginative projection? Bacon held the use of poetry to consist in giving "some shadow of satisfaction to the mind of man in those points wherein the nature of things doth deny it." Centuries later, in the era of Freud, Théodule Ribot (who exalted scientific creativity far above art) maintained that "all invention presupposes a want, a craving, a tendency, an unsatisfied desire." When on a later page in the same *Essai sur l'imagination créatrice* he declares the origin of all imaginative creation to be "a need, a desire," the effect is mainly to give scientific caste to proverbial notions— necessity has been the mother of invention for two thousand years just as the wish has been the father to the thought. Desire if impeded may begin a visionary action of thought; but the origin, says Ribot, can also be a need. The word "desire," which is understood to be the attraction toward something we want to possess or to do or feel or know, is broad enough to include almost anything, and the same may be remarked of "need." But the two are not the same unless we choose to make them the same. And if we do, we shall have to take account of the *modes* of desire-need that are associated with creativity and its productions.

At this point the distinction made at the close of Chapter 3 becomes decisive. One mode will be seen to consist of what it is that the creator of the poem desires-needs to possess or do or feel or know as embodied in the references of his lines to experiences (feelings, ideas, objects, events) within the culture. A wholly different order of desire-need arises from his human condition as a creature inhabiting the earth: a specific type of creature (as noted earlier) in whom the desire-need expresses itself as a burden upon his organism—malaise, irritation, tension, even torment, which finds relief in the act of composition.

Creativity cannot emerge without an unburdening of the organism whether the disturbance be remarked or not and regardless of degree. Alongside Byron's bravura passage on "the lava of imagination whose eruption prevents an earthquake," Donne's couplet is comparatively calm:

> Griefe brought to numbers cannot be so fierce,
> For, he tames it, that fetters it in verse.

And Wordsworth's lines are plain:

> To me alone there came a thought of grief;
> A timely utterance gave that thought relief,
> And I again am strong.

In fact, Newman's prose remark that "poetry is a means of relieving the overburdened mind" might be mistaken for a paraphrase. Odd as it may seem, few people have gone so far as Newman's contemporary, the High Anglican cleric and professor John Keble, who argued in his *Oxford Lectures* and reviews that to innumerable persons poetry "acts like a safety-valve to a full mind," at times "preserving men from actual madness."[4] Whether or not one accepts the last phrase, there can be no ignoring of the fact that the pressure exerted by these desires-needs upon the organism may at intervals be sufficient to direct much of its behavior. Or that they may continue to do so over long periods of time despite the counterpressure of its livelihood desires-needs. All too many careers of musicians, painters, writers, and scientists show the sign of obsessive dedication, often at the cost of deprivation and suffering and with little or no likelihood of worldly reward.

To wring one's hands at the adulation some of them receive only posthumously is irrelevant if their kind of creating involved little choice. In a sense, volition plays the same part here as in composing. At least, most typically creative persons do not seem to be able to help themselves from doing what they "have to" do, susceptible as they are to those accumulating burdens whose arrivals cannot be predicted or controlled. Much like other events which upset the balance of the organism, these particular desires-needs demand to be disposed of . . . by the classic means for regaining stability. We are back to "The Body Makes the Minde," to the cycle of creative accumulation and release, to the inspiration that sets it in motion (Chapters 1, 2).

We are also back to the second paragraph of the present chapter: to the paradox and to the need omitted from the lists. Whatever may be their total number, each basic drive must show its own disturbances, periods of crisis, directions, effects, and so on, but no one could pretend to have perceived more than a miniscule amount of the manifestations of all that must drive the organism, or to expect the enormous complexity of these phenomena to exhibit parallel behaviors. On the other hand, no one doubts that the drive to perpetuate the species manifests itself in the desire for sexual union with another human body. And if there are any discernible manifestations of the drive to recover primary organic unity with the rest of creation, one of them surely is adducible in the public objects produced by creative imaginers: in the act by which they are created as well as in the supposed recapitulation of this act as re-lived in the re-experiencing of the object. The foregoing pages of this book have focused on the creator; the remainder of the present chapter is concerned both with ourselves as participants in what the creator has made and with the creature-drive for unity instinct within us. Analogies here may be difficult to find, yet it would seem that if the reproductive drive can fulfil itself when it finds release through union with another human body, this other human-creature necessity, when it finds its release through imagination's symbols, can unite us with the "body" of the world.

How is such a statement to be justified? What is there about the creative symbol that makes possible any union with the world? In all that has preceded I have referred to various forms of creative productivity, but in facing this question I limit myself to the form I know best, which is poetry, while continuing to assume the essential nature of all creative imagining to be the same.

Fusions of Resemblance

A poem is made of words as a musical composition is made of tones: words are the public materials composing the private, irreducible entities—the metaphors, similes, other figurative structures; the questions, exclamations, propositions, other statements—and the terms denoting their relationships. No single one of these expressive units is itself a *sine qua non*. If Western readers show surprise at discovering that a poem can be effective without any figures of speech, it is because they have grown used to regarding metaphors and similes as indispensable. And, of course, the metaphor is not only the commonest figure in verse; as the naming of an imaginative fusion of resemblance which has already occurred in the poet's mind, it is emblematic of the poem itself. Personifications and imaginative similes (basically varieties of metaphor) are also functions of resemblance. As for the so-called "tropes of connection—the synecdoche ("blind mouths"), the metonymy ("When I consider how my light is spent")—though technically fusions of contiguity, they are obviously also expressions of resemblance, and of a highly compressed kind.

One might expect that figure-less verse must, by contrast, be weak in impact. So narrow a notion of poetic condensation can be tested by trying to bluepencil Goethe's "Wanderers Nachtlied, II," the poem by Wu-ti quoted on page 100, H. D.'s "Lethe," Eliot's "Rhapsody on a Windy Night," or longer works such as Cavafy's "Waiting for the Barbarians," the best of the Scottish ballads, some of the *Cantos* of Pound. Structure proves as various in figure-less verse as elsewhere—as poetic logic itself. And if, as noted earlier, each picture in Wu-ti's poem acts as a term of a multiple fusion, much the same can be said of figure-less poems in general: each expressive unit holds together with the force of resemblance to the totality they form, as a part of the work or as the whole. That is, each poem is a total unification composed of smaller unifications; through its fusions of resemblance, it identifies a relational unity. To say that a poem which fails to do so fails as a poem, is a circular way of reaffirming the demand we make that a work be a whole. So we speak of the organic unity of a successful poem, attributing to it the power of a life of its own within the reader. Can such life fail to stir in him empathetic feelings of unification, since (whatever the fusions employed) its action proceeds by bodying forth similitude?

British writers of the last century, fascinated by imagination's gift for identifying resemblances, discovered in it the essential of poetic thought. "This intuitive perception of the hidden analogies of things," wrote Hazlitt, "or, as it may be called, this instinct of the imagination, is, perhaps, what stamps the character of genius on the productions of art more than any other circumstance; for it works unconsciously like nature, and receives its impressions from a kind of inspiration." Moreover, the making of "strange combinations out of common things" (Shelley) is an act of emotion. "Imagination, purely so-called, is all feeling; the feeling of the subtlest and most affecting analogies" (Leigh Hunt). And so on. Some of these writers remarked on an accompanying disturbance, as noted earlier in citations from Byron, Wordsworth, and especially Keble; yet nowhere is it viewed as bringing on a type of assault to which the brain responds with its characteristic drive to "make sense" of it. In assimilating the new to what it already knows, it may seize on things that turn out later to make bad sense, if sense at all. The organism's resumption of balance in itself cannot assure validity. There is no telling what its headlong action to contain the assault may lead to. Indeed no pathways conceal so many pitfalls as the ones that the mind may take in its "intuitive perception of hidden analogies." The distinguished French *philosophe* J. B. Robinet declared that life's principal effort is to make shells, and his *Philosophical views on the natural gradation of forms of existence, or the attempts made by nature while learning to create humanity* was for a time regarded as a scientific contribution. The world's recorded verse must be populated with images of every range which are as valid as this large one of Robinet's, and since the same doubtless holds true in other provinces of creative imagining, it makes all viable intuitive perceptions the more astonishing and precious. Moreover, the drive toward similitude reflects itself not only in linguistic fusions of resemblance but in countless other actions within the poem—obviously, for example, in parallelism, refrain, antithesis. Poems in fact are steadily engaged in the work of con-fusing, for the paradigm of poetry—metaphor—pervades its every act.

If, as Oliver Goldsmith remarked, metaphor is a kind of magical means "by which the same idea assumes a thousand different appearances," it is also the means by which the same appearance stands for a thousand different ideas. The two actions are simultaneous and indivisible. We "understand" by perceiving-feeling likenesses and unlikenesses, by bringing some things together and, in so doing, setting other things apart—assimilating/distinguishing. This amounts to regarding likeness and difference as reflexive parts of the process of relational thinking, the one implying the other. They are aspects, not antitheses. That likeness is not identity nor difference always contrariety, is generally—and curiously—ignored despite the glaring fact that much less than we suspect in experience can be fitted into neat little packets of black-and-white. The engulfing universe exemplifies variety in uniformity, as Plato had discovered long before British poets and critics rediscovered its significance for art. Coleridge said "poetry produces two kinds of pleasure . . . the gratification of the love of variety, and the gratification of the love of uniformity," which correspond to the "two master-movements or impulses of man." Wordsworth, in pointing to the second ("which the mind derives from the perception of similitude in dissimilitude") as the drive at the center of poetry, anticipated the view of the contemporary scientist. "A man becomes creative, whether he is an artist or a scientist," says Bronowski, for example, "when he finds a new unity in the variety of nature . . . finding a likeness between things which were not thought alike before. . . . An innovation in either field occurs only when a single mind perceives in disorder a deep new unity."[5] For Wordsworth the necessity for such perceiving flows out of the depths of the organism. It is "the great spring of the activity of our minds, and their chief feeder. From this principle the direction of the sexual appetite, and all the passions connected with it, take their origin. . . ."

Ultimately such a view would seem to differ little from the one I have offered with the introduction to this chapter, though on the plane of overt behavior only. What of anterior causes, what of the great spring's sources? Man's actions and thoughts could hardly be impelled by and drawn toward the interrelatedness of all that surrounds him unless at the depth of his organism he believed in its unity and felt and knew it to exist, as ancestral man had felt and known it in his capacity as a participant. At these innermost creature levels of feeling and knowledge, the arbitrary cannot find room. Nature's buzzing and blooming confusion that engulfs our senses is not suddenly ordered and unified and interinvolved in all its parts merely because post-Eden creatures would wish it to be. Such statements as Anaxagoras' (that everything is latently involved in everything else) or Emerson's (that everything is convertible into every other thing) are but feeble and partial intuitions in latter-day symbols of the primary organic unity of a creature who himself had been part of the seamless unity of the "All."

If the sciences, like the arts, are busy with new unifications, in their encompassing physical laws as in minor equations, every such enactment of the imagination is a mirror-image of the all-involving unity whose existence it affirms and toward which it reaches out with the only means we possess: the microcosm of a symbol. The passion impelling such creations underlies not only transcendent dramas and murals of paradisal grandeur; even in casual-seeming sculptures assembled from industrial debris its forces are at work, manifesting the same uniquely human need for perceiving kinship among the disparate, wholeness beneath the chaos. And if every such created object is a unification, it is so not only in its totality but equally in the smaller fusions that make it one. So it happens that when, in experiencing a poem, we respond within us to such large and small embodiments of language, we participate in a re-enactment of unification, whether we know it or not—and by the means (the symbols of language) provided by the very capacities of mind that were and are involved with divisiveness.[6]

That only certain types of imaginative creation can impart a sense of cosmic identification has sometimes been insisted on by philosophers and poets in particular. The greatest of all of poetry's attempts "to say one thing in terms of another," writes Frost, "is the philosophical attempt to set matter in terms of spirit, or spirit in terms of matter, to make the final unity." The duality is quite as plain in Karl Jaspers' remark that "We call great art the metaphysical art which reveals, through its visuality, Being itself." The differences in the terms employed by Frost and by Jaspers count less than the common belief that both statements avow:

Poetry begins in trivial metaphors, pretty metaphors, "grace" metaphors, and goes on to the profoundest thinking that we have.

—Frost

Fundamentally, just art and therefore skill bare of philosophic signifi-cance is the non-transcendental manner of representing, of decorating, of producing the sensuously attractive, in as much as it exists in isolation and has no metaphysical bearing.

—Jaspers

In a conversation with Wilhelm Furtwängler, the philosopher was still more insistent. "In art there are two layers: one is metaphys-ically sincere, the other, while showing vital creativeness can at best please but it cannot impress itself in an essential manner. This sharp division cannot be made with objective certainty, but I con-sider it of fundamental importance."[7]

Division of art into a hierarchy may also grow from quite different thinking—from a "new ontology of the imagination," for example, as described by Gaston Bachelard in *The Poetics of Space*. Renouncing both his earlier "objective" method and his "interpretation through depth," the French philosopher-historian of science distinguishes formal from material imagination, the second of which bodies forth poetic "purity." In an attempt to help others recognize in the image *being is round* "the primitivity of certain images of being," he pursues "the phenomenology of roundness" with the addition of statements on roundness collected from La-Fontaine, Michelet, Van Gogh, Rilke, and others. Bachelard's "pure imagination"—which he names "metapsychological"—is neither the "profoundest thinking" of Frost nor the "revelation of Being" of Jaspers but the experiencing of being itself ("we find ourselves entirely in the roundness of this being").

For each of these thinkers there are two different species of poetry, variously defined. Yet how would one go about separating poems which fuse spirit with matter, matter with spirit, from those which do not? Or poems which are metaphysically sincere from those in the underlayer which show vital creativeness only? Or poems which are metapsychological from the lowlier others? In all such cases, two different species presuppose two different births or sources. Are there, then, two different creative processes? Or, at the level of sources, two different sets of impelling needs, drives, compulsions? Furtwängler rejected Jaspers' dichotomy as a miscon-struction of the genesis of art. Even the most insignificant tune, he assured him, originates in the same indivisible source of creativity.

Both musician and philosopher clung to their convictions, neither succeeding in proving that the other was wrong.

Proof in matters of this kind seems all but unreachable. (How validate Auden's assertion that "every poem is rooted in imaginative awe"? As Mark Van Doren "answered," in a similar discussion, "If you have to prove it, then it can't be very important.") Furtwängler, however, might have added that any attempt such as Jaspers' to rank imaginative works into a higher and a lower species rests on a misconception of subject matter in art. To look, with Jaspers, for the metaphysical—or with Matthew Arnold, for the solemn-serious—is to ignore what a poem *does* in favor of what it seems to be "about." As remarked many times in this book, the experiencing of a work of art is indivisible; hence any thinking about, any focusing upon, a partial aspect of the whole can take place only within our analytic heads. Nevertheless we have no instruments for dealing with matters of rank except for our analytic heads; and when we use them to cope with this question a number of conclusions confront us.

First, every successful poem, regardless of whatever else it is and does, embodies similitude. It embodies it, as we have noted, through the action of its language, through its fusings of resemblance, in the whole and in the parts, irrespective of how each happens to be formed grammatically and irrespective of the experiences, objects, events, and/or ideas in the culture to which it happens to refer. This is to say that regardless of what any poem may happen to be "about," all the resemblance-making actions begin and end with unification. Furthermore, we may even conceive of these unifications of poetry as comprising a generic mode of love. This would be doing the kind of thing that Plato, Jean Baptiste Lacordaire, and Freud, for example, have done in attributing its multiform manifestations (love of woman, of parents, of a cause, etc., etc.) to a single generative force. For the Greek philosopher, it was mind; for the French theologian, love of God; for the Viennese psychoanalyst, instinctual impulse. To conceive of each poem as "an act of thinking love" implies an even vaster emotion, one which takes these three great forces as themselves but partial expressions of man's organic desire for reunion with creation itself.[8]

Resonance and Reverberation

Whether all human feelings flow out of a single source, whether, as Otto Rank believes, "every emotion which is admitted in its totality manifests itself as love,"[9] poetic thought, no matter which aspects of reality it embodies, proceeds by enacting union. Viewed thus in terms of what it does, every successful poem is a binding-together. And since binding-together is fundamentally what every poem is "about," we meet a seeming paradox. The substance or referents of a poem appear to serve as the vehicle for the making of unifications; or, in more familiar terms, it is a poem's "form" (structuring) that constitutes its ultimate "subject" (unification) —the act of unifying forms the poem, its referents subserve this action. But it is in this sense only that every poem must embody the identical theme, for "form" is always a structuring of particular referents. And *what* a poem binds together are elements drawn from the writer's private experiences, elements possessing public meaning and interest, which are therefore able to resound in the experience of the reader.

These *resonances* depend on and evoke the world of their culture, its events, ideas, objects, and so on. Unlike the "ultimate subject," which transcends human time and place, the resonance-world is walled in always by the specific culture it arises from and speaks to. A less apparent limitation inheres in the speech it is borne on. "In a symbol," says Carlyle, "there is concealment yet revelation" —and for this reason it is a "wondrous agency." One of the sources of the conflict was noted earlier, in the disparity between the terms of a metaphor and the counterpull away from resemblance (p. 91). A second relates to one of the modes of desires-and-needs discussed earlier in this chapter. That an impulse to reveal encounters an impulse to conceal is an axiom of behavior within the culture. And that the poet may be unaware of their effect upon his thinking also may be taken for granted, as well as their conflict, for the characteristic ways by which poetry speaks make its presence plain. We have already noted the tendency of poetic language to obscure the directness of reality, to throw over it a sort of half-consciousness of unsubstantial existence—to reveal the fervent emotions of the mind under certain veils and disguises. Revelation yet concealment —and, as a consequence, a tension which marks the very nature of poetic resonance, adding to the other forces it exerts upon the reader a further power: that of a message which "still seems to be trying to express something beyond itself."[10]

What can be found of the reader's response to the poem's *act* of uniting? Hopeless though it may seem to ask where or how, some light yet glows from the crucial fact that this action does not address itself to bits and pieces of nameable cultural experience. It speaks purely as a force of feeling. And when this force "sounds" upon the feeling-capacities within the reader, his organism vibrates with responsive aliveness; it fills with *reverberations*. F. W. H. Myers, like a good many others, acknowledges the apparently "mysterious power by which mere arrangements of sound can convey an emotion which no one could have predicted beforehand, and which no known laws can explain."[11] And despite the great attention given by scholars to the linguistic structures of poetry, one essential effect—if not the profoundest effect—has been ignored. That a poem embodies rhythm together with other patterns of recurrence (rime, assonance, parallelism, antithesis, and so on, as the case may be) has been taken for granted. But taking for granted totally misses the emotional symbolism—and consequent import—of recurrence, associated as it is with other cycles of recurrence, with diurnity, the seasons, and the deep creature reassurance that they bring. Similarly, taking for granted fails to appreciate what the presence of these expectation-patterns implies for the reader as structural reflections and embodiments of uniting in the over-all action of uniting that is every poem.[12]

None of the foregoing observations so much as implies any possible notion of separating the meanings of any word in a poem from its sounds.[13] So far as I can see, every attempt to do so has greatly confused by suggesting, when not asserting, that a word actually leads two separate lives. At times the sequence of sounds in a poem of an unknown tongue can be so "musical" as to delight a listener who has no idea of their meanings; and if the word "musical" can ever be applied to verse, it is here: to a sonal pattern with no denotation at all. A special kind of meaning, however, is held by some writers to exist in certain words. F. E. Halliday, for example, speaks of an "aural symbolism lying deep in the unconscious and fully operative and evocatory only when experienced in the semi-hypnotic condition induced by verse, and to a lesser degree by rhythmical prose such as that of the Bible and Sir Thomas Browne." This "elemental significance" would be possessed by only certain sounds and sound-combinations "which are echoed and partially reproduced in words like *lie, light, foam, sea, beat, grave, stone, day, glory*."[14] But even agreement with this writer that "Far more words are onomatopoeic in origin than is generally realised" could not affect the fact that every word is a complex of sounds and of meanings which acts upon the reader as an indivisible totality—just as his response to a poem is an indivisible experience of what I have called resonances and reverberations. In the same passage (on the "poetic state"), Valéry gives his own characterization of the first:

Under these conditions familiar objects and persons somehow undergo a change in values. New affinities are felt to exist between them, new relationships never observed in ordinary circumstances.

and of the second:

There is a tendency to discover a complete new system of relationships in which men, things, and events . . . also seem to have some indefinable though marvelously exact relation to the modes and laws of our general being.[15]

The most telling and neglected aspect of the reverberative process must now be considered, one which was foreshadowed in the opening words of this book. As Collingwood in his *Principles of Art* says of "psychical expression," it consists in the doing of involuntary and perhaps wholly unconscious bodily acts, related in a peculiar way to the emotions they are said to express. Not only are the two "elements in one indivisible experience" but "every kind and shade of emotion which occurs at the purely psychical level of experience has its counterpart in some change of the muscular or circulatory or glandular system . . . which expresses it." Thus, "the mere sight of some one in pain, or the sound of his groans, produces in us an echo of his pain, whose expression in our own body we can feel in the tingling or shrinking of skin areas, certain visceral sensa, and so forth."[16]

This involuntary expression of "sympathy" by the organism

is central to Spire's massive study of the biological foundations of poetry, *Plaisir Poétique et plaisir musculaire*. By its organization of rhythm, says Spire, which is so different from that of the verbal structure in a typically logical sentence, and by its more or less strong accents, the affective word-order of verse "echoes" the internal physiological motions of the poet during composition as well as those of the reader during his experiencing of the poem. "Indeed, it models itself on these internal motions; it is their external and communicative aspect. The movements and attitudes of our muscles— those hidden in our organs and in the rest of the body as well as those of the face (especially the mobile and sensitive muscles associated with responses of sight and taste)—*translate* the ideas and feelings experienced in the poem." ("I read sentences of Goethe as though my whole body were running down the stresses"— Kafka.)

Since the poem produces patterns of motion in the body which parallel those set forth by the words, one might almost be tempted to say that in its own way the organism "reads" these motions. In any case, it clearly participates in them. As counterpart, as psychical expression, they are re-presented—and therefore "known"—by the organism in ways that antedate by millennia the life of the culture. For reaction-with-the-body is an archaic type of identification; hence to be expected in the expressions of a type of person who is (as Eliot calls him) "more primitive, as well as more civilised, than his contemporaries," one whose imagination can draw him toward the very depths of his creature nature—and his reader with him.

Knowledge

To respond to a poem is to know its resonances-reverberations— but do they equal knowledge? The question touches on categories, leading away from all knowledges which complete themselves in abstractions whose validity must be verified, regardless of the thinking processes out of which they had been born. Science, of course, is the exalted example. Every truth it proposes must survive testing by "value-free, objective" analytic procedures before it can gain acceptance. By contrast, certain types of knowledge become true or untrue according to criteria which are "subjective." And here the exalted example is religion—toward which our question of knowledge is inevitably magnetized.

So often and so surely has the closeness between religion and poetry been stressed that most people who think of the relationship probably suspect that the two must ultimately be one. Or agree with Arnold that most of what passes for the first will in time be replaced by the second.[17] If all poems are rooted in imaginative awe, so are all religious experiences, the most voluble witnesses to which are the mystics. But as they never fail to avow, the feeling-knowledge that they behold in their ecstatic visions simply cannot be conveyed. Though poetic inspiration may already be on the decline when composition begins (as Shelley maintained), great poetry nevertheless succeeds in affecting readers profoundly, even if it is (as Shelley added) only a feeble shadow of the poets' original conceptions. This basic difference in capacity to impart does not in itself clear up the question of knowledge. To do so, one has first to define religion—if one can.

Sir James G. Frazer's definition, which was generally shared—that it is "a propitiation or conciliation of powers superior to man which are believed to direct and control the course of nature and of human life"—has been despatched for filing in the dustbin of history by replacements both legion and ingenious. Yet while the new verbal arrangements may rule out the supernatural, even the type that proposes "an expanded new religion based on the new materialism" makes room for a kind of divinity—for example, one that is "not truly supernatural but transnatural," growing out of ordinary nature but transcending it (Julian Huxley). Thus the poetic knowledge conveyed in Wordsworth's Immortality Ode and numberless other intimations in verse of cosmic-identifications-cum-beneficence must be nothing else or more than religious knowledge. Although this reasoning does not lead us quite back to archaic cultures, where poetry was at one with prophecy and other rituals, it dismisses all the distinctions that emerged when (as noted before) the single personage who was a poet-possessed, God-smitten, and a seer gradually split into the specialized figures of the prophet, the soothsayer, the mystagogue, and the poet as we know him.[18] We should have to shut our eyes to the outcome: to the fact and all its compelling implications that the primordial composite type, the *vates*, evolved into different persons who must use different means for achieving their ends. For a person who believes that means and end are ultimately inseparable, that the one cannot help but condition the other, the relation between poetry's knowledge and religion's knowledge is decisively settled. The road available to poetry is not a road available to religion. Nor is it necessary to belabor differences in interest and temperament. "I cannot answer for the experience of others," wrote Ruskin, "but I have never yet met with a Christian whose heart was thoroughly set upon the world to come, and so far as human judgement could pronounce, perfect and right before God, who cared about art at all."

Though poetry's knowledge (no matter how viewed) is neither trans- nor super-natural, some of its advocates, constrained to make it respectable, try to prove it able to compete with or even exceed the knowledge of science. A critic sets out to establish "the empirical status of the work of art" (Read), a poet argues the basis for teaching poetry (MacLeish), a philosopher analyzes the "truth-value" of art (Feibleman) or art as knowledge (Ross). . . . With their dependence on analytic reasoning, some of the demonstrations make a curious spectacle since science itself is unable to justify its existence by analytic reasoning. While value-free, science is based on values, freedom from value-judgements being one of the first, as Eric Weil points out. And since "science and consistency are unable to justify fundamental values, and particularly themselves, as necessary," "logically, scientific thought seems to have undermined its own basis."[19] Moreover, unless the theorems of Kurt Gödel and of Alfred Tarski do not hold, the very ideal that science pursues will continue to be hopeless. As for complete objectivity, one of its most precious principles, it is now acknowledged to be unattainable even in the segment of existence to which science applies. The apologists for poetry's knowledge may lay down their arms.

The understanding that poetry brings I call by the name of "creature knowledge" in the hope of suggesting the entirety and profundity of the reader's involvement with the All. The poem's resonances-reverberations submerge the aspects of divisiveness that qualify his ordinary thoughts and feelings. Nor can future or past, of time or of place, exist in this here-and-now. "All possible objects of the ordinary world, exterior or interior, beings, events, feelings, and actions, remaining normal as far as appearances are concerned, suddenly fall into a relationship that is indefinable but wonderfully in harmony with the modes of our general being" (Valéry).[20] For the poem as a whole and in its units is, above all, an act of uniting. And to respond by experiencing its act of uniting is to relive, for the duration and with the whole of one's being, an indefinable sense of organic creature unity such as pervaded our creature-existence when it "knew" itself part of the seamless web of creation. That a man is an alien, that divisiveness burdens his nights and days, that his organism is instinct with the drive toward primary unity, make his need for re-living acts of this kind more crucial than he can know. For isolate man, as he lives ever more in himself, from others, and apart from the world that contains him, creature-knowledge has become no less than a necessity for his survival.

NOTES AND COMMENTS

1. This, Langer says (*Mind*, pp. 98 f.), is the second thesis of Jean Philippe's *L'image mentale (évolution et dissolution)*, Paris, Alcan, 1903, p. 5. Malinowski, *Coral Gardens and Their Magic*, Indiana, 1967, vol. 2, pp. 236-237, *cf.* p. 213.

2. "They continuously and bitterly complain of the utter inadequacy of words to express their true feelings but, for all that, they glory in them; they indulge in rhetoric and never weary of trying to express the inexpressible in words. All writers on mysticism have laid stress on this point. Jewish mysticism is no exception, yet it is distinguished by two unusual characteristics which may in some way be interrelated. What I have in mind is, first of all, the striking restraint observed by the Kabbalists in referring to the supreme experience; and secondly, their metaphysically positive attitude toward language as God's own instrument."—Gershom G. Scholem, *Major Trends in Jewish Mysticism*, Schocken, 1961, p. 15; see also pp. 58, 135. • Not every mystical experience must remain unaffecting for others: the "visions" re-presented

by the creative imagination in certain poems of St. John of the Cross, Traherne, Dickinson, for example.

3. Karl Popper, *The Logic of Scientific Discovery*, London, Hutchinson & Co., Ltd., 1958, preface, cited in A. M. Taylor, *Imagination and the Growth of Science*, Schocken, 1967, p. 1. • To the examples given earlier (Chap. 2) may be added the account of composition presented by Mozart: "[M]y thoughts come in swarms and with marvelous ease. Whence and how do they come? I do not know; I have no share in it. Those that please me I hold in mind and I hum them, at least so others have told me . . . and all these morsels combine to form the whole. Then my mind kindles, if nothing interrupts me. The work grows,—I keep hearing it, and bring it out more and more clearly. . . . I then comprehend the whole at one glance; and my imagination makes me hear it, not in its parts successively as I shall come to hear it later, but, as it were, all at once (*gleich alles zusammen*)."—Paul Chabaneix, *Le Subconscient*, Paris, Alcan, p. 94, quoting *Mozart* by Jahn, vol. III, pp. 424 f. • After "Kubla Khan," the most celebrated work assigned to composition during dream may be "Il Trillo del Diavolo" by Giuseppe Tartini ("I heard [the Devil] play with consummate skill a sonata of such exquisite beauty as surpassed the boldest flights of my imagination. . . ." • Jacques Hadamard, *The Psychology of Invention in the Mathematical Field*, p. 7, gives an authenticated report of the mother and sister of a prominent American mathematician, who had spent a long, futile evening over a certain problem in geometry: "During the night, [the] mother dreamed of it and began developing the solution in a loud clear voice; the sister hearing that, arose and took notes. On the following morning, she happened to have the right solution which the mother failed to know."

4. For the earliest American discussion of Keble's theories of poetry, see Prescott, *op. cit.*; for the most recent, Abrams, *op. cit.* (Keble's *Lectures on Poetry* were delivered in Latin in 1832-1841, published in 1844, and translated into English by E. K. Francis in 1912.)

5. "The Creative Process," *Scientific American*, Sept. 1958, p. 63.

6. Symbols of language, in literature; and by extension, in the other arts, by their respectively different symbols.

7. Robert Frost in "Education by Poetry," *Amherst Graduates' Quarterly*, Feb. 1931. Karl Jaspers in *Von der Wahrheit*, Munich, 1947, as translated by J. P. Hodin, *Prism*, No. 1, 1962.

8. ". . . Wherefore the syllables/ Reach outward from the self in an embrace/ Of multitudes. The poetries of speech/ Are acts of thinking love. . . ."—Burnshaw, *Caged in an Animal's Mind*, p. 109.

9. Rank's sentence continues: "yes, one might also identify love with totality, just as fear, and all its negative emotions, are one with partiality."—*Will Therapy*, Knopf, 1936, p. 197.

10. The last two sentences of this paragraph are a mosaic of quotations cited earlier, from Wordsworth (Chap. 4, p. 126), Keble (Chap. 4, p. 138), and A. C. Bradley (Chap. 3, p. 106).

11. F. W. H. Myers, "Essay on Virgil," precedes the words that I quote and preface with an adverb: "[Poetry] as a system of rhythmical and melodious effects—not indebted for their potency to their associated ideas alone—it appeals also to that mysterious, [etc.]."

12. "The rhythmic oscillation becomes the distinguishing mark of the functions of life-structures. The pulsations, the rhythmic flow of the functions of cells form the law of life. . . ."—J. C. Smuts, *Holism and Evolution*, Macmillan, 1926, p. 175.

13. Gerard Manley Hopkins, in a student paper of 1865, says the following: "The structure of poetry is that of continuous parallelism [which I should call recurrence here as he does later], ranging from the technical so-called Parallelisms of Hebrew poetry and the antiphons of Church music up to the intricacy of Greek or Italian or English verse. But parallelism is of two kinds necessarily—where the opposition is clearly marked, and where it is transitional rather or chromatic. Only the first kind, that of marked parallelism, is concerned with the structure of verse—in rhythm, the recurrence of a certain sequence of syllables, in metre, the recurrence of a certain sequence of rhythm, in alliteration, in assonance and in rhyme. Now the force of this recurrence is to beget a recurrence or parallelism answering to it in the words or thought and, speaking roughly and rather for the tendency than the invariable result, the more marked parallelism in structure whether of elaboration or of emphasis begets more marked parallelism in the words and sense. . . ."—*The Journals and Papers*, London, 1959.

14. F. E. Halliday, *Shakespeare and His Critics*, London, Gerald Duckworth & Co., 1949.

15. Valéry "Poetry," in *The Forum*, April 1929, p. 251.

16. Collingwood, *op. cit.*, pp. 229-231 *passim*. Remy de Gourmont: "Le véritable problème du style est une question de physiologie." Kafka quotation from his *Diaries, 1910-1913*. • "Echoes" is a poor word here because of its denotation of a time interval, which would raise a question which does not affect these psychical expressions (do we blush because we are ashamed? vice versa? "The common-sense view is right, and the James-Lange theory wrong," says Collingwood). • See discussion of the unity of perception and movement in Ernest G. Schachtel, *Metamorphosis*, Basic, 1959, Chap. 9, esp. p. 213. • The quoted passages from Spire are slightly revised from the highly telescoped translation I made for Cleanth Brooks and Robert Penn Warren, *Understanding Poetry*, 3rd edition, Holt, 1960, p. 124. • "In laughter the whole body becomes, to a varying degree, an 'apparatus for expression'; archaic pleasure in movement is reactivated and is socially permissible."—Kris,

op. cit., p. 225. Eliot's phrase ("more primitive . . .") recalls the suggestion of F. W. H. Myers that men of poetic genius may be progenerates—may not "their perturbation mask an evolution which we or our children must traverse when they have shown the way?"—*Human Personality and Its Survival of Bodily Death,* London, Longmans, Green, 1903, vol. 1, p. 56. See also Prescott, *op. cit.,* Chap. XV.

17. See above Chapter 4, pp. 128-131. J. G. Frazer's definition is from Chapter 4, *The Golden Bough,* Macmillan, 1949.

18. Here, as in the passage on the *vates* type (p. 129), I follow the phrasing of Huizinga in his *Homo Ludens.* I am indebted to Sir Kenneth Clark for the Ruskin quotation from *Stones of Venice,* vol. 2, Chap. 4, par. 58. Poems on religious subjects tend to be handicapped to the measure in which they evoke objects and events connected with a specific creed, in having appeal only to readers who are able to accept and believe in the referents.

19. Eric Weil, in *Daedalus,* Winter 1965, pp. 183-186 *passim.* According to Gödel's theorem, the consistency of any system cannot be proved within the system itself, yet unless it has consistency it cannot be a system. Tarski's theorem shows why there cannot be a universal description of nature in a single, closed, consistent language. • "The power of modern man is based on 'objectivity.' But look closer and you'll see that this power is possessed by objectivity in itself—and not by man himself. He is becoming the tool—or slave—of what he has discovered or evolved . . . a way of looking."—Valéry, *Idée Fixe,* Pantheon, 1965, p. 79. See also "Passion in Clear Reason," by David Krech, *The Nation,* March 28, 1966. The outcome for "complete objectivity" of the work of Werner Heisenberg and Niels Bohr requires no restating. For the hopelessness of the scientific ideal, see "The Logic of the Mind," American Association for the Advancement of Science Lecture, by J. Bronowski, *American Scientist,* Jan. 1966, p. 4.

20. Valéry, *Poésie et pensée abstraite,* Oxford 1939, p. 8. (Cf. translation in *The Art of Poetry,* Pantheon, 1958, p. 59.) Creature knowledge, regardless of the source from which it is drawn, is not supernatural, transnatural, or divine. It is a reliving of the indefinable sense of organic creature unity at the *creature level,* not "above" or "beyond," though the rules by which human thinking organizes the brain tend to endow any such indefinable and timeless sense with the transcendental, with divinity of some sort. There is, of course, no correlation between the significance of the creature knowledge that a person may draw in experiencing works of creative imagination and the quality of these works as art.

N.B.—page 183, last 6 lines: see Conrad Aiken's "the miracle of interconnectedness" in his poem "The Crystal" (*Sheepfold Hill,* New York, Sagamore Press, 1958, p. 18; also *Selected Poems,* Oxford, 1961).

III

Art-Experience

7 · Object

Recurrent prophecies on the death of art would be entitled at the least to a hearing if esthetic processes were not rooted in human biology. When it was that they first may have manifested themselves, we have not the slenderest notion, but that they were long indeed in evolving seems quite beyond doubt. The incredible productions of Upper Paleolithic sculptors and painters imply biological origins at least as ancient as those of speech—and probably also as common. In any case, anthropology has yet to discover a human society where art expression is unknown.

What for the lack of a clearer name we call esthetic processes does not seem to be limited to man; on the contrary, it is almost impossible to perceive certain animal behaviors except in some relation to art. Among the well-observed instances, none is more striking than that of the male bowerbird of Australia and nearby islands, so named for the structure he builds, into which he tries to lure the female for mating. Whether it resemble a tunnel, a tepee, or a roofed hut, near the entrance he sets up a display area filled with bleached bones, feathers, shells, pieces of stone, of metal, shining coins, or similar objects. Some bowerbirds arrange the display with brightly colored fruits, which are not eaten, or with flowers and silver-sided leaves, which are replaced when withered, sometimes daily. Members of one species color the interior walls of the bowers with a paste of fruit pulp or powdered charcoal, using dried grass for a brush. Others (the satin bowerbirds) make a painting implement out of a small wad of inner tree-bark and dip it into "pigments" such as berry juice. Not only are these decorated areas attractively maintained but the bird insists on a specific color scheme. One experimenter placed flowers of different hues onto the area only to watch the bird remove all but a red orchid, which it finally deposited on top of a group of pink flowers. Similarly a bird using blue flowers will take away a yellow one added there by an observer, and a bird choosing yellow flowers will not tolerate a blue one.[1]

Immediate questions spring to mind. Might these striking actions include something in addition to what we know about fertility? Easy as it is to read human mental processes into the behavior of other creatures, it is even easier to reject the possibility of relationship. In view of the common ancestry of vertebrates, such reasoning hardly makes sense. Moreover, our first question threatens to grow respectable when we realize that this bower is not used by the female for laying eggs; that she builds her nest and raises her family without the father's help; and that only when the birds are fledged will she "consider" taking them to the bower. Meanwhile, the male, who may have spent four or five months putting together the original construction, has continued to maintain it. Every day over the weeks he gathers new flowers and places new leaves on the ground according to his "design." And he cannot even be sure that the female will come back. Some mothers eventually bring the young birds to the bower—and the family goes through a type of ritual display—but others never return.

The post-mating behavior of this father calls to mind the singing performed by birds long after it had served in the cause of sex or territoriality. Is this "playing with sounds"? Does it represent the beginnings of true artistic activity? As Thorpe, whose *Bird Song* studies "The Biology of Vocal Communication and Expression in Birds," points out:

the twilight song of the wood pewee appears to have no territorial function and is said to be independent of the breeding cycle, and the daytime song also continues long after the end of the breeding season. Experienced observers state that the song of late summer and autumn is, in many American song birds, superior to that of the breeding season. The duration of the skylark's song in Europe is greatest in September and October. Similarly, in many species of American song birds, the lengthening, elaboration, and sometimes complete change in the song after the end of the nesting period is noteworthy, and these changes often seem, to our ears, to take the form of aesthetic improvement.

Moreover, some songs "show evidence of spontaneous rearrangement of phrases and the invention of new material which suggests something similar to real musical invention." Finally, he asks, since "the fundamental intervals of human and bird song are the same," "is it not reasonable to suppose" that man, with bird song impinging on his ears, "developed a musical signal system by imitating birds"?[2] However we dispose of this question, we are left with a stubbornly non-speculative fact: that the songs of various species of birds imitate those of other birds.

What accounts for this kind of expression? What motivates the morning song of the gibbons of Thailand who, after climbing to the highest branches as soon as the sun touches them, send their chorus sounding across the canyons to be answered by neighboring gibbon families from opposite ridges? They all sing the same tune, beginning in the key of E, rising by halftone steps to an exact octave, and introducing each with a grace note. (The songs were transcribed by G. R. Waterhouse, whose conclusions were confirmed by recordings made later by biologists.) Though these gibbons seem to be the only nonhuman creatures with voices organized like ours, a number of other mammals have been found to sing, alone or in chorus. One of them, a mouse who performed a solo varied in pitch, sometimes for as long as ten minutes, apparently was not motivated either by sex or territoriality as he sat in a closet in an overshoe filled with popcorn.[3]

To turn now from music to drawing is to concentrate on our nearest relatives, the anthropoid apes. Their productions have not only been fostered and widely observed in the last fifty years; some of them—chimpanzee fingerpaintings by Betsy of the Baltimore

Zoo and Congo of the London Zoo—when exhibited at the Institute of Contemporary Arts in London in 1957 were bought up by collectors, among them Picasso and Read. Drawing in particular has been searchingly studied, and it now seems established that chimpanzees and human children make the same progress in art and by the same stages till the latter reach three or four years of age, at which point they begin to sketch faces and other representations. None of the apes produced drawings in the wild; and yet, while allowing for the possibility of unintended cues from their observers, one cannot help being astonished by the behavior of these artists. That they paint or draw without any assistance or guidance, without any rewards of food or favor, now stands beyond question—Julian Huxley at three different times observed one of his young gorillas in the London Zoo tracing with his forefinger the profile of his shadow on the wall. Moreover, the chimpanzee artist works with extraordinary concentration. When stopped, he grows angry; when prevented from completing a drawing, he flies into rages; and he cannot be forced to continue working on a picture once he regards it as finished. A capuchin monkey quite obviously recognized her own sketches when they were shown to her again after a lapse of time.[4]

"Apes, both young and old," says Desmond Morris in *The Biology of Art*, "can become engrossed in picture-making to the point where they may prefer it to being fed." Most immediately striking are the unity and design in these drawings—"where compositional factors are concerned, this control is more active and better organized in the apes than it is in the young human." They will put their configurations in the center of the sheet; balance one side against the other; fill in all the corners if any are already filled in; surround a center configuration with new ones. When sheets of paper with a centered square were offered to certain apes, each of them proceeded to fill it in or to surround it with marks. Others, finding that the square on the sheet they received had been set off center, drew forms of their own on the empty side. Has the ape-artist an inborn sense of composition?

If he has, he is not unique, assuming composition to be consubstantial with symmetry, order, and other feelings for "esthetic relationships" which spontaneously mark the responses of the human organism.[5] A number of nonhuman creatures show a similar preference for "form": a jackdaw, a crow, a capuchin monkey, a guenon monkey. Rensch carried out more than 300 tests with white cardboards presented in pairs: one displaying black-and-white elements in orderly patterns, drawn with a steady line; the other, disorganized arrangements, roughly drawn. (For example:

3 parallel vertical bars spaced equally apart—and 3 bars of the same thickness, twisted and spaced irregularly

a circle superimposed by equal triangles radiating out of the center-point—and a circle with triangles strewn helter-skelter within it

a number of squares inside one another—and a jumble of scribbling.)

The capuchin monkey scored a perfect record; both jackdaw and crow, 6 out of 8; the supposedly more primitive guenon monkey, 5. What we have is a confirmation of preference—based on statistically significant responses of two species of monkeys and of birds —for steadiness, symmetry, repetitive rhythm, pattern. In the eye that beholds an object as in the hand that shapes it: an ape's or a human being's.

And no less to be preferred, no less essential: variation on the rhythmical theme, the organism being self-driven to escape from mechanical sameness, from exact repetition.[6] A creature-need to "differentiate," by exploring, experimenting—by serious playing, if you will. The earliest student of nonhuman art (Nadjejeta Kohts, 1916) discovers that chimpanzee scribbles can change and develop. Analysis by others proves that the marks and lines develop into distinct shapes in a slow process of pictorial growth with both children and apes. No doubt the same process is also to be observed in more sophisticated form among adult human painters as an integral part of the modification of old images and styles and of the evolution of new ones.

"Styles" among nonhuman artists? One chimpanzee favors short dashes; another, long curves. One concentrates on short, straight strokes; another makes bold horizontal sweeps from left to right. As more and more primate artists are studied, individual styles become more and more striking. Indeed, when a careful test of individual variation was made a decade ago, each of the six chimpanzee subjects became quickly identifiable by its own distinctive style of drawing. As might have well been expected at this level of expressive behavior in a complex creature, where every biological structure of the organism owes its existence in part to the genetic inheritance, in part to its interaction with the environment.

Although for human beings, where individual difference is taken for granted, disagreement persists as to which of the two factors is the greater, there can be no possibility of discounting the effects of the culture. Nor does one have to believe that each epoch has a defining "spirit," a *Zeitgeist,* to recognize that a particular society at a particular time shows predilections and disapprovals that set it apart. Neither writer nor reader will quite escape them. In any case, pressures of taste, of judgment, and above all of other attitudes shared within a period work on a reader's responses. (On a poet's also. Could César Vallejo's funeral liturgy for a hero of the Republic "Pequeño responso" or James Dickey's "The Fiend" have been written in earlier epochs?) Whatever the time of the culture, its inhabitants are steadily assaulted by avowed or implied hierarchies of values—hence, of interest also. Donne's poetry, virtually unread for more than two centuries, captivated Swinburne, Browning, and Rossetti but not till generations later was it popularly revived. Our own century has seen several kinds of poetry adulated and then rather quickly scorned, all in the wake of an early anti-Romanticism which at one stage of the seventh decade spawned a much-praised dead-end Romantic celebration of self-confessing morbidity.

Poetic abreaction of this sort could readily be related to active trends in the culture, but too many scholars and critics would not listen, being concerned above all with esthetic values objectively verified and as absolute and timeless as possible. Why they are thus concerned is another tale of the *Zeitgeist,* mainly of intimidation —set among the minions of scientism—whose theme is an anxious passion for depersonalization. Inevitably, very much critical writing (as Stephen Spender noted with some ire) has become "so analytic, so intellectual, so *knowing,* that it tends to insinuate conscious or self-conscious critical intention into the work of the poet at the very moment of creation, at the root of the dream." He was writing twelve years ago; his terms might now be less extreme. Yet readers continue to be told that a poem not only can but ought to be studied, examined, inspected, with detachment. It should be analyzed with the help of dependably impersonal instruments. If all types of "findings" can be verified by scientists, why not try something similar with poems? Meanwhile, in their turn, scientists show great interest in their newfound affinities with the arts. More has happened than the histories of both "disciplines" take account of since Kekulé had cried out to his colleagues, "Let us dream, gentlemen! . . ."

Poems are, of course, experienced in personal ways. The life they take on in the reader depends ultimately on his individual responses, on the uniqueness of all that he brings to his encounter with the poem. Altering preferences, growth, even critical insights can affect him—on occasion profoundly—but even then his uniqueness must determine the nature and the outcome of all that happens between himself and the poem. Three sentences of Jules Laforgue were never more cogent:

> Chaque homme est selon son moment dans le temps, son milieu de race et de condition sociale, son moment d'évolution individuelle, un certain clavier sur lequel le monde extérieur joue d'une certaine façon. Mon clavier est perpetuellement changeant et il n'y en a pas d'autre identique au mien. Tous les claviers sont légitimes.[7]

Which is to say that each person, as a result of his particular moment in time, of his racial and social milieu, of the specific point in his individual evolution—each human being is a kind of keyboard on which the outside world plays in a certain way. My own keyboard changes incessantly, and there is no other keyboard exactly the same as mine. All keyboards are "légitimes": they are equally justified, they have an equal right to their existence.

A Virtual Object Made of Words

Throughout this book I have referred to products of creative imagining as objects added to the landscape, without so much as adding an epithet to set them apart from what is usually meant: things that can be touched or seen. But a poem is never actual as the

odor of a flower or the warmth of the sun is actual. "After all,"
as W. H. George remarks,

to the external observer a book starts as an elaborate series of "overt
responses" evoked from an animal pushing a pen over many sheets of
paper. Without a reader it remains a lot of irregular black marks on a
regular pile of papers. If it means more than that to a reader, then that
something more is his contribution.

Works of art are, obviously, virtual objects. The sonata that Tartini
hears in a dream comes from a virtual musician and his virtual
violin; the tree beheld on a canvas is a virtual tree. Either may
possess what is sometimes described as "livingness—a sense of life
deep and intense" which would make it seem "more real" than ordinary reality. The virtual objects that are works of art present
semblances, not actualities, and are experienced as such by reader,
gazer, listener.

Suzanne Langer refers to this drawing-out process as "abstracting"; and "in this elementary sense all art is . . . an abstraction
from material existence." "This fundamental abstractness belongs
just as forcibly to the most illustrative murals and most realistic
plays, provided they are good after their kind, as to the deliberate
abstractions that are remote representations or entirely non-repre-
sentative designs."[8] The average, representative man "Walt Whitman" who is portrayed in *Leaves of Grass* is not the unaverage,
unrepresentative author who bears the same name; nor the "I" of
Walden the New England citizen Thoreau. Virtual objects have
been added to the landscape; and in the poem (as remarked in
an earlier chapter), the action such objects give rise to resembles a
"dramatized-speaking-to-some-other." Neither speaker nor listener
plays a role. The presences form the characters for self-enactment
within the reader where they can spring to life with a fullness
which does not depend wholly on the poem. What the object
offers the reader is potential experience only part of which he can
realize at any one time. Not only is every reader unique as a keyboard but every keyboard incessantly changes.

Something emerges from the virtual object which had not been
present before in the reader's experience. "Something" emerges from
the language—"Ce n'est point avec des idées qu'on fait des sonnets,

Degas, c'est avec des mots." Mallarmé's reply has by now become scripture, yet a word is also an idea. A word conveys "a notion, thought, or mental impression," something "known, believed, or supposed." These dictionary definitions come close to the usage of recent psychology in which an idea is any thought or conception of an object not actually present to the senses. Which is to say, a word signifies, serves as the sign or the name, having two distinct traits: "It *denotes* the idea which good use agrees that it shall stand for; it *connotes* the very various and subtle thoughts and emotions which cluster about the idea in the human mind" (Barrett Wendell).

But words are also biology. Except for a handful of poets and scholars, nobody has taken time to consider the feeling of verbal sounds in the physical organism. Even today—despite all the public reciting of verse, the recordings, the classroom markings of prosody —the muscular sensation of words is virtually ignored by all but poets who know how much the body is engaged by a poem. That words are physical events for the organism, even when experienced in silence, others will of course quickly acknowledge. Indeed, it is obvious and, taking it for granted, they "naturally" pass it by.

Not so with the histories of words. Treatise after treatise appears, for the specialist, layman, occasionally for both. But the ordinary adult, except when forced to use a dictionary, assumes that he knows all he needs to know about the words in a poem to respond to their fullness. Of course he does not nor, strictly speaking, can anyone. But what is fullness? How much does one need to know of each word's history? Michel Bréal, the founder of semantics, warns against "too vivid a recollection of etymology." Not only does it often "spoil the expression of thought"; it brings the danger of disturbing it by all kinds of false reflections. Must fullness in time arrive of its own as the outcome of wide random reading, of meeting with obstacles, of plain curiosity about the careers of many words, the formation of classes of words, and the like? Footnotes are sometimes essential to save a reader from pointlessly "deep" interpreting, from attributing, for example, to "silly" in line 20 of Burns's "To a Mouse" something other than "weak," which it meant to Burns and his readers. Similarly, a gloss by a critic—for a Dickinson lyric, which begins:

Of Bronze—and Blaze—
The North—Tonight—
So adequate—it forms—
So preconcerted with itself—
So distant—to alarms
An Unconcern so sovereign
To Universe, or me. . . .

A dictionary fails to explain that "adequate" at the time when the poem was written had not yet taken on the diminished sense that it has today but retained the full root meaning of "in exact proportion," an attribute, says Charles Anderson, "that can attach only to God."[9]

Scholars, to be sure, are expected to give such aid. But where can one turn with literature too recent to be part of their quarry? At least one admired contemporary, Edward Dahlberg, scorning the demand that writers be confined to the "live speech" of their epoch, by his studied use of such words as "caitiff," "adust," "drumbling," "niggish," even "deliquium," seeks to give them a second life:

I cull what I can from the Elizabethans, from Nashe, Deloney, or go to Congreve, and somewhere he tells: "he flea'd me alive." It is better for what I need than "flail" or even "flense," and there is far more nutriment in it than "strip". . . . Rabelais says that to offer words is love. It has never been my intention to be archaic, or to use an antiquated ice-breaker for a quill. One should sauce a sentence with a surprising word, be it birthed in the 14th century, why not?[10]

Certain words, though in constant use, are beyond reviving, even by writers. "God," for example. "The thought it suggests to the human mind," says Shelley, "is susceptible of as many varieties as human minds themselves." Much the same applies to "truth" and "beauty." Yet other words just as commonly used do not fail as words. Roethke was fond of remarking that some, "like hill, mother, window, bird, fish, are so drenched with human association that they sometimes can make even bad poems evocative." Certainly "God" (perhaps "truth") is no less drenched. A word's poetic vitality, however, depends not only on human association but on reactions of dissent or belief—whence the "complicated problem" which some writers (myself excluded) regard as quite insoluble (p. 299).

Words give rise to other issues-disagreements, as they must, with their mysterious pressures on the listener, at times acting with little effect, at other times striking with the thrust of a physical blow. One can only guess at the events in a person's response to a poetic image, for example. Is it "a word picture with emotion or with passion" (Day-Lewis)? Is it quite as much an image-with-sound? A "resonant metaphor," says George Whalley,

is not static in the way a picture is; neither can it be "taken in at a single glance." For the poetic image is not so bounded with a wiry line; and a whole poem is not bounded by a discrete frame, but by an ocean of reverberant silence.[11]

Hence his new term "sone" (from French *son* [sound] and English *tone*). But a great many sones or poetic images are non-literary creations and constantly serve as "live speech" till they wear themselves out. Is the residual cliché quite without power to picture-with-sound? For some people (I am one) even a dead metaphor may be able to produce a presence. When they hear "half-cocked," a pistol set for firing is somehow seen-heard-known—however faintly—together with the meaning it stands for. Such a word, however, does not evoke the fresh meaning it would have to evoke in order to come to life in a poem, for at once the feeble picture-with-sound disintegrates, leaving only the univocal idea. Lacking the support of context, it falls apart, each word having nothing to suggest, no meanings which the hearer can intuit for himself. Such glimmer and whisper that each might have had fades into a type of nonexistence which makes an ideal negative paradigm of a poem. For ideally when a word is used in a poem it should be, to quote R. P. Blackmur, "the sum of all its appropriate history made concrete and particular in the individual context." In poetry all words "act *as if* they were so used, because the only kind of meaning poetry can have requires that all its words resume their full life: the full life being modified and made unique by the *qualifications* the words perform one upon the other in the poem."

Since only within their particular poem they can act in this manner, the consequence for translated verse must be all to plain. However, if a verse translation is itself a good poem, the identical as-if principle will be found in the action of its words. Meanwhile the words of the original poem remain there, wholly unaffected, looking in several directions at once, giving and receiving echoes, suggestions, and the other qualifications that create the uniqueness of their life. In *The Poem Itself* I point to this fact as the first of the many that makes it impossible for anyone to experience an original poem in a different tongue. A verse translation takes the reader away from the foreign literature and into his own, away from the original into something different. And the instant he departs from the words of the original, he departs from *its* poetry. Regardless of the virtues it may possess as a poem, an English translation is always a different thing: it is always an English poem.[12]

In this fact about words lies the source of all the slanderous remarks that have been made about translators, from Frost's well-known sentence (poetry is "that which gets lost from verse or prose in translation") to the notorious Italian pun *traduttore-traditore* ("translator-traitor"). Says Renato Poggioli: "Both original and translation deal with a single substance, differentiated into two unique, and incommensurable, accidents"; and Nida: "There can never be a word-for-word type of correspondence which is fully meaningful or accurate." When Coleridge proposed as "the infallible test of a blameless style" "its *untranslateableness* in words of the same language without injury to the meaning," he took care to "include in the meaning of a word not only its correspondent object, but likewise all the associations which it recalls." For every "meaningful" word is a unique totality—unique as denotation, connotation, picture, sound, history, biology, and doubtless much more.

The order that the words make is no less crucial to the translator than the words themselves. For when they appear in their sequence (as in a poem) they begin to mean in a special way—their uniquenesses act, as it were, selectively. The position that each word holds in relation to the others causes parts of its total content to be magnified and other parts diminished. Yet even though some meanings recede as others come to the fore, most of them are to some degree also active—whence the multiform richness of feeling and thought conveyed (the "suggestions, ambiguities, paradoxes, levels of meaning" of current critical terminology). These facts may be read into Coleridge's definition of poetry as "the best words in the best order," especially into his famous remark about "a more than usual state of emotion, with more than usual order." Nowadays we speak of the affective phrase or sentence, whose word arrangement differs from that of prose; we say that each poem is an organization of such phrases. But (as noted in the preceding chapter) each affective phrase is also a rhythmic metaphor—a poem is a series of rhythmic metaphors—which evokes a physical response in the reader's body, in his internal and external muscles. More than the mind: the total organism moves with and mirrors the rhythmic pattern of the words. For a translator to evoke *this* response with his *different* words and word order is of course impossible. But, all corporeal concurrences aside, could a translator even dream of trying to carry across into a different language the "more than usual order" of the original words?

In this preface to *The Poem Itself*, I had no occasion to mention the metalinguistic problem that inheres in the very notion of translation. Besides, all the languages used there were part of one family. Yet as Von Humboldt had realized—long before Benjamin Whorf (p. 115)—the character and structure of a language express the inner life and knowledge of its speakers: its "inner form," as he called it, reflects the manner in which its users regard the world. Some specific obstacles traceable to inner form proved not only severe but unmanageable to the poets and scholars with whom I worked on *The Modern Hebrew Poem Itself*. For these and other reasons, the more I work with *The Poem Itself* method, the more I feel the need for dealing with words individually rather than with clauses or lines. For only when each word in the original is accompanied by its attempted "equivalent"—that is, pertinent denotative and connotative alternates and, when needed, remarks on its other relations of meaning and of sound—can a foreign reader begin to know what each may be doing in the phrase, in the line, in the whole.[13] Only then can he hope to follow the texture and the shape of the poem's substance. For example, of a poem in Latin—a highly inflected language which, as Rolfe Humphries explains,

makes possible effects that are impossible in our word-order English. Words not in agreement can be placed side by side for ironic effect; images can carry from one word to the next, the memory, the linger-

ing overtone of the first making a chord, or a prism, with the second
line; the line, or the stanza, can be full of ambiguities or surprises, matters
held in suspense, judgment on them changed as we go along, and the
resolution not coming till the very end. Horace is the master of these
effects, and the utter despair of all translators (except those who make
him out a light-verse comic).

The exacting procedure I propose would bring a foreign reader
closer to Horace than he could come short of learning the Latin
language. He would at the least be learning the language of the
poem, perhaps getting it almost by heart as an effortless outcome.
He would in some degree be experiencing the original poem in the
words of its author.

For what does a reader wish but to get to the poem itself, to
know it at first hand? And where can he turn but to the author's
words—to Dante's if he wishes to read *Inferno*, not to Binyon's or
Sayers' or Ciardi's or other rewriters'. Verse translation is the art
of composing a second-hand poem from a foreign model; hence a
person unable to read the latter has to take the former on faith.
Like the author himself, he is wholly at the translator's mercy, the
quality of which by the nature of the task must be strained. At
times very little but at other times so greatly as to range beyond
translation into something else. The contemporary examples by
Robert Lowell he himself refers to as "imitations." Dropping lines,
moving lines, moving stanzas, changing images, altering meter,
and so on, they are neither translations nor original poems but a
species of improvisation. The reader of Lowell's rewriting of "La
primavera hitleriana," for example, cannot fail to be shocked when
he turns to the original by Eugenio Montale. He may even ask,
with John Simon, whether a translator, though self-licensed as an
imitator only, has the right to change the entire mood and import
of a serious poem by an authentic poet. Such a question seems to
invoke morality—which is not always so far from the creative
act as is supposed (surely not when involving re-vision [p. 64] or
obscurity [p. 275]). In any event, nobody can protect a work
in the public domain from its friends, let alone its foes. The person
who wishes to get to a foreign poem has the self-obligation to read
what the poet wrote before reading an interpretation by someone

else. If a foreign poem, like any other creative work, is a virtual object, in verse translation it can be at best but a semblance of a semblance.

Shapes of "Substance"

Words, with all their elusiveness, seem much more tangible alone than when combined to form the units of a poem. And since both the units and their modes of combining differ from work to work, "the structure" of poetry is no more adducible than "the logic" or "the order" of its words (Chap. 3). Moreover, popular terms for defining do not help in accounting for the shapes with which each poem structures its action. Some of the terms mislead—"content," for example, when denoting one part of all that is "contained" by the language without naming which part it is. (This type of confusion can be readily cured by adding the appropriate qualification. In fact, to speak of a poem's "formal content" or "sonal content" or "narrative content" or "pictorial content" or "philosophical content"—the list can go on—has the virtue of showing that you can abstract any thing you please if you look at the work with that particular thing in mind.) All too often, however, the unqualified term "content" is used for only one of many possible interests: the thoughts or ideas. And when this sort of content is opposed to a group of other interests defined by the single-word "form," fundamental confusions develop. Not only is this so-called "content" and "form" then dealt with as though they composed "the two parts" of a poem; but, to judge from the effects they are assumed to produce, each has an actual and independent life in the reader's response.

Fifty years ago, A. C. Bradley asked the pertinent question and followed with the clearest reply:

When you are reading a poem, I would ask—not analyzing it, and much less criticizing it, but allowing it, as it proceeds, to make its full impression on you through the exertion of your re-creating imagination—do you then apprehend and enjoy as one thing a certain meaning or substance, and as another thing certain articulate sounds, and do you somehow compound these two? Surely you do not, any more than you apprehend apart, when you see someone smile, those lines in the face which express a feeling, and the feeling that the lines express. Just as there the lines and their meaning are to you one thing, not two, so in poetry the meaning and the sounds are one: there is, if I may put it so, a resonant meaning, or a meaning resonance. If you read the line, "The sun is warm, the sky is clear," you do not experience separately the image of a warm sun and clear sky, on the one side, and certain intelligible rhythmical sounds on the other; nor yet do you experience them together, side by side; but you experience the one *in* the other. And in like manner when you are really reading *Hamlet,* the action and the characters are not something which you conceive apart from the words; you apprehend them from point to point in the words, and the words as expressions of them. Afterwards, no doubt, when you are out of the poetic experience but remember it, you may by analysis decompose this unity, and attend to a substance more or less isolated, and a form more or less isolated. But these are things in your analytic head. . . .

In your analytic head—not in the poem. For the poem produced a unitary experience. And if you want to have the poem again,

you cannot find it by adding together these two products of decomposition; you can find it only by passing back into poetic experience. And then what you recover is no aggregate of factors, it is a unity in which you can no more separate a substance and a form than you can separate living blood and the life in the blood. This unity has, if you like, various "aspects" or "sides," but they are not factors or parts; if you try to examine one, you find it is also the other. Call them substance and form if you please, but these are not the reciprocally exclusive substance and form to which the two contentions *must* refer. They do not "agree," for they are not apart: they are one thing from different points of view, and in that sense identical.[14]

One need hardly add that these strictures apply to all aspects or sides of all works of art. Hence with full awareness of what we shall be doing and where it can take place, we may decompose any poem to our mind's content. We can analyze aspects of "substance"— thoughts, ideas, images, and the like when isolated—and speak of their structural "shapes." We can do the same thing with "sound."

Analogies sometimes vividly suggest the over-all structure of a work as it appears to a critic. Anderson describes *Walden* as a circle and a web. Tate calls the *Cantos of* Pound "talk, talk, talk; not by anyone in particular to anyone else" but "conversation," with the length of canto, "the length of breath, the span of conversational energy." Abrams brings together "Five Ways of Reading *Lycidas*," only to add a sixth of his own, while noting that there are as many possible descriptions of the poem as there are diverse premises and procedures. The statement is unexceptionable only when applied to a reader's vision of a work in its entirety. The cataloguing in Whitman's "I Hear America Singing" or in Kenneth Fearing's "Dirge" has nothing to do with diversity of critical premises. Nor does the phrase repetition in the opening of *Ash Wednesday*, the word repetition in Othello's "Put out the light . . . ," where "light" recurs five times in seven lines. Structures of this kind are not discoveries of critical insight. Their distinctiveness is as obvious as the difference in over-all shape of substance in these two lyrics by Dickinson:

[1] I never saw a moor,
    I never saw the sea;
    Yet know I how the heather looks,
    And what a wave must be.

    I never spoke with God,
    Nor visited in Heaven;
    Yet certain am I of the spot
    As if the chart were given.

[2] The heart asks pleasure first,
    And then, excuse from pain;
    And then, those little anodynes
    That deaden suffering;

    And then, to go to sleep;
    And then, if it should be
    The will of its Inquisitor,
    The liberty to die.

If you take eight other poems of two rimed quatrains and diagram the motions that the prose meaning traces in each, you will end with ten dissimilar patterns of notation:

[3] Lay a garland on my hearse
    Of the dismal yew:
    Maidens, willow branches bear;
    Say, I died true.

My love was false, but I was firm
From my hour of birth.
Upon my buried body lie
Lightly, gentle earth!   —[John Fletcher]

[4] Ah, Sunflower! weary of time,
     Who countest the steps of the sun;
Seeking after that sweet golden clime
     Where the traveler's journey is done;

Where the Youth pined away with desire,
     And the pale virgin shrouded in snow,
Arise from their graves, and aspire
     Where my Sunflower wishes to go!   —[Blake]

[5] When lovely woman stoops to folly
     And finds too late that men betray,
What charm can soothe her melancholy?
     What art can wash her guilt away?

The only art her guilt to cover,
     To hide her shame from every eye,
To give repentance to her lover,
     And wring his bosom, is—to die.   —[Goldsmith]

[6] Ah, what avails the sceptred race!
     Ah, what the form divine!
What every virtue, every grace!
     Rose Aylmer, all were thine.

Rose Aylmer, whom these wakeful eyes
     May weep, but never see,
A night of memories and of sighs
     I consecrate to thee.   —[Landor]

[7] The way a crow
     Shook down on me
The dust of snow
     From a hemlock tree

Has given my heart
     A change of mood
And saved some part
     Of a day I had rued.   —[Frost]

[8] A slumber did my spirit seal;
     I had no human fears—
     She seemed a thing that could not feel
     The touch of earthly years.

     No motion has she now, no force;
     She neither hears nor sees;
     Rolled round in earth's diurnal course,
     With rocks, and stones, and trees.   —[Wordsworth]

[9] With rue my heart is laden
     For golden friends I had,
     For many a rose-lipt maiden
     And many a lightfoot lad.

     By brooks too broad for leaping
     The lightfoot boys are laid;
     The rose-lipt girls are sleeping
     In fields where roses fade.   —[Housman]

[10] I know my soul hath power to know all things
     Yet she is blind and ignorant in all.
     I know I'm one of Nature's little kings,
     Yet to the least and vilest things am thrall.

     I know my life's a pain and but a span;
     I know my sense is mock'd in everything;
     And, to conclude, I know myself a Man—
     Which is a proud and yet a wretched thing.—[Sir John Davies]

You can go as far as you like with this choreographic analyzing and wherever your fancy takes you.[15] Into types of sentences,
clauses, phrases. Into types of figures of speech. You can look for
repetition, antithesis, accumulation, inversion of order; grammatical
arrangements which intensify, which minimize; and so on. Fowler's
section of "Technical Terms" (by no means exhaustive) runs to more
than 30 double-column pages of definitions at least 40 of which
relate to the shape of substance. Though many are too familiar to
seem technical at all, others bearing Greek names have the use of
discovering for a reader the terms for constructions by which he
has sometimes been charmed. Yet I doubt that he would gain by
becoming expert in all these matters. Does he need to be told that
these lines from Shakespeare exemplify balance:

Music to hear, why hear'st thou music sadly . . .
In praise of ladies dead and lovely knights . . .
Most worthy comfort, now my greatest grief . . .

the first by simple repetition, the second by parallelism, the third by antithesis? Do the terms help when he responds to passages which hold together by contrast and comparison, cause and effect, accumulation of detail, subordination? He cannot read the first seven lines of *The Waste Land* without noting that all but the fourth and last are patterned in a phrase + participle, and that the phrase of the first and fifth differs obviously from the others. No one has to call his attention to the word order in Milton's famous description of Satan's fall:

> Him the Almighty Power
> Hurled headlong flaming from the ethereal sky
> With hideous ruin, and combustion down
> To bottomless perdition, there to dwell
> In adamantine chains and penal fire,
> Who durst defy the Omnipotent to arms.

Nor to the violations of normative syntax in poems by E. E. Cummings or Mallarmé. Though never having heard of zeugma, he recognizes in Shakespeare's "Kill the boys and the luggage!" and in Pope's

> Here thou, Great Anna! whom three realms obey,
> Dost sometimes counsel take—and sometimes tea.

the structural effect it stands for.

For certain people, no doubt, a cultivated awareness of litotes, chiasmus, hypallage, tmesis, hyperbaton, and more specialized matters may deepen their response to poetry. Roman Jakobson goes so far as to brand the literary scholar who is "indifferent to linguistic problems and unconversant with linguistic methods" a flagrant anachronism. Although no comparable demand has as yet been made on the "serious" reader, one can hardly be sure of the permanence of his immunity. In any case, readers who have cared for the technical parts of the present chapter may be stimulated, perhaps even charmed, by much that Jakobson says in his essay "Linguistics and Poetics," especially in analyzing "into plain linguistic fictions" Marc

Antony's famous lampoon of Brutus' speech. I doubt, however, that the detailed scansion at various linguistic levels of Baudelaire's "Les Chats" (by Jakobson and Lévi-Strauss) will greatly enrich or enlarge the response of any reader.[16] One cannot, of course, even guess how the new disciplines—statistics, information theory, grammars, etc.—may affect a future reader's experience of literature. Will he have to become a literary scholar also? Will their various approaches produce very much more than consensual reinforcement of what he already knows: that a viable work of art has incredible structural qualities?

Shapes of Sound*

Structural linguistics has contributed enough to certain aspects of prosody to enable everyone to see them with clearer eyes. A half-century ago Pierre-Jean Rousselot and his associates at the Laboratory of Experimental Phonetics at the Collège de France were able to establish the "validity" of *vers libre* by showing, through photographic recordings of intensity, duration, pitch, and timbre, that even their strict *alexandrin* does not consist of the 12 syllables it was assumed to possess. Of the 1100 lines recited by master *diseurs*, 650 contained 9, 10, 13, or 14 syllables. Much as these findings led poets to question the traditional basis of French verse, recent mechanical recordings have raised doubts about theories of English metrics.[17] If the ears of the machines do not lie, there can be no such "foot" as a spoken spondee (húmdrúm) or a spoken pyrrhic (— —), for no two successive syllables, either stressed or unstressed, can be identical in loudness (intensity). There may be as many as 6,236 different kinds of iambs (— '), 2,376 of trochees (' —), even more of three-syllable feet. And if the variations in strength of stress in any single recitation are impressive, when the same poem is given a number of recitations the disparities between the meter and the spoken rhythm

---

* One cannot go very far into any work of art as an object without continuing to deal with certain so-called technical matters. To undertake this type of inquiry with the art of painting or of sculpture or of music is out of the question since examples of works must also be made available. Hence I continue with the poem, inquiring into the shapes of its sound with the aid of examples on the page. Many of the quotations will be familiar to the reader as well as some of the elements that enter into the shapes of sound.

grow overwhelming. Why, then, bother with this method for arranging the rhythms of verse into a system based on theoretically stressed-versus-unstressed syllables?

Do poets compose in meter? In the light of what we know of creativity, such a question is as meaningful as one that asks if poets compose in grammar. Both matters form parts of their knowledge at certain times of their lives, to be drawn on thereafter as needed. Eliot's experience no doubt is typical: "I have never been able to retain the names of feet and meters, or to pay the proper respect to the accepted rules of scansion. . . . But certainly, when it came to applying [them] to English verse, . . . I wanted to know why one line was good and another bad; and this, scansion could not tell me." As, of course, it should not be expected to do. Scansion by metrical feet takes account of only one of the several elements that compose the shapes of sound (albeit the most prominent). Nor would it suffice to regard English verse as based on the relationship between the stresses and the number of syllables in a line. The enlarged definition ignores the role of quantity, for one thing; for another, the "strong-stress" modern rhythm; for a third, free verse; and so on.

Faced with the question "What is the basis of English verse?" a cautious scholar names four. But two of them—(1) Quantitative, (2) Syllabic—conflict with the natural (accentual) way by which English creates its rhythms. To be sure—with regard to (1)—some syllables take more time to pronounce than others, but quantity in English is not long or short but relatively one or the other. As a consequence, experiments in classic measures (of duration only) cannot satisfy the rhythmic demand of the English ear except when the sequence of longer syllables coincides with or seems to play against a rhythm of stress—which is to say, when the rhythmic base is not quantitative at all. "Johannes Milton, Senex" is the splendid example:

Since I believe in God the Father Almighty,
Man's Maker and Judge, Overruler of Fortune,
'Twere strange should I praise anything and refuse Him praise. . . .[18]

The same impression occurs sometimes in verse presumed to be based on Syllabic count (2). Each stanza of Auden's "In Memory of Sigmund Freud" is composed of four lines of 11, 11, 9, and 10 syllables:

> ...Only Hate was happy, hoping to augment
> His practice now, and his shabby clientèle
> Who think they can be cured by killing
> And covering the gardens with ashes.
>
> They are still alive but in a world he changed
> Simply by looking back with no false regrets;
> All that he did was to remember
> Like the old and be honest like children. . . .

Reading these lines, one forgets syllabic count; the "strong-stress" beat takes over (4, 4, 3, 3). Here the rhythmic pattern is as regular as it is erratic in the much more typically syllabic stanzas of Marianne Moore, which do not, however, hold together by number only. Rime, often assonance, reinforces the patterning of her lines, together with conspicuous typographic indentations.

> My first—an exceptional
> an almost scriptural—
> taxi-driver to Cambridge from Back Bay
> said, as we went along, "They
> make some fine young men at Harvard." I recall
>
> the summer when Faneuil Hall
> had its weathervane with gold ball
> and grasshopper, gilded again by
> a -leafer and -jack
> till it glittered. Spring can be a miracle . . .

These stanzas appear in her "In the Public Garden," which, as it moves from a fairly strict initial pattern of analogous lines, alters in its shape and rime scheme. To find a paradigm for the rhythm of her syllabic poems, one turns to prose, with its unpredictable, shifting stresses. For our example above, one thinks of conversational rhythms, but of a kind very far removed from those in the *Cantos* of Pound, where the regularity of the beat insists.

As it does in the works that compose the mainstream of English poetry whether classified as (3) "Accentual" or (4) "Accentual-Syllabic." Frost's ultrasimple yardstick—that our verse is either strict or loose iambic—might also serve for most poems of the last five centuries.

> I sit in one of the dives
> On Fifty-Second Street
> Uncertain and afraid
> As the clever hopes expire
> Of a low dishonest decade. . . .

One writer would call this Auden passages "loose iambic," another would call it "accentual." Both would count only the prominent stresses, disregarding the number of syllables (6, 7, 8). Yeats's lines,

> Some have known a likely lad
> That had a sound fly-fisher's wrist
> Turn to a drunken journalist;
> A girl that knew all Dante once
> Live to bear children to a dunce;
> A Helen of social welfare dream,
> Climb on a wagonette to scream. . . .

whether of 7, 8, or 9 syllables, fall into the same category. This despite the initial beat in four of the lines; for an iambic line, even when strict, often starts with a heavily stressed syllable (with what metrists call "substitution": "*Un*der the greenwood tree/Who loves to lie with me").

"Strong-stress" rhythm, which derives from the four-beat alliterative verse of Old English, is also loose iambic or accentual:

> *Sing* a song of *six* pence,   *pock*etful of *rye*,
> *Four* and twenty *black*birds   *baked* in a *pie*

Two groups of two heavily accented syllables usually (sometimes fewer or more), divided by a marked pause; and always without restriction as to number and location of other syllables (including those of secondary stress; e.g., "song," "twenty," "birds"). Pound's *Canto 1* holds close to the Old English model, even to its alliterative system:

> . . . Bore sheep aboard her, and our bodies also
> Heavy with weeping, and winds from sternward
> Bore us out onward with bellying canvas,
> Circe's this craft, the trim-coifed goddess.

At another extreme stands Hopkins' free-ranging "The Windhover." Its rhythm clearly reflects its relationship to Old English verse:

> I caught this morning morning's minion, king-
>   dom of daylight's dauphin, dapple-dawn-drawn Falcon, in
>   his riding

> Of the rolling level underneath him steady air, and striding
> High there, how he rung upon the rein of a wimpling wing . . .
> In his ecstasy! then off, off forth on swing, . . .

With certain other poets, "strong-stress" rhythm, when not sustained through an entire work, may precede or follow rather strict iambic (as in sections of *The Waste Land*). The reader unconcerned with technicalities moves effortlessly from one into the other, from strict iambic into loose and back into strict. The metrist, however, analyzes the shifts. But if he tries to scan, his metrical feet will make great complication when applied to the unrestricted syllables of the "strong-stress" passages.[19]

Analysis into metrical feet becomes much more manageable with (4) Accentual-Syllabic ("strict iambic") verse, for the relationship between syllable number and placement of stress forms a pattern. A pattern which marks the majority of English poems, whether written in rising or falling rhythm, rimed or unrimed, in stanzas or irregular line-groups. Blank verse may be taken as typical. The metrists' iambic pentameter; five feet, each bearing a strong stress on the second syllable—the line is quite obviously accentual:

> The cúr | fēw tólls | the knéll | of párt | ing dáy

But what of the number of accents and their position in such iambic pentameters as these from *Othello*, *The Duchess of Malfi*, and *Paradise Lost?*

> It is the cáuse, it is the cáuse, my sóul
> But hóld some twó dáys cónference with the déad
> Rócks, Cáves, Lákes, Féns, Bógs, Déns, and Shádes of Deáth

What makes these lines blank verse? What holds them together? Would it be better to think of them as a decasyllable in ascending rhythm?

The metrist, of course, explains that iambic pentameter measures only the abstract pattern of stress that the reader *expects* to hear. Moreover, as a purely theoretical sequence, it is not to be confused with the reader's phrasing of a poem. Indeed, it could not possibly be so confused; for not only is every such phrasing different from every other, but no usable system of notation could begin to take account of the three or four distinguishable degrees of stress. In his theoretical way, the metrist brushes aside these distinctions that are crucial to readers; he scans as if all syllables were either strong or weak, which he knows quite well they are not. As one metrist (Gross) puts it, "meter *is* a simple, even crude element in poetic structure. . . . Any scansion, of course, is a convenient fiction, abstracting certain phonetic elements and ignoring others. But the scansion must describe what is without doubt *really there*." And it must be there, says another (Thompson), because "the metrical pattern is a copy, a mimicry, a counterfeit without intention to deceive, of the basic elements of our language and of their order."[20]

But is it really there—a metrical pattern implied? Many writers assume the presence of two different patterns of stress, at least when trying to account for the actual rhythm of a poem. One poet will speak of "both meter and the expressiveness on it," of the "strain of the rhythm against the meter"; another, of "the rhetorical pull-back against the anapaestic movement" in Blake's Sunflower poem (p. 215). Is meter, then, something more than a conveniently fictive means for explaining the actual rhythms of a poem by projecting upon it a sort of metronome which its language has to violate? Does every reader of

Silent upon a peak in Darien

—whether he knows it or not—hear the metrist's "Silént" pressing against his normal pronouncing of the word and, as a result, a tension between theoretical and natural speech? Such a paradigm is more than just congenial to an intellectual tradition which thinks in terms of dualisms. So perhaps for its writers and readers the actual rhythm of the poem has to be explained as a synthesis of meter-*thesis* and expressiveness-*antithesis*. The rules by which we have organized our brains are not easily altered. One may wonder, however, what kind of poetic rhythms we should find if we could enter a poet's or a reader's head. All three types? Or simply his own phrasings of all the verses he remembers? Whatever their shape, we may be sure that these rhythms in each instance grew out of very much more than a tension between the meaning of the words and an abstract pattern of stress.

To see what these rhythms are, we turn from the metrical foot and consider the line. To be sure one is always uneasy in using Greek names of quantity for English accent, but this is scarcely a reason. Nor does it greatly matter that the scanners themselves cannot always agree as to which feet are "really there." Nor even that recordings of acoustic instruments deny that the syllable exists. The foot at best is deceptive as a unit of measure. The same type varies depending on where it occurs in the line; its relation to the meaning; whether it is made of monosyllables, polysyllables, or both; timing; quantity; and other matters. Verse, moreover, can exist without feet—there are numerous poems without them, but obviously none without lines.[21] Deriving from Latin *vertere*, *versum*, to turn, to turn round, *versus* is a furrow, a row, a line in writing, and in poetry a verse. One turns round at the end of a furrow to plough the next. The poet turns round at the end of one line to the next. Whether the last words stop or run on, each line is an entity for the reader as for the writer. Whether forming one row in passages of long, of short, or of varied line-lengths, or in uniformly patterned blocks or stanzas, *a line asks to be seen and heard as a unit of meaning-full sound*. And the shape of that sound is marked by a rhythm unmistakably its own, determined as it always is by a particular complex of sonal forces found only in that line. A few of the elements that exist there fairly leap from the page, some can come forth by disclosing, others no doubt elude or defy analysis. There could be no such thing as a science of sound in poetry any more than—or apart from—a science of meaning. All we can try to distinguish are a few of the "forces" that produce the type of meaning-full sound we might find inside a poet's or a reader's head.

Meaning-full Sound

"Meaning-full sound" is not accurate, though it is better than Pope's formulation that "the sound must seem an echo to the sense" (sound does not echo that of which it is part). A poem, like a word, is a single complex of sense and sonality. And bearing always in mind that in reading a poem, we experience the one *in* the other, we may proceed to decompose this unity within our analytic heads. And while doing so, we must also keep in mind what Jakobson characteristically calls "the poetry of grammar, and its literary product, the grammar of poetry"—the "poetic resources concealed in the morphological and syntactic structure of language."[22]

Aware that the over-all shape of sound is also the shape of the word-arrangement that shows the semantic relationships, we can attend to the fact that in free verse poems, for example, with their lack of regularity in rhythm and in line-length, the sonal aspect of syntax tends to be much more than conspicuous. Often the grammatical movements, we can say, seem to constitute the rhythmical pattern, to hold the structure of the varying line-lengths together—whether by command, as in H.D.'s tiny "Oread";

> Whirl up, sea—
> Whirl your pointed pines.
> Splash your great pines
> On our rocks.
> Hurl your green over us—
> Cover us with your pools of fir.

by enumeration, as in Smart's ode to his cat Jeoffry; by parallelism, as in Whitman's "When Lilacs Last in the Dooryard Bloom'd"; or by various other distinguishable structures (some of which have been touched on earlier in this chapter). Of course, traditional verse frequently veils the semantic figure under the assertive presence of regularity in rhythm, line-length, stanza, pattern, rime, etc. Yet the shape of the sound in each of the lyrics printed on pages 214 ff. will be found as respectively different as the shape of substance, once the reader considers the variety of sonal forces that contribute to the "music" of poetry in English.

Our verse is obviously accentual. English is a tonic language: it has no such word as "bécause"; "cóntent" means something quite different from "contént." "Inquisitor" has at least three different degrees of stress; and those in two-syllable words frequently vary ("never" as compared with "heartbreak" and "humdrum"). English also abounds in words of one-syllable, whose relative emphasis depends entirely on context. Because stresses on monosyllables "actually are a function of the meaning" there is no limit to the range of rhythmical patterns that such words can produce. Calvin S. Brown's invaluable discussion of "Monosyllables in English Verse" (from which I quote) presents numerous well-known, memorable passages which exemplify both common and "fancy meters" composed wholly of one-syllable words. And as he also points out, these may occur anywhere in a poem—at the climax, at the close, even at the beginning, where the "meaning-full rhythm" of the monosyllables establishes the pattern for the lines that follow.[23] Among his examples of the last:

> When I have fears that I may cease to be. . . .   [Keats]
>
> Fair stood the wind for France.   [Drayton]
>
> I struck the board, and cried, "No more."   [Herbert]
>
> Toll for the brave!   [Cowper]
>
> Fair and fair, and twice so fair. . . .   [Peele]
>
> Break, break, break,
> On thy cold gray stones, O sea.   [Tennyson]
>
> Let us go hence, my songs; she will not hear.   [Swinburne]
>
> Look at the stars! look, look up at the skies.   [Hopkins]
>
> Let us go then, you and I.   [Eliot]

The "obvious accentuality" of English is, however, generally remarked where words of all lengths and patterns intermingle freely. Here the rhythm of the line grows mainly out of both tonic accent and meaning. In the opening of Shakespeare's Sonnet 55, the reader's phrasing will have been determined to the extent of the line's three primary tonic accents (*mar, gil, mon*) along with others whose force will be created by the meaning for him:

> Not marble, nor the gilded monuments. . . .

Similarly in the opening of Landor's "Rose Aylmer," but with a different resolution:

> Ah, what avails the sceptred race,
> Ah, what the form divine!

The first two syllables (with their lengthy vowel) demand virtually equal emphasis before giving way in the rest of each line to the regularly rising beat that derives from *both* tonic requirement (scéptred, divíne) and parallel structure. A negative view of the same interdependence of elements can be had by reversing one word in Dickinson's line: "I saw never a moor."

But to speak of rhythm as I have done above is to slight other forces which are always at work in the line. Pitch is one of them, pause a second, the timbre of consonants and vowels a complicated third. With the first, one cannot go far without taking account of individual phrasing—a subject which cannot be exhausted or even managed. Does pitch coincide with accent usually? Only at times? Does it always constitute one of accent's elements? All we can say is that relative highness and lowness of tone is part of every passage of verse as an effortless expression of emphasis. It is naturally there; yet the pattern it makes alters with each interpretation, even in so classic an instance as the cry of Lady Macbeth:

> The raven himself is hoarse
> That croaks the fatal entrance of Duncan
> Under my battlements. Come, you spirits
> That tend on mortal thoughts, unsex me here,
> And fill me from the crow to the toe top-full
> Of direst cruelty! make thick my blood; . . .

Pause, however, in a number of its aspects, is virtually dictated by the text: by punctuation, division into lines, falling stress, obvious grammatical breaks.[24] These and the more crucial occasions for pause are most readily seen in connection with tempo (pp. 231 ff.). For they also issue from the complicated third force mentioned above: the effects of vowels and of consonants. For example, the effects that they make by recurrence—which is to say, by the various modes of rime in English.

Consonants alone account for two familiar ones: alliteration and consonance. The close repetition at the beginning of words or of accented syllables ("Full fathom five thy father lies") is called head rime or initial rime; as the close repetition at the end of words with differing vowel-sounds ("bids-loads; nearer-horror") is loosely referred to as slant, oblique, near, half, approximate, partial, or para rime. Many complicated patterns of alliteration can be found in traditional verse, such as:

The baiting place of wit, the balm of woe   [Sidney]

I sigh the lack of many a thing I sought   [Shakespeare]

And weep afresh love's long since canceled woe   [Shakespeare]

The sad account of fore-bemoaned moan,   [Shakespeare]

Which I new pay as if not paid before.   [Shakespeare]

It can even be found with the vowel sound repeated, as in Herrick's "That *brave* vi*bra*tion"; also in combination with consonance, as in Hopkins' "The Golden Echo":

O then, weary then why should we tread? O why are we so haggard at the heart, so care-*coiled*, care-*killed*, so fagged, so fashed, so cogged, so cumbered, . . .

From consonant to vowel, no better transition could be wanted than Shakespeare's Sonnet 12, a prodigy not only of alliteration but also of assonance: the repetition of identical vowel-sounds. For the sake of the reader's eyesight, I italicize only the latter; but even when one ignores the alliterations, it is hard to identify all the assonances (or "vocalic rimes"). Notably in lines 1-5, where the identical vowel (*I*, *time*, etc.) occurs eight times, and 5-6-7, where the same is found (*-ty*, *trees*, *see*, etc.); in 8-9

When *I* do count the clock that tells the t*i*me
And see the br*a*ve d*a*y *sunk* in hide*ou*s n*i*ght;   2
When *I* behold the v*i*olet past pr*i*me,
And sable curls all silvered *o'er* with wh*i*te;   4
When l*o*fty tr*ee*s *I* *see* barren of l*ea*ves,
Which *erst* from h*ea*t did canop*y* the h*er*d,   6
And summer's gr*ee*n all g*ir*ded up in sh*ea*ves
Borne on the b*ie*r with wh*i*te and bristly b*ear*d,   8
Th*en* of th*y* be*au*ty *do* *I* quest*i*on make, . . .

(*white-thy-I*); in 4-5 (*o'er-lofty*); in 6-7 (*herd-erst-girded*). While italicizing vowels regardless of stress, I have not done so with every pattern of recurrence (5-6: *barren-canopy*; 4, 6-8: *silvered-which-did-in-with-bristly*). For vocalic rime has been a feature of English verse from the time of Shakespeare, except in the 18th century. With the 19th, it occurs in great abundance, notably in Keats,

from *Hyperion* through the *Odes*,[25] and in Hopkins, who inter-
weaves it with alliteration—

I c*au*ght th*is* m*o*rn*i*ng m*o*rn*i*ng's m*i*nion, king-
    dom of daylight's d*au*ph*i*n, dapple-d*aw*n-dr*aw*n F*a*l*c*on, *i*n h*is* riding

as some recent poets have also done (for example, Robert Lowell in
the last three lines of "For the Union Dead").

Coming, finally, to "true," "full," "perfect," or "sufficient"
rime, which the English ear (unlike the Spanish or the French) has
preferred above all other rime, one can add very little to what a
reader knows—that the final stressed vowel and all succeeding
sounds must be the same while those that precede must differ (*bone-
flown*, n*ever*-for*ever*). By these terms, neither a *rime riche* will suffice (way-weigh), nor one for the eye only (dove-move). Although
perfect rime on occasion may appear at the start or the middle of the
line, its characteristic place is at the final point, where it completes
a rhythmical unit. And whether it coincides with a pause in meaning
(as in Davies' poem, p. 216) or runs over (as in Frost's), it calls attention not only to its special force as the final utterance. For as a
single complex of sound *and* meaning, each word of a rime participates in a twofold act: of sonal and semantic pairing. Aware or not,
the reader responds to *both* meaning and sound in rime since both
are involved.[26]

This general effect also issues—in much smaller degree, to be
sure—from the "lesser" kinds of rime we have followed; for when
sounds are stressed by repetition in a poem they cannot help but
imply other modes of resemblance, other levels of relationship, the
import of which a reader will not "know" so much as "feel," at the
very least as an overt element in the over-all act of uniting that is
every poem. By contrast, phrases or words repeated are explicit in
the extreme—whether found in verse within or outside the tradition
or somewhere between: Othello's "Put out the light . . ." passage,
H. D.'s "Oread," the opening of *Ash Wednesday*. We are back to
"meaning-full sound."

Hence we might look, for a moment, at presumably meaning*less*
sound—those effects said to be produced solely because each vowel
and consonant has its own distinctive timbre. But what is one to do
after hearing that *u* and *o*, for example, belong with roundness, hol-

lowness, and depth, with softness, liquidity, solemnity, and gloom, whereas *e, i, y* are best suited to thinness, intensity, delicacy, purity, as well as mobility—and that *u* and *i* also belong with tenderness and mystery? One recalls the curious things that hues are said to stand for: yellow for brightness, determination, and also cowardice; blue for hope and happiness as well as depression. And so, without waiting to hear comparable things concerning consonants, one re-reads Milton's Piedmont Massacre sonnet,[27] in which all but three of the rimes end in *o*, and moves onto somewhat firmer ground, where mention is made of euphony versus cacophony.

And doubtless *l, m, r, v, y, w*, for example, do bring more ease to articulation than *k, g, kts, ts, gt, nkt, gs*; doubtless the longer vowels flow more smoothly than the shorter. Who would argue that Browning's

> Irks care the crop-full bird? Frets doubt the
> maw-crammed beast?

is as pleasing to the ear as Tennyson's classic

> The moan of doves in immemorial elms
> And murmuring of innumerable bees.

But having granted the obvious, one comes back to the fact that consonants and vowels do not exist as independent entities. Does the euphony of Keats's line come from meaningless sounds?

> And lucent syrops, tinct with cinnamon;
> Manna and dates, in argosy transferred
> From Fez; and spice dainties, everyone,
> From silken Samarcand to cedared Lebanon.

How much of it derives from the images? From all they connote? And, to go a step further, into onomatopeia, is a word capable of duplicating the noise it describes? Without the supplement of association, the acoustic effect in itself could scarcely suffice, being never more than a suggestion which the reader accepts as a substitute. Moreover, some closely similar sounds bring different meanings to the same human ear (English *rot*, German *Rath* [councilor]). But is it only the auditory structure that accepts as onomatopeia *miaow* in English, *miauler* in French, *maullar* in Spanish? If the ear alone did the interpreting, verbal sounds might exist for a reader as esthetic experience independent of the meanings they are part of.

We are back, as always, with the word as sense-and-sonality, to consider timbre as related to both, and specifically through its effects on the tempo of verse. English syllables (unlike those of Spanish) vary freely in duration: but their differences do not issue from the quality peculiar to each vowel or diphthong despite their dictionary markings as long, half-long, and short. To be sure, "met" is shorter than "m*a*te" and "m*ee*t"; and "b*oo*n" is longer than "b*a*n," which in turn is longer than "b*i*n." But the same "short" vowel of "bin" alters when combined with different consonants: "rip" is a shorter syllable than "ring" or "swing"; and "seas" is longer than "seed," which in turn is longer than "seek." Quantitative difference thus derives from timbres-in-combination, and English has more than a score each of vowel and of consonant sounds! Combination of timbres—in the word, hence also in the phrase and the line. A number of poets, among them Sir Philip Sidney and Robert Bridges, have been fascinated by the possibilities of duration as the basis of English prosody; others, by its contributions to verbal "music." Keats discourses on the relations between longer and shorter vowel sounds. Tennyson claims to have learned the quantity of every word in the language ("except perhaps 'scissors' ").[28]

Now if quantity qualifies the rate of movement of the words, it does so in concert with other elements, notably of sonal and rhythmic repetition, grammatical structure, diction, meaning. Like a work of music, a poem is an event in time. But, lacking an *adagio, andante, allegro, presto,* or similar instruction, the interpreter decides for himself. Yet despite this freedom of choice as he reads aloud or in silence, the tempo of his phrasing in relation to the pace he has chosen is in large part dictated by the score. Compare two quatrains of similar pattern: the close of Wordsworth's "To the Cuckoo" and the anonymous lyric on the next page.

> O blessèd bird! the earth we pace
> Again appears to be
> An unsubstantial, faery place,
> That is fit home for thee!

Ignoring grammatical structure, diction, rhythmical stress, and other elements, we find only three sounds that can slow up the movement: the continuing vowel of "O"; "bird"; and "earth." A marked pause occurs after "bird!" and another at the end of line 3. Otherwise the quatrain moves quickly, despite its "long" vowels (in the rimes and in "home"); and except for "home" and "thee" these timbres have little quantity. Moreover, one word flows into the next without any retardation. The timbres combined in the phrases and lines give rise to verse that if anything may be read too quickly. Which cannot be said of the lines that follow, especially of the first:

> O Western wind, when wilt thou blow
> That the small rain down can rain?
> Christ, that my love were in my arms,
> And I in my bed again.

Almost every word within lines 2, 3, 4 flows into the next, except for the pause after "Christ." In the opening, however, the sound of *w* prolongs every word: seven in all; in the first and the last two as vowels. In between, several "short" vowels occur but combined as they are they have marked duration. Similarly the consonant in "thou." Also the added prominence of "blow" from its riming with "O." In addition to the pause at the comma, three junctures hold back the movement of the words: "wester*n*-*w*ind," "Whe*n*-*w*ilt-*th*ou."[29] It is simply not possible to phrase this line—or lines 3 and 6 of "Ah, Sunflower," (p. 215)—with anything like the pace of the Cuckoo quatrain. In reading "golden" and "virgin" in Blake's poem, one is almost compelled to add a rhythmical beat to the three that the other lines call for.

Still another presence can act to slow down the tempo. Compared with "An unsubstantial, faery place" of the Cuckoo quatrain, "O Western wind, when wilt thou blow" is a tight massing of stresses. Although here the retarding occurs in concert with other forces we have noted, the demand made by the words of a poem that results in a crowding of accented syllables in itself can prolong the line. The beginning of Frost's "Directive," ten monosyllables of which eight are "short,"

> Back out of all this now too much for us

reads much more slowly than his

> There is a house that is no more a house

despite the word repetition. As the last part of Wyatt's "It was no dream: I *lay broad wak*ing" with its three prolonged stresses reads much more slowly than the first.[30] Relative swiftness, then, may also come from sparseness of stress and relative slowness from density, in the line or part of the line; from shift in position of accent, and so on—examples are easy to find. But statements of this type suggest an independence of action which has no relation at all to the inter-involved working complexity of every good poem, to say nothing of the mechanistic notions about "conscious artistry" which were hopefully laid to rest on an earlier page (60).

Compared with these relativities in flow of movement, pause is the critical element in the tempo of verse—and beyond. Pause is a patterning of silences. Lust in action, says Shakespeare's Sonnet 129,

> Is perjured, murderous, bloody, full of blame,
> Savage, extreme, rude, cruel, not to trust, . . .

A reader would stop at each juncture marked by a comma even if it were not there—as it is not in the line from Eliot's "Marina":

> Bowsprit cracked with ice and paint cracked with heat.

He would also pause, irrespective of punctuation, in Donne's "Batter My Heart"—

> That I may rise and stand, o'erthrow me and bend
> Your force to break, blow, burn, and make me new.

slightly after "rise" and "force"; perceptibly longer after "stand," "o'erthrow me," "break," "blow," "burn"; and scarcely at all after "bend." It may not be particularly enlightening to trace all temporary cessations of utterance to divisions in grammatical structure, in rhythm, in rhetoric; but little more will be discovered of this endlessly varied complication of tempo. For pause, as much as choice of words, reflects the unparaphraseable attitude of the poem toward all it says-and-suggests as well as toward the person who listens. Its presences lie waiting to reveal (as Frost might have put it) the way the poem "takes" itself and the reader. And the converse holds as true for the latter's response to these presences—in the way he "takes" the poem.

Thus, while the object varies with each interpretation, it also retains an unaltered virtual existence beyond them. For the words, facing in all directions at once, have given and received glancing blows of sound-and-meaning. And the "tones" gathered from this striking of one upon the others coalesce into a total saying-and-suggesting that still seems to be attempting to express something beyond itself.[31] Total meaning seems to expand into something boundless which is only focused in the words. One becomes deeply aware of this during certain suspensions of audible sound when the "tones" cease and then somehow continue, looking back, as it were, on themselves. Silences of this extraordinary sort insist occasionally within the poem and always at the close. Audible sound is followed—or, better, replaced—by a filled silence which is neither tonal echo nor reflected presence. Perhaps what the poem has been trying to but cannot express speaks to us here.

NOTES AND COMMENTS

1. See A. J. Marshall, *Bower-Birds*, London, Oxford, 1954; Sally Carrighar, *Wild Heritage*, pp. 224 ff.; S. D. Ripley, *Trail of the Money Bird*, Harper, 1942; W. H. Thorpe, in Eccles, *Brain and Conscious Experience*, pp. 486 ff. Some bowerbirds build structures 9' high which they ornament with living orchids. Some bowerbirds are "quite exceptional mimics of other birds" (Marshall).

2. "There is no question that some manifestations of 'beauty,' particularly of the human body, are related to sex; the aesthetic is, undoubtedly, affiliated with the erotic."—T. Dobzhansky, *Mankind Evolving*, Yale, 1962. See also Kenneth Clark, *The Nude in Art*, Bollingen, 1956. • It is "plausible to think that at least some of man's artistic activities, notably his dances and displays involving headdresses and other ornaments, may have been stimulated by watching the ceremonial displays of birds. Here, perhaps, the fundamental problem is why, in so many cases, the patterns which have been produced in evolution as recognition marks for sexual behavior (quite apart from bird song) strike us as beautiful. (Quite apart also from beautiful sound patterns, one must remember the display plumes of many birds and the subtle and magnificent colors and patterns of Lepidoptera.) Does it all imply some fundamental unity between the mind and perceptual systems of groups as far apart as the Insecta, the Aves, and mankind?"—Thorpe, in *ibid.*, pp. 487. • Elephants, according to Rensch, have the gift of absolute pitch; they can also identify the basic line of a short melody through various transpositions and variations. Dogs, according to Pavlov, can distinguish the single notes that compose a chorus; etc. • W. H. Thorpe,

Bird Song, Cambridge, 1961; quotations from Eccles, *op. cit.,* pp. 487, 488, with its reference to the findings of P. Szöke, *Studia Musicologica,* pp. 33-85, 1962.

3. Gibbon: Carrighar, *ibid.,* p. 228. Mouse: report by W. O. Hickey, *American Naturalist,* cited there.

4. Desmond Morris, *The Biology of Art,* Knopf, 1962, pp. 39, 165, 144, 151, 113, 162.

5. See D'Arcy Thompson, *On Growth and Form,* Cambridge, 1966 ("the finest work of literature in all the annals of science recorded in the English tongue"—P. B. Medawar); Portman, *op. cit.;* Dubos, *American Scholar, ibid.;* Bernard Rensch in *Zeitschrift für Tierpsychologie,* 1958, vol. 15, pp. 447-61. Certain "misses" were the result of the creature's inability to make up its mind.

6. In animal play (as noted earlier) when novelty wears off, interest diminishes; hence, a tendency to introduce variations. Cf. "There are too few obscure writers in French," wrote Remy de Gourmont; "We accustom ourselves like cowards to love only writing that is easy and that will soon be elementary." • N. Kohts: *Infant Ape and Human Child,* Moscow, Museum Darwinianum, 1935. W. N. and L. A. Kellogg, *The Ape and the Child,* McGraw-Hill, 1933, and Rhoda Kellogg, *What Children Scribble and Why,* San Francisco, Author's Edition, 1955. My discussion of differentiation is based on Morris, *op. cit.,* pp. 161 ff.; similarly, of styles: pp. 33, 30, 38, 162 ff.

7. Laforgue is echoing Taine's explanation of art and most of English literature.

8. William H. George, *The Scientist in Action,* London, Williams & Norgate, Ltd., 1936, p. 11. Suzanne K. Langer, *Feeling and Form,* Scribner, 1953, pp. 50 ff.; for virtuality, Chaps. 3, 4. My first two paragraphs appropriate some of her phrases in addition to those I have set within quotation marks. • Degas: cf. " 'Yours is a hellish craft. I can't manage to say what I want, and yet I'm full of ideas. . . .' And Mallarmé answered: 'My dear Degas, one does not make poetry with ideas, but with *words*."—Valéry, *The Art of Poetry,* p. 63. The thought, however reported, is not new; e.g., Ibn Khaldun (1332-1406), Arab historian: "The Art of Discourse, whether in verse or prose, lies only in words, not in ideas" (E. G. Browne, *A Literary History of Persia,* Scribner, 1902-1906, vol. 2, p. 85).

9. Rhythm is only one aspect of the biology of words in poetry. But even with rhythm, though it "tends to increase the vivacity and susceptibility both of the general feelings and of the attention," the effects are "themselves unnoticed," *Biographia Literaria,* Chap. 18, p. 51. "What we take for granted rarely comes into our awareness," Milton Mazer, in *Science and Psychoanalysis,* IV, 1960, p. 1. Michel Bréal, *Semantics: Studies in the Science of Meaning,* Dover Publications, Inc., 1966. The original Scottish meaning of "silly" was "weak in intellect."

In English, "silly" may go back to *selig* (German for "blessed"); the sequence perhaps from blessedness to unworldliness, innocence of the world, to unsophistication, simplemindedness as well as helplessness, frailty, with some variation owing to geography, and an Anglo-Saxon meaning of happiness and goodness—Michael Girdansky, *The Adventure of Language*, Prentice-Hall, 1963, pp. 110 ff. Dickinson's "adequate": Charles Anderson, *Emily Dickinson*, Holt, 1960, p. 49.

10. Dahlberg: personal letter to me, July 19, 1968.

11. Whalley, *op. cit.*, pp. 161 f. See also Barfield, *Poetic Diction, op. cit.*, pp. 131-133. R. P. Blackmur, *The Double Agent*, Arrow Editions, 1935, pp. 1-29. • See also pp. 84-85 above.

12. I summarize from *The Poem Itself* and *The Modern Hebrew Poem Itself*, S. Burnshaw, T. Carmi, E. Spicehandler, eds., both Schocken (paperback) editions, 1966. Because a word in a poem is always a single complex of sound and meaning, these books present the original text together with guides for pronunciation. It would be ludicrous to expect to experience a foreign poem (or any other) without experiencing to some degree its physical sound. • See also the discussion of prose translation in my *Varieties of Literary Experience*, pp. xiii f. • See Edmund Wilson, *Red, Black, Blond, and Olive*, Oxford, 1956, pp. 389 ff.

13. Rolfe Humphries in *On Translation*, Reuben Brower, ed., Harvard, 1959, p. 61. • Robert Lowell, *Imitations*, Farrar, Strauss, 1963. pp. xi ff. Compare "La primavera hitleriana," pp. 113 f., with plain prose translation in George Kay, *The Penguin Book of Italian Verse*, 1958, pp. 397 f. (For a contrary view: D. S. Carne-Ross, *Delos*, 1, 1968, pp. 210. f., 165-175.) John Simon, *Hudson Review*, Winter 1967-68, also touches on translating the effects of sonality. • "Public domain" is not meant here in the technical sense (out of copyright). • I believe every verse translation should be accompanied (not necessarily on the same or facing page) with a literal one in prose or a trot, for the protection of the reader and the author. • Semblance of a semblance, or as I call it elsewhere "a second-hand poem" (*Caged in an Animal's Mind*).

14. A. C. Bradley, "Poetry for Poetry's Sake," *op. cit.* Marshall McLuhan's assertion about the relation of the medium to esthetic experience has only aggravated the content-form confusion (see, *e.g.*, review by Richard Gilman, *New Republic*, Nov. 18, 1967).

15. Choreography: I am indebted to Gregor Sebba for calling my attention to the attempts made by Vilma Mönckeberg in *Der Klangleib der Dichtung*, Hamburg, 1946 (with poems by Goethe, Möricke, Rilke, and Hölderlin, pp. 59-81).

16. See discussion by Michael Riffaterre of Roman Jakobson and Claude Lévi-Strauss, "*Les Chats* de Charles Baudelaire" in *Yale French Studies*, Sept. 1966, which begins with a summary of the Jakobson "formula" as set forth in "Linguistics and Poetics," in *Style in Language*, T. A. Sebeok, ed., M.I.T. Press, 1966. See also my "Three Revolutions of Modern Poetry" in *Varieties of Literary Experience*, pp. 145-9, 157 ff.

17. Rousselot: André Spire, *Plaisir Poétique et plaisir musculaire*, pp. 11 ff.; Burnshaw, *André Spire and His Poetry*, Philadelphia, Centaur Press, 1934, pp. 131-5. The stress (loudness, intensity) with which a sound is spoken is mechanically measured by the amplitude of the sound waves. Similarly: the quantity (time required for speaking it), by the duration of the waves; pitch, by the wave frequency; the timbre (quality peculiar to each sound), by the wave form. Unlike the timbre, the stress, quality, and pitch vary greatly in degree. • I use "quantity" and "duration" interchangeably for the length of time required to pronounce a syllable. I also use "stress" and "accent" synonymously though some writers regard stress as the emphasis demanded by the metrical pattern and accent as inherent in a word ("tonic accent," as in *silent*). • In metrical feet, a syllable is stressed (′) or unstressed (–); relativity of emphasis is completely ignored. The commonest feet either rise or fall: iamb (– ′) or trochee (′ –); anapest (– – ′) or dactyl (′ – –); also the uncommon bacchius (– ′ ′) and antibacchius (′ ′ –). Spondee (′ ′), molossus (′ ′ ′), pyrrhic (– –), and tribrach (– – –) do neither. Amphibrach (– ′ –) and amphimacer (′ – ′) do both.

18. Cited by Harvey Gross, *Sound and Form in Modern Poetry*, who speaks of the "normative coincidence of vowel length with syllabic stress; we hear syllabic-stress iambics underlying, and occasionally combating, the quantitative measure" (pp. 62 f.). See Jakobson in Sebeok, *Style in Language*, pp. 361 f.

19. For example: "Foúr añd twēntȳ, | bláckbiřds | | báked iñ ā | píe" will break down into a paeon (of which there are four different forms) and a trochee followed by a dactyl and a nameless foot of one syllable— or by a nameless foot of one syllable and an anapest ("báked | iñ ā píe")—or by a trochee and an iamb ("báked iñ | ā píe").

20. Gross, *op. cit.*, p. 31. John Thompson, *The Founding of English Metre*, Columbia, 1961, p. 9. The "rhetorical pull-back" in Blake's Sunflower poem: John Crowe Ransom in Brooks and Warren, *Conversations on the Craft of Poetry*, p. 29.

21. For a discussion of the work of the Russian formalists in shifting the metrical basis from the foot to the line, see Wellek and Warren, *Theory of Literature*, pp. 170 ff.

22. Jakobson, *op. cit.*, p. 375. "Meaning-full sound" has nothing in common with view that "meter, and prosody in general, is itself meaning"—Gross, *op. cit.*, pp. 12 ff. Free verse lacks regularity in *both* rhythm and line-length. This usual explanation of its difference from formal, traditional verse makes sense only when the twofold lack is seen as a matter of degree. Alongside Dryden's "Alexander's Feast," with its irregular line-lengths, Arnold's "Philomela" is free verse; yet almost half of the lines are blank verse and most of the others have the same ascending rhythm. The Chorus of Milton's "Samson Agonistes" is "freer" verse still; the blank-verse pattern, though visible, is farther away. Rhythms reminiscent of traditional English poetry do not, however, mark such works as Smart's "Of Jeoffry, His Cat," "Whitman's

"When Lilacs Last in the Dooryard Bloom'd," Lawrence's "Snake," or Jeffers' "Post Mortem." These manifestly free verse poems, though not associated with patterns of traditional verse, may call to mind certain rhythms of traditional prose, for example, in the King James Bible and Browne's *Hydriotaphia.*—Which leads to another question of degree: in the line of demarcation between verse and prose.

23. Calvin S. Brown, in *Studies in English Literature:* 1500-1900, Autumn 1963: "I am not arguing that there is any particular virtue or guarantee of excellence in monosyllables. In fact, my basic thesis is that there is no point to be made about them either way in English verse. Whatever theorists may say about them, poets use them naturally and unconsciously, and readers accept them in the same way" (p. 489). Note: "The native stock of English words consists largely of monosyllables, and a monosyllable always demands a separate accent, however slight."—Northrop Frye; see Brown, *op. cit.,* pp. 476-477. • One of the "other forces which are always at work in the line is, of course, the "tendency to reduplicative phonetic patterns [which] seems innate in man. They occur in infant babbling; in certain languages; in strong feeling; in spells; in oaths; in proverbial expressions [etc.]"—D. I. Masson in *Encyclopedia of Poetry and Poetics,* A Preminger et al., eds., Princeton, 1965, p. 784. • Dickinson line: a dissimilar outcome develops in lines which invert normal word-order for the sake of (a) rime or (b) rime and rhythm. For example, Jonson's "To Celia":

'Tis no sin love's fruit to steal   (a)
But the sweet thefts to reveal. . . .   (b)

24. Compare: "There are many performances of the same poem—differing among themselves in many ways. A performance is an event, but the poem itself, if there is any poem, must be some kind of enduring object"—Wimsatt and Beardsley, quoted in Jakobson, *op. cit.,* p. 366.

25. Keats, as noted in W. J. Bate, *John Keats,* Harvard, 1963, pp. 414-5. A technical discussion would distinguish subtypes of alliteration (e.g., augmentation diminution, etc.) and assonance (e.g., full, hidden, semi-, etc.); the vowel triangle; along with bodily structures (mouth, larynx, throat, lungs, diaphragm, abdomen) which create the qualities of consonants and vowels.

26. This fact of a poem's life hardly needs documentation. However, see Jakobson, *op. cit.,* pp. 367-8, for a linguistic view. See Henry Lanz, *The Physical Basis of Rime,* Stanford, 1931: rhythmical theories, pp. 180-194; physiological effects of rime and rhythm, pp. 195 ff., 284-294. That English is comparatively poor in rime has long been recognized. None exists for a number of words (month, circle, etc.); only one, for certain others (babe, mountain, etc.). Mayakowsky called rime "the tightening nail," but other sonal-semantic actions contribute no less to reinforcement of unity. "Repetition in word and phrase and in idea is the very essence of poetry. . . . Rhythm is the entire movement, the flow, the recurrence of stress and unstress that is related to the rhythms of

the blood, the rhythms of nature. It involves certainly stress, time, pitch, the texture of the words, the total meaning of the poem"—Theodore Roethke. • "A rhythm involves a pattern, and to that extent is always self-identical. But no rhythm can be a mere pattern; for the rhythmic quality depends equally upon the differences involved in each exhibition of the pattern. The essence of rhythm is the fusion of sameness and novelty. . . . A mere recurrence kills rhythm. . . ."—A. N. Whitehead, *The Principles of Natural Knowledge*, Cambridge, 1925, p. 198.

27. If the single rime in Mallarmé's "Le vierge, le vivace et le bel aujoud'hui" sonnet "illuminates white bird, frozen winter, spiritual intensity, sterility" (Preminger, *op. cit.*, p. 857), how define the comparable function of the two rime-sounds (*run, more*) in the 18 lines of Donne's "A Hymn to God the Father"? Consonant combinations *sp, sw, sl, st, sh* are said to have movement and excitement—as in *spit, swish, slit, stab, ship*. But in *spoon, swale, slow, stone, shard?* Though the sound of a word is most assuredly "related" to what it stands for, nobody so far as I know has been able to explain how. • Keats's quotation: see M. H. Abrams, *A Glossary of Literary Terms*, Holt, 1957, pp. 33 f.

28. Sidney: see John Thompson, *op. cit.*, pp. 128 ff. Keats: Bate, *op. cit.*, p. 414. Tennyson: Hallam Tennyson, *Alfred Lord Tennyson*, Macmillan, 1897, vol. 2, p. 231.

29. Another variant version, preferred by some anthologists:

> Westron winde, when will thou blow,
> The smalle raine downe can raine?
> Christ, if my love were in my armes,
> And I in my bed againe.

30. Pope's lesson in the *Essay on Criticism* exemplifies something else:

> When Ajax strives some rock's vast weight to throw,
> The line too labors, and the words move slow; . . .

It labors with consonants as one word moves into the next. The end of the couplet, however, has sparseness of stress:

> Not so, when swift Camilla scours the plain,
> Flies o'er th'unbending corn, and skims along the main.

31. I am echoing Bradley (p. 106 above).

8 · Reader

Every human being is unique,
unprecedented, unrepeatable.
—Dubos

Since every poem differs from every other poem and no two readers
are the same, what use can there be in referring to "the poem" and
"the reader"? Regardless of whatever else may be true of an object of
art, the steady state of its physical form sets it apart from the plane
of the living: it does not change. Whereas (as doubtless I have said
too often) even the same human being cannot continue to be entirely the same. Any reference, then, to "the reader" implies a
theoretical person marked by multiple and altering capacities of
thinking-and-feeling. Like any such composite, this creature can be
found only in our analytic heads. But he is all we have to place
against "the poem" for a paradigm of the encounter; and enough has
already been said of his nature and his history to invest him with a
semblance of life.

Reader as Person

Although everything he is taught enters through the filters of his
own particular nature, their presence is commonly ignored, their
decisiveness questioned. Yet every reader's innate capacities ulti-

mately qualify all that he can learn to respond to. You may be able to persuade another person to accept your ideas but you will not teach him to feel in a passage of verse something which his range of capabilities does not equip him to feel, any more than you can teach him to make movements which call for muscles which he lacks. Though each newborn human is assembled from a limited group of chemicals, no two individuals enter the world with the same gene complex. And, as noted before, genetic uniqueness makes for differences in the organism's range and type of reactions and consequently for differences in development. Hence every person can respond with only the functional remnant of his original capacities —the remnant made functional within the influences and accidents of all he has encountered (p. 32).

Which is to say: with preferential capacities. How many, how various, how limiting they are in each instance, no one needs to establish, since their presence can be seen in the kind of response that Laforgue defined with his "keyboard" (p. 204). They operate on every level of response, from the most elusive down to the most obvious, where a specific word-sound or word-arrangement may produce an aversion. I am thinking, for example, of Keats's personal dislike of the Petrarchan sonnet stanza (because of its "pouncing rimes") and the Shakespearian (because "the couplet at the end of it has seldom a pleasing effect"). Or Tennyson's wanting to do away with sibilations ("kicking the geese out of the boat . . . I never put two 'ss' together in any verse of mine"). Or my own inability to hear Dylan Thomas' celebrated line "Do not go gentle into that good night" without being disturbed by the prevalence of *t* and *d*. Frost found that he could not make "certain word sounds go together —sometimes they won't say. . . . I've changed lines because there was something about them that my ear refused." Whether one could trace the etiology of every such instance to particular shaping events in the original capacity matters less than that predilections arise at every level of response out of the esthetic potential at work in every human organism.[1] That esthetic processes are a normal endowment is certain if only from the spontaneous way in which children create and respond to the arts. And while creativity may mature into a normative bodily function with but relatively few, with a great many others it takes different forms of expression—in the arts or elsewhere. Or like other endowments exposed to the pressures of the culture, it withers, ceases to be part of a functional remnant. Progress is no more inevitable in the arts than in history—for those who respond or who create.

At this point nothing more need be said of our inborn endowments, for even if they were the same—which we know they are not—the uniqueness of each person's inner and outer environments should produce extraordinary differences in the nature and power of response. How remarkable, then, that despite the disparity, our separate reactions to a given poem have enough in common to allow us to discuss it as though we had had the same experience. Despite the fact that our behavior implies another as-if, the forces of the culture cannot fail to produce certain similarities in the ways we organize our separate brains—and hence in our "exchanging" of ideas. For even though, as Keats was able to see, "The greater part of Men make their way with the same instinctiveness, the same unwandering eye from their purposes, the same animal eagerness as the Hawk," their time-and-place in the culture forms part of their fate. And when they come upon a work of art, it delimits their field of vision, at least at the beginning.[2]

Owen Barfield's illustration, while it speaks of philosophy, holds true of poetry as well. A modern European

can read Plato and Aristotle through from end to end, he can even write books expounding their philosophy, and all without understanding a single sentence. Unless he has enough imagination, and enough power of detachment from the established meanings or thought-forms of his own civilization, to enable him to grasp the meanings of the fundamental terms—unless, in fact, he has the power not only of thinking, but of *unthinking*—he will simply re-interpret everything they say in terms of subsequent thought. If he merely seeks to deduce the meaning of words like *arche, logos, psyche, dynamis,* . . . from the general context, if he cannot rather *feel* the way in which they *came into being out of the essential nature of the Greek consciousness as a whole,* he may read pages and pages of Greek letterpress, and enjoy them, but he will know no more than the shadow of Greek meaning. One could add many other words, but it would take us too far afield. Spengler is excellent on the untranslatableness of these "root-words," as he calls them, and in insisting on the consequently unbridgeable gap between the souls of any two great cultures.

The delimitation is of course most evident in expressions of taste. Mario Praz, for example, reminds us that Petrarch's line "Fior', frondi, erbe, ombre, antri, onde, aure soavi" ("Flowers, leafy branches, grasses, shades, caverns, waves, delightful gentle breezes") used to send sixteenth-century Italian readers into ecstasies. "Who among us at the present day," would be capable of responding to it as "the loftiest, the most sonorous, and the fullest line in modern or ancient writers"? But we need not go back so far. Writing of Keats's *Isabella*, W. J. Bate declares:

It relies too heavily on the reader's predisposition; one either brings a readiness to enter into the direct pathos of a poem like this (in which case specific criticism is irrelevant; for it is then a moving, a "sincere" poem, which, as Lamb said, "should disarm criticism"); or else, if one cannot come prepared with that predisposition, the poem seems absurd and embarrassing. The nineteenth century delighted in it . . . and the poem continued to be praised throughout the Victorian era. Sir Sidney Colvin (1917) still felt that in *Isabella* Keats "reaches his high-water mark in human feeling, and in felicity both imaginative and executive." In another seven years, Amy Lowell, speaking perhaps a little abruptly for a very different generation, found the poem a deplorable, unexplained retrogression in Keats's writing.

If the history of taste must be in part a record of changed delimitations, each epoch cannot help but correct the mistakes of its forebears and in doing so expose predilections of its own which will soon enough be judged absurd, naive, all wrong. For their own time being, to be sure, they are utterly right. He who says otherwise is simply out of step with his peers and with their mentors—whoever and whatever they may be. George Santayana holds that

Taste is formed in those moments when aesthetic emotion is massive and distinct; preferences then grow conscious, judgments then put into words will reverberate through calmer hours; they will constitute prejudices, habits of apperception, secret standards for all other beauties. A period of life in which such intuitions have been frequent may amass tastes and ideals sufficient for the rest of our days. Youth in these matters governs maturity.

That youth in these matters governs maturity may be true with a great many people, but with a great many others—for whom reading is a meaningful part of their existence—the taste that has been formed continues to be formed and re-formed. Eliot in time rediscovers

Milton and Tennyson. The reader, possessed of multiple and altering capacities, one day finds himself surprisingly stirred by a poem which had always left him cold. Or surprisingly unmoved by another which he once could turn to with delight. Curious shifts in the meaningfulness of these poems, themselves unchanged, occur as maturity takes over the governance from youth, possibly in time to relinquish it to age.

Much impressed by such instances in my own experience, I took some care in defining a book of my verse as "offered to people in their middle years by one of their contemporaries," with the following prefatory statement: "Very young and very old readers will probably find the greater part of this book pointless, dull, or misguided—and in their own terms they will be right; for each of us holds different matters to be important. What practiced reader has not at some time squirmed before a piece of writing that once shook him with delight? The writing hasn't changed but the reader has moved into new ranges of feeling and belief. For each age is a subculture group of its own, and some day the phenomena of this stratification will be explored and its meanings for esthetics debated. Criticism continues to talk of books that appeal to readers of all age levels, yet a man in his twenties cannot truthfully agree with a man in his forties and another in his sixties on what is really important or interesting or true. Not only ten-year-olds but every emotional-age stratum has a subculture of its own to whom the celebrants of a different group are inevitably outsiders—promulgators of a barbarism *pro tem.* More than the cells in the body are changed every cycle of years."[3]

Though I felt these remarks to be self-evident, a number of readers assured me that I was wrong. Yet, like Pound, I could see "no reason why the same man should like the same book at 18 and 48." And even assuming for a moment that he did, could the book have been actually the same? Though a certain poem may speak to people of disparate age-groups, can it bring them a comparably similar "message"? While the poem's language remains intact, to the degree that the hearers differ in living experience, great gaps must exist in what each will be *able* to hear. The poem, then, is not the same poem—nevertheless to each reader for whom it is markedly different it may be able to bring a certain type of poetic experience.

The question here leads back into the two great "fields" of response as distinguished at the close of Chapter 3 and elaborated in Chapter 6 (pp. 187 ff.). What was set forth there on the subject of a poem's "resonances" and "reverberations" does not need to be considered again except in relating the first field to the "great gaps" I speak of in the paragraph directly above. To respond to a poem is to know its resonances-reverberations, and if the former are bound to the reader's life in the culture, the latter are not except in one decisive respect: the resonances must have meaning[4] enough for the reader to allow him to enter the poem. This is to say that unless the ideas, feelings, objects, events, and other referents make some acceptable type of sense to the reader he will probably turn away from the poem before allowing its acts of uniting to take him toward its "ultimate subject" (p. 187). More often than not, the culture-knowledge of a poem is the gateway to its creature-knowledge. A poem before it can "be" for a reader must "mean."

This reversal of scripture-according-to-MacLeish does not condone the abuses he sought to redress but simply keeps what

> A poem should not mean
> But be

would appear to remove. For it goes without saying that both meaning and being are attributes of every successful poem, including this one by MacLeish from which I quote. And if I focus on meaning here it is only because of its gateway position—because readers feel constrained to abandon a work when the resonances tend to exclude them. Nevertheless to a good many people my insistence may seem misplaced. A poet creates an autonomous object which must stand or fall on its own. "The work of the artist," as Plekhanov declares, "is for him an end in itself." A poet is no longer "a man speaking to men" (Wordsworth). The poem does all the speaking, and if a reader wants to hear what it says, he must pay no attention to anything lying outside it. Indeed many critics forewarn him against cluttering his mind with extrinsic concerns—the poem's relation to history, the writer's biography, his presumed intent—and especially against listening to someone who tries to paraphrase the poem. As his mentors explain, this is something that cannot be done.

All the same, even they will sometimes attempt it, taking care to make fine apologies for their sin. Eliot's rationalization—in which other critics at times seek refuge—all but denies the relevance to poetic experience of what he nonetheless undertakes to provide by a paraphrase: "one needs to quiet the housedog of the mind with any meat so that the poem may do its work," says Frank Kermode, before offering his version of what a work by Stevens is "about."[5] That "it may well be an inaccurate account" he is sound in warning; but the issue transcends both rightness and wrongness of any specific paraphrase. It takes us back into the matter of "ordinary-extraordinary meanings" as discussed in Chapter 3. Furthermore, if Plekhanov's assertion is valid, so is Wordsworth's provided we think of it not in terms of a man but of a poem speaking to men.

It "speaks to" men with its common-and-uncommon kinds of sense, with the seemingly incompatible forces of its meanings, certain aspects of which can be described (paraphrased) in the hope of bringing the reader *toward* the total meaning which, obviously, no words other than those of the poem could embody. In each instance, however, the speaking is a dramatized-speaking; it is not a direct address, communication. Neither speaker nor hearer-reader plays a role; both maintain a certain distance. And yet their encounter, when valid for the latter, is above all else a relationship—better still, an axis of relationships.[6] The dramatized-speaking enacts the materials for the reader to interpret in the terms of his private experience; and when by an act of sympathy he goes out from the self toward the poem, something akin to communion may come into being. But his private experience cannot always know (recognize) what the dramatized-speaking embodies. Full response calls for various sorts of cumulative learning out of numerous attempts of sympathy. And at times in the course of this learning it must call out for help.

Reader "Versus" Hearer?

One kind of learning that is almost always prescribed consists in closing the eyes and opening the ears. Reading cannot possibly match the rewards of listening.[7] In fact, no poem can come alive except when it is spoken and experienced aloud! Proof for this claim can be readily adduced—the reader's advisers can always quote from the letter of Hopkins:

Of this long sonnet ["Spelt from Sibyl's Leaves"] above all remember what applies to all my verse, that it is, as living art should be, made for performance and that its performance is not reading with the eye but loud, leisurely, poetical (not rhetorical) recitation, with long rests, long dwells on the rhyme and other marked syllables, and so on. This sonnet shd be almost sung: it is most carefully timed in *tempo rubato*. [*Letters* I, cxliii]

Then they may go on to reinforce the point by reciting the lines— rather by trying to recite them with the aid of the accents, grave and acute, and the mark | that calls for what the poet defines as "a rest of one stress":

Earnest, earthless, equal, attuneable, | vaulty, voluminous, . . .
    stupendous
Evening strains to be tíme's vást, | womb-of-all, home-of-all,
    hearse-of-all night.
Her fond yellow hornlight wound to the west, | her wild hollow
    hoarlight hung to the height
Waste; her earliest stars, earl-stars, | stárs principal, overbend us,
Fire-féaturing heaven. For earth | her being has unbound, her
    dapple is at an end, as-
tray or aswarm, all throughter, in throngs; | self ín self steepèd
    and páshed—quíte
Disremembering, dísmémbering, | áll now. Heart, you round me right
With: Óur evening is over us; óur night | whélms, whélms, ánd
    will end us. . . .

If Hopkins' conviction is unqualified, so is that of another eminent modern poet whose manuscripts are also filled with sonal markings: Emily Dickinson. But her belief is completely opposed: "a Pen has so many inflections and a Voice but one."

Whether or not such a thought could have come to many of our ancestor-poets, its cogency is inescapable for us after all that has taken place in English verse over the last six centuries—with

its increasing emphasis of the sense pattern rather than the sound pattern; its gradual assimilation to conditions of the printed, rather than the spoken or chanted, word; its exodus from the crowded hall to the quiet library, from public performance to private perusal.[8]

The third assertion in this statement by a scholar, published in 1944, needs correction, for to judge by the numbers of people who pay to hear public readings (not to mention verse recordings), we are living in a Second Bardic Age. So popular are recitals today that almost any author of a volume of verse can expect at least one engagement. And doubtless there are already more poems on tape than any one person would care to confront in a lifetime. Though all this activity must be counted as "good for poetry," vastly more people pay to listen to verse than to read it in books. Furthermore, listening does not equal reading—nine out of ten contemporary Americans have been found to be eye-minded. Thanks to their steadily greater dependence on writing and print, Western people have lost the listening talent they had once possessed. The kind of audience has long ceased to exist that a bard could hold in a spell through scores of stanzas.

To speak to his hearers, to keep their attention, a contemporary poet-reciter has to think more than once about the work he selects to perform. Poems of subtle indirection, of oblique suggestion? Veiled contemplative stanzas—or passages bright with dialogue, incident? Lines of low-keyed reflectiveness—or others that might possibly be sung or chanted? . . . More likely than not, whatever he has written will be close in texture, allusive, compressed. And though his verse may abound in recurring structures, it is probably not of the kind that most listeners will be able to follow, particularly during their initial encounter with a poem. How much, in fact, can any audience experience from a single hearing of any new poem which may call for thoughtful study? Limited as he is by these and other conditions, the poet-reciter does well to choose poems which his auditors will best be able to stay with in their minds. To do otherwise invites the embarrassments of their half-hearing, hence of half-listening—which can also arise with the best-chosen text. For even poems suited to the platform are hard to perform well. They demand an extraordinary talent which—as any devotee of recitals soon discovers—very few poets possess. And why should one expect them to possess it? Opera composers are not coloraturas. Composition and performance are different arts; rarely does the gift for both inhabit the same body.

But whether poetry is performed badly or well is beside our

question, which concerns the kind of help one might gain from hearing aloud. That there can be no simple or single answer must be evident to anyone familiar with the sources of Modernism, or even with only one of its greatest makers, Mallarmé. His final work, "Un Coup de Dés," may have reached the ultimate in the arrangement of words and spaces. And yet at least in one respect Cummings pioneered even further. How recite to anyone at all the opening lines of his grasshopper poem:

r-p-o-p-h-e-s-s-a-g-r

who

a)s w(e loo)k

upnowgath

PPEGORHASS

Here, says a critic in a passage which Cummings reviewed,

the spacing is governed by the disruption and blending of syllables and the pause and emphasis of meaning which produce a figurative equivalent for the subject of the poem, as the reader reads in time.

Experimental typography, however, is merely an aspect of all that is meant by "the writing of poetry for the eye," and perhaps the least significant. Obviously it is the extreme compression, textural subtlety, veiled allusiveness, innovated syntax, private reference, resonant ambiguity, "denotative" or at least "connotative sonality" —in sum, the entire widened range of linguistic structures—that have made modern poetry a poetry that requires to be *seen*. Homonyms, word-groups, lines, stanzas, spaces, punctuation, spelling swarm with clues and signs, with suggestions and with expectations which "speak to" the eye. The fullness of all such meanings cannot possibly come to the reader through his ear alone.[9]

Nevertheless, Hopkins' "The Golden Echo and the Leaden Echo" and a good many other modern poems virtually demand to be heard aloud. They demand it, however, as a necessary part of the total experience for the reader. Within such a context, eye-versus-ear as a question begins to make sense; and answers can follow once we note the difference between a first and a later encounter; between a poem which is new for the reader and one which he has known. For with the latter, no one can doubt the possibilities that a heard recital may provide out of all that another reader had discovered for himself. Indeed no one could begin to define the countless and subtle assertions of meaning that the spoken poem can convey to a well-attuned ear. We need consider only one of the interfused sources: pause, the disposition of which cannot fail to reflect the unparaphraseable attitude of the work toward all it says-and-suggests as well as toward the person it speaks to.

"A Pen has so many inflections and a Voice but one." The rhetorical markings on Dickinson's manuscripts may have been an anxious attempt to help her reader to hear—but to hear aloud? Whatever her private intent, the reply for the art of poetry to the questions implied must be sought in its genesis. And if it is true that to experience a poem is to have an experience analogous to the poet's when he composed it, then the listening must take place within. "The completest existence of a poem," says Mark Van Doren,

is in that inner ear where no sound ever comes. The harmony is in the reader's brain, or better yet, his soul. And if he is a good reader he cannot bear anybody else's voice between him and the words.

For in the poetic encounter, neither the person who speaks nor the person who listens is actual. It is rather the creative self of the poet addressing the responsive self of the reader: imagination calling to imagination with the only voice they know—the voice of silence. Only with the inward ear is it possible to hear simultaneously all the keys in which the words are sounded, all their multiple emphases, modulations, overtones, undertones, turns—all the inflections of the poem. So constrained am I by this limiting fact that after speaking or hearing any poem aloud, I feel a need to reread it in silence, thus to regain it in its "completest existence," to recover the missing voices. The specific poem does not matter, nor the distinction that Barfield, for example, makes between the kinds of poetry that he calls "architectural" (Milton's, the Metaphysicals') and "fluid" (Chaucer's, Shakespeare's):

[I]t is much harder to convey the *full* effect of poetry of the architectural type with the *voice*. The eye seems to be necessary as well, so that the shape of a whole line or period can be taken in instantaneously. The actual sounds have grown more fixed and rigid and monotonous; the stresses accordingly are more subtle, depending upon the way in which the emotional meaning—as it were—struggles against this rigidity; and this produces a music different indeed, but none the less lovely because it is often audible only to the inward ear. The fluid type of verse, on the other hand, is made for reciting or singing aloud and probably gains more than it loses by this method of delivery.

My reaction has much in common with that of Stravinsky as suggested in his altered attitude toward "embalming [his own] performances [of his works] in tape"; "one performance represents only one set of circumstances, and . . . the mistakes and misunderstandings are cemented into traditions as quickly and canonically as truths." The analogy to a single recital of a poem would substitute for "mistakes and misunderstandings" an enormous inadequateness— the absence from "only one set of circumstances" of all the other inflections that come to the reader when he listens to the poems in "completest existence." For poetry is speaking heard, not through the ear as speech is heard, but taken in by the eye to be heard in the mind.

The Anxious Helper

Is literary criticism possible? It is "perpetually necessary . . . and perpetually impossible" Tate concludes in an essay on the question. Out of reasons different from his and in a secular context, one can be brought to the same double thought. For example, with respect to judgment, in which history shows it to have been unusually wrong; it is not the failures that make criticism impossible but its being deprived of fixity in its grounding. The poems we deplore may prove admirable to our heirs. Meanwhile among the works of literature there are many, old as well as new, which resist understanding, not to mention others which seem more accessible than in fact they are: with both, aid must continue to be kept available. Nevertheless, while serving this scholarly purpose, criticism cannot help but act as a self-elected instructor. At times for the better, at others for the worse, for except when supplying disinterested bits of information, it does not proceed without pressing and propagating taste and opinion. Yet all that a serious reader can need is aid-by-elucidation, being a keyboard peculiar to himself, and having to learn and experience for himself.

He may, of course, be eager to know what others have said about works he has known or intends to know. And if he reads some accounts of writers and their critics, he will surely be shocked when he discovers what Dryden thought about Shakespeare; Johnson about Swift and Milton; Goethe about Hölderlin and Byron; Pope about Milton; Wordsworth about *The Ancient Mariner;* or Byron about Keats. But "the failures of criticism" are not told by these random examples, as Henri Peyre makes evident in a book by this title:

The list of misunderstood writers, who were charged with obscurity, madness, decadence, and immorality [not to mention other failings], would include practically all the great English writers whom we admire today. To be sure, not all their contemporaries were equally blind or mistaken: there have been a few voices crying in the wilderness, proclaiming the originality of new talents. But the more dignified and respectable the periodicals and the more imposing the critics, the more preposterous the misjudgments, the more influential the mistakes.

That such things no longer can happen, each age takes for granted. But why, when the weight of experience compels us to assume that contemporary judgments are almost sure to be reversed within fifty years, sometimes even before their victims are dead? Perhaps there is something naive in our expectations. Perhaps there must be two sorts of critical judgment: one that reflects the immediate response or lack of response to every writer as he speaks to his time;[10] the other, that develops gradually as a consequence of change in the time itself. Such a notion, of course, has its comforts; yet it also arises from faith—in the possibility of criticism, in the better sense of posterity, in the "progress" of taste.

Meanwhile, it is plain that all critics are more or less dangerous insofar as whatever their judgments imply affects and conditions the responses of readers. This evident principle has even been proved—in the field—by studies of reactions to a painting: what people physically see turns out to be closely related to what they have been told or taught. Or, as Leo Spitzer remarked three decades ago—in a library—the person "who has digested Lanson's antithetic statement '*Voltaire pense, Rousseau sent*' may never discover the emotional in a diatribe of Voltaire, nor the intellectual in a harangue of Rosseau."

After digesting Dahlberg's "*Moby-Dick: An Hamitic Dream*" some people may not be able to respond to Melville as they had before. To be sure, exposure to criticism has always brought risks, though a reader has rarely felt uneasy. Not so today, intimidated as anyone might be by the sheer pervasiveness and power of the critical assault, with its inexhaustible profusion of exegeses, handbooks, canons, revivals, reconsiderations, and self-perpetuating forums.

Gazing about at the prevalence of anxious helpers, one has trouble in believing that this late Alexandria came out of a movement largely of creative artists who distrusted any criticism not produced by a fellow artist. The skies of Britain before World War I sang with manifestoes and polemics as the editors and writers of *Blast* and *The Tyro* echoed the tones they had learned from the literary battles of Paris. So Wyndham Lewis could flatly announce that no criticism about a painter was worth a glance if the critic was not also a practicing painter. And Eliot, that "the *only* critics worth reading were the critics who practised, and practised well, the art of which they wrote."

The confession, however, with its proper repudiation, did not appear till 1923, and when it appeared it formed part of an essay which exalted "the capital importance of criticism in the work of creation." No gift of insight is required to find in the panegyric the germ of the rationale of those who would later try to press to perfection that "part" of the creative process which Eliot declared to be "probably, indeed, the larger part." But while the assertions I am about to quote flow out of those of Eliot, they also contradict his strictures on "creative criticism."[11] No matter; say the editors of *Reading Modern Poetry* of the commentaries accompanying their anthology:

The explanations are in many cases almost as important as the poems. It is a characteristic of our times that the criticism of poetry has reached a level where it is often as imaginative an act as the writing of the poem itself.

It is fashionable to charge the "New Critics" for excesses of this kind, yet nothing could be more careless. The term, first used by Spingarn in 1910, did not come into currency till thirty years later when Ransom published *The New Criticism*. Rather than hailing Eliot, Richards, William Empson, and Yvor Winters as the new dispensation, he objected to what they shared in common; he called out instead for an "ontological" critic to supply the philosophic basis for poetry's being. Nevertheless, in the years ensuing, "New Criticism" has been used to mean virtually anything at all despite the fact that it constitutes a distinctive school whose tenets have been plainly set forth.[12] "Essentially," said Auden a decade ago, "The New Criticism has been an attempt to train people to read carefully." No doubt; but with what in mind? For the New Critics, not with the poet's personality or biography, not with the reader's emotions, certainly not with the socio-historical backgrounds. They are mainly concerned with the texture, the structure, with the poem as a literary object in itself, and—in theory if not always in practice —with the meaninglessness of trying to separate form from content. In short, a deliberately restricted approach toward each word and the place of each word within the poem, consequently also toward irony, ambiguity, paradox, plurisignation—toward the literary complication of verbal meaning.

How such an approach could lead to enlargements *ad absurdum* need hardly be shown. Any number of parents have looked at the classroom papers carried home by their gleeful or solemn children, and parodists have had the time of their lives with the jargon of literary scientism. Even critics have at times felt obliged to restrain their colleagues. Ransom, referring to Empson's analysis of "Annihilating all that's made/To a green thought in a green shade," complains of his "almost inveterate habit of overreading poetry," adding:

But I think at any rate, we do well just to observe it and let it pass, rather than build it into some big system of knowledge to load upon the consciousness of Marvell, who was merely a poet.[13]

It is all too easy to get carried away by a poem's connotations, suggestions, associations beyond one's sense of proportion. But I think that for many the explanation is connected with the workaday task of critics, most of whom have to earn their living in schools. For as anyone knows who has done it for long, "teaching" literature two or three hours a week makes large demands on ingenuity as well as on energy. One solution, of course, is to follow the lead of Empson and expound on the possibilities. Another—which has the virtue of class "involvement"—is to make one's charges ransack a work for discussable materials. A recent syllabus, for example, proposes that high school seniors and college freshmen read the *Odyssey* on

1. The Literal Level: *The Odyssey* as an Adventure Story;
2. The Moral Level: The *Odyssey* as a Definition of the Gods, the World, and Man;
3. The Symbolic Level: The *Odyssey* as Archetypal Experience;
4. The *Odyssey* as Atonement of Everyman and God the Father.

When MacLeish arrived at Harvard (around 1950) to teach literature, he assigned his class to report on a story which they had not read: "Big Two-Hearted River." Hardly a story at all, it is rather, as Harry Levin remarks in his discussion of the episode,

simply a sketch about a boy who goes fishing. Its striking quality is the purity of its feeling, its tangible grasp of sensuous immediacy, the physical sensation that Mr. Hemingway is so effective at putting into prose. The students did not seem to feel this quality. They liked the story; they wrote about it at length; but in their protocols, to a man, they allegorized it. Each of those fish that Nick Adams had jerked out of Big Two-Hearted River bore for them a mystical significance, which varied according to its interpreter—Freudian or Jungian, Kierkegaardian or Kafkaesque. . . . Literature is not a game of charades.

Yet the restless search for symbols would make it so—restless and quite as serious as that of the medieval monks who looked for Christian symbols and Christian allegories in the pagan poems of Ovid, Virgil, and Homer. Naturally, they were able to find them— any work of art can be found to mean more than it says or suggests and, besides, one can always invest it with whatever one feels it has to possess. Nothing can stop such a process; the writer has no recourse. Fortunately, the reader has. He can close his ears to any symbolical, allegorical, anagogical construct which interferes with his own experience of the poem. And if he gives himself to what Levin calls its particulars—that "whatness" which characterizes a work of art, the truth of an object to its peculiar self—the rest may come of its own. In any case, nothing will prevent him from returning again and again to the poem to see if the loftier or profounder meanings that others prize will have relevance for him as well.

But he may have neither the patience nor stomach to read through their pages, jargon being one of the grimmer gifts of Alexandria. Not that it arises from caprice—the language of a critic never does. Nor that it could be recast in more readable terms; to do this would violate the attitude of those who use them. Publishing in journals and calling to the many, they form no official school, but what and how they speak are sufficient to define them. Two excerpts, at random:

[Referring to *Paradise Lost*:] Poetic strategy was involved; it always is, when a poet starts upon a grand campaign. The performance tells us whether the strategy has succeeded.

[Referring to an anthology:] Extraordinary advances in critical method make the inspection of a poem today by a first-rate critic as close and careful as a chemical analysis.

One could take even better examples, but I am as aware as anyone else of the difficulty of finding words for discussing the arts: "Critical terms are rare pearls born of the irritation that the mind feels at not being able to account to itself for something it repeatedly encounters." Jacques Barzun is speaking of the visual arts, whose repertory in this respect is smaller than literature's, but literature is far from possessing terms that are faithful to the many and subtle complexities of composition and response. And possibly this lack explains in part why some critics reach out into alien fields. Possibly. But could they expect to take over the terms of technology, for example, without also taking over the assumptions? A reader, repelled by some of the results, can simply glance and turn away. A writer will not be forebearing. "The time has come," said Spender, ten years ago,

when we ought to challenge every single one of the assumptions which are so confidently put forward by the critics when they "examine" the texts before them. Otherwise the new intellectualization may finally become an even greater menace to the development of new original talent than the old stupidity.

Though they both are surrounded by the same laden orchards of Alexandria, the reader is luckier than the writer: he can pick and choose or not pick at all. In any event, if he decides to taste the fruits, he soon learns which trees to avoid. But the writer feels occupationally tempted to sample them all, and though he also may end in dismay and confusion, the reader is better able to see both the trees and this forest; and when he does, he realizes that any and all can be had for the taking. He does not have to decide between, for example, the formal-esthetic qualities of a poem and the socio-cultural worlds to which it belongs. He can have both and many other things as well. He can, in a word, be unintimidated—as indeed he will have to be if his life as a reader is to thrive.

He can turn to whatever responds to his interest or need. And even if he is that rarity, a "well-trained reader," he will be irritated most by his own inadequacies. Though steadily assured that a work can be read in and of itself as an object, he soon enough realizes how much its words also live by reason of the outside worlds that they bring transformed into the poem. I refer not merely to things that can be found in handbooks—specific references within the poem to persons or events associated with their originals in myth or in history, or the chronology of writers and of works. Any number of "aids" can be used. Any number of accounts can tell him that Burns preceded Shelley, that Hölderlin wrote almost a century before George, that Jarry's play about the King of the Absurd had been witnessed by Yeats as well as Mallarmé. Rather I refer to all that inheres in a literary work by reason of its place in the courses of recorded experience—its historicity. A poem is born in and of a historical moment—as Blake might have said, it is one of the productions of time. And because its language is also of that moment, text and cultural context are indisseverable. So it is that a reader who experiences a poem of whatever period also confronts this fusion, whether he knows it or not.[14]

Whence the peculiarly double historicity suffusing works of art of another epoch, regardless of how near they may seem by virtue of their way of speaking or their mythic timelessness. A reader can never hope to know even familiar poems—Herbert's "The Collar," Gray's "Elegy," Wordsworth's "Ode"—as they were known by their contemporaries. He cannot even by imagining wholly become such readers. Necessarily he sees aspects they could not see, misses some, overstresses certain passages, fails in his feeling for others. In such an encounter, perspective—the supposed prerequisite for perfect seeeing—distorts. It also deceives. As C. S. Lewis discovered from observing his students, a poem of the 16th or the 19th century may need as much elucidation as one written hundreds of years earlier. Actually it may need it more. With an earlier text, we rather expect to want help when confused or uncertain, whereas with later texts we assume that we follow all the words. As a result, when we feel ourselves "content with whatever effect the words accidentally produce in our modern minds" we may be reading, rather than the poet's poem, one that to some extent has been remade by our time.

In his zeal to come close to a work of another period, can the reader find anything of use in the poet's biography—in the plain facts, the verified incidents? Speaking as a reader, I may ask what I have gained from learning that "Le Cimetière marin" is a meditation by the sea at Sète where Valéry's family lived and died; or that eels were a common sight in the boyhood country of Montale, author of "L'anguilla"; or that Frost's "Out, Out—" was written after the accidental death of a sixteen-year-old boy with whom the poet and his children had been friendly; or that Stevens' "Anecdote of the Jar" refers to an actual jar; or that Wordsworth composed "It is a beauteous evening . . ." while in France on a visit to his ten-year-old illegitimate daughter; or that a love affair with a girl of nineteen inspired the seventy-four-year old Goethe to write his Marienbad elegy; or that Vallejo's "Pequeño responso . . ." was one of fifteen poems of this Peruvian writer which were set up and printed during the Spanish Civil War by members of the Loyalist Army.

I cite these haphazard items in the generally increasing order of their personal interest for me, but so far as I can tell, none of them has added to my knowledge of the poem or to my response. If anything, to the contrary,[15] at least in some instances. But with Ungaretti's "Tu ti spezzasti" or Brecht's "An die Nachgeborenen," for example, the outcome differs. The effect of the young Italian child's motions and the cry of grief largely depend on the reader's awareness of where he came from and the setting of the alien landscape. With the German poem, lacking knowledge that the author speaks as an active Communist, the reader could make only vague emotional sense of its confiding plea to posterity. In instances of this kind, the biographical fact is a needed element which the poet omitted from the poem. As he may have felt compelled to do. Rilke says as much in a letter. He "did not want to make a note" on the one addressed in his sixteenth *Orpheus* sonnet (Part I). "Any indication would only have isolated him again, singled him out." He admits, however, that the reader "has to know—or guess" that the sonnet is addressed to a dog.

Knowledge of this kind is knowledge that a reader has a right to expect from scholar-critics—and which makes them perpetually necessary. Facts and matters of fact, whatever their source, in the writer's life or outside it, which restore, for example, to "La Belle Dame Sans Merci" the opening line that Keats accepted at last. Or to Yeats's "Among School Children" the word that had been steadily misspelled through a dozen editions (as "Soldier" instead of "Solider"). Though aids of this "minor" kind ideally ought not to be required, they frequently are; and at times they may come into existence only because a scholar-critic makes a final appeal to the author as the "logical person" to give the last word. Luciano Rebay provides a fascinating account concerning the pivotal word "diàspori" in Montale's *Elegia di Pico Farnese*, which had bewildered critics along with readers for almost thirty years. Writers who discussed the passage in which it appears simply quoted the word as Montale wrote it and went on, one translator going so far as to remark in a footnote "another chemical notation," which he followed with the dictionary meaning. In fact it meant nothing of the sort. Until the spring of 1967 the possibility of an orthographic error in the woman-love phrase had not entered anyone's mind—or that Montale could have missed both the Italian word "diòspiri" and the Tuscan "diòsperi" and had ended with "aluminum hydroxide" instead of "persimmons."[16]

Many poems, even those in a poet's perfect text, need the complement of other kinds of knowledge. How close can one get to Nerval's later sonnets without some guide to the privacies of their allusions? Or to Donne's cryptic passages, unless he uses one of the short or long glosses which arose in the wake of Grierson's comments? With works of this type, the difficulties do not issue from time or place so much as from the nature of their ways of speaking to a reader and the consequent gaps in what he hears. How to go about closing them is seldom a matter of choice. Gaps of this sort will not fill up of themselves or in response to a reader's will or desire. As he finally learns, help anxious or patient, if it can light up an allusion, an ellipsis, a tangle of syntax, has no reason to be scorned. More than one poet has been eager to receive it—also to give it, even if it meant providing footnotes. In some instances, extensive material is needed; with contemporary Hebrew verse, for example, in which much depends on a buried tradition. Granted that, at times, after reading through recondite paragraphs of scholarship-criticism, one gets but a doubtful conclusion or a guess. In our decades—following *The Waste Land* and *Little Gidding*—such efforts will have to be made if only to discover when a poet has embodied in a work of his own some other writer's imaginative act with the force of an edited meaning.[17]

"Works of art are of infinite loneliness," wrote Rilke, "and with nothing to be so little reached as with criticism. Only love can grasp and hold and fairly judge them." Rarely will a reader confuse the critical response that was inspired by affinity with the one that was not. What is harder to tell—and matters more—is the part played by this force that Rilke calls love; for the staying power of all critical writings depends on its relation to judgment. Proust had no doubts on this matter. "The moment our reasoning intelligence tries to judge works of art," he warned, "one can prove anything one wishes to." Let analytic thinking take over and judgment sinks into pointlessness.

Readers respond to the critic's impassioned involvement as much as to the insights that he helps them to make their own. When he lacks the first and must strain for the second, the straining will show. When he lacks the second, he can offer little more than the high enthusiasms that made a bad word of "Impressionism." Yet he needs something more than these two abilities, along with sensibility and learning. Tact, perhaps, is a close enough term for defining the quality without which even loving criticism usually fails to affect a reader deeply. I think, at random, of an essay (on Hardy's "Nature's Questioning") in which the interweaving of positive and negative findings communicates a breadth and a depth of conviction which can seldom come out of mere admiration.[18] While believing that criticism must occupy itself with the literary merits of a work, I am far from suggesting that the only kind worth having must amount to praise. The point of my concern is the source of the critic's responses, for even an attack—unless it is demeaned by contempt or condescension—can issue from compassion deeper than its statements might imply.

We have been looking at the rosy side of the relation between reader and critic whereas they actually cohabit in uneasy peace. Much as they need each other and know that they do, critics are the constant aggressors. More than just willing and eager to guide, they tend to tell the reader what and how to read, urging, instructing, insisting, often hinting at wonders he will otherwise miss. With their yearning to give unto others every possible thing to be found in a poem, the most anxious of the tribe would stuff the mind of the reader till it bursts. Luckily lacking the wish to hear all that they cry to him, the reader develops a compliant deafness. Yet the chorus may become too loud. Enjoy, enjoy, they beseech him. Take what we offer! Until he flees for cover from the should's and the don'ts to nurse his uncatholic taste. The caricature could be harsher. It makes no mention of the language of a good many critics, their tone, their gratuitous moralities. It says nothing at all of "insights" which are plainly absurd.

But even the most lovable of critics are abandoned by the reader when he makes his encounter with the poem. As in all other learning, he performs this act for himself. If up to this point, criticism has often helped him and often failed, it resembles the rest of his living relationships for which no cure can be found. Coming to the poem, he is what he is as a reader not only by having already known a good deal of verse and of criticism. "Men do not understand books," said Pound, "until they have had a certain amount of life." Whether he had reason to add that "no man understands a deep book, until he has seen and lived at least part of its contents" raises another question. But it is not one which will seriously trouble a reader. In the immediacy of his encounter with the poem, he thinks only of the stranger's words speaking through verbal symbols which come to life in his mind. That these symbols can seize and hold him is surprising enough. That they sometimes have the power to change his sense of the world is the possible miracle. Sometimes, for many of these encounters must come to little or nothing. Though each of us sees himself as eager and able to accept every work of art that is truly authentic, the image deceives. Not every poet can be heard by every reader. The person who listens remains in his way as unique as any poet, de Gourmont notwithstanding: few readers, if any, are constitutionally capable of "accepting as many esthetics as there are original minds."[19]

NOTES AND COMMENTS

1. The "esthetic potential" is rooted also in groups of organisms, united by place, time, region, language, etc. For example—again, on the most obvious level—with the consonant p as silenced in English but sounded in French (*psyche*).

2. Time-and-place delimits more than just their field of vision. Renoir considered the ugliness of buildings and the "vulgarity" of design in articles in common use toward the end of the last century as more dangerous than wars: "We get too accustomed to those things, and to such a point that we don't realize how ugly they are. And if the day ever comes when we become entirely accustomed to them, it will be the end of a civilization which gave us the Parthenon and the Cathedral of Rouen. Then men will commit suicide from boredom; or else kill each other off, just for the pleasure of it."—Jean Renoir, *Renoir My Father*, Little Brown, 1962. Mario Praz, *The Romantic Agony*, Oxford, 1951, pp. 15 f., quoting line 5 of Petrarch's "Canzoniere, CCCIII." Barfield, *Poetic Diction*, p. 133. Bate, *John Keats*, p. 314.

3. "Age does not exist in a 'pure state' for sociologists. Linked as it is with other traits, age seems less significant than membership in a group that has certain folkways, attitudes, beliefs. One need not be a sociologist to add that childhood, senescence, and (to a marked extent) adolescence are each homogeneous enough for forming three subcultures of their own" (John H. Mueller).

4. "Sense" is to be understood here in a very broad way. See Calvin S. Brown, "Difficulty and Surface Value," for example: "What is required is that there be some easily accessible attraction, some value for the reader on the surface of the poem, to induce him to return to it and eventually to look deeper. • These surface values may be of many kinds. They may even be superficial values, though they are not necessarily so. They are not to be identified by their nature, but rather by

their availability. . . ." in *The Disciplines of Criticism*, P. Demetz et al., eds., Yale, 1968, p. 51.

5. Frank Kermode, *Wallace Stevens*, Grove Press, Inc., 1961, p. 45.

6. These are almost the words of Jorge Luis Borges: "A book is not an isolated being; it is a relationship, an axis of relationships."

7. I mean to imply here a crucial distinction between two kinds of experience: one in which you make the sounds of the poem for yourself, aloud or in silence; the other, in which you overhear someone else as he makes the sounds for himself. To be sure, neither kind need exclude the other. Yet the point cries out to be made against the popular fallacy that this opening paragraph reflects. In my discussion of "Reader 'versus' Hearer" listening means listening to a recital by someone else, overhearing someone else. My discussion makes no mention whatever of the kind of listening that also occurs when the reader speaks the poem aloud to himself and for himself, whether others be present or absent. Need anyone argue the importance of this part of the total act of experiencing a poem or the value for the reader of getting any poem by heart?

8. Harold Whitehall, *Kenyon Review*, Summer 1944. • Nine out of ten . . . eye-minded: Carrighar, *Wild Heritage*, p. 207, who informs me that this finding, obtained not long ago from exhaustive market researches and other sources by a very large American corporation, formed the basis on which it allocated millions of dollars worth of advertising. • Unlike the play-actor, who is not responsible for his lines, the poet-reciter stands in double jeopardy, to be judged for both what he says and the way he says it. For other things also, which reach his beholders through unspoken *Gestalten*, at times to the sharp discomfort of his friends among them. At one time or another I have witnessed the effects of every imaginable infelicity of diction, enunciation, nasality, pitch, intonation, tempo, to say little of undue boldness or restraint and nothing of interpretation. So I am never surprised when I overhear someone whispering, "I liked his poetry better before I heard him." Such confidences rarely reach the writer's ears. Poetry audiences are more generous than most. • Since most members of his audience are not habitual readers, do they come exclusively to hear? A recital is always an event of a peculiar type, in which a private citizen willingly appears to "confess" to yearnings, fantasies, fears, etc., standing in a spotlight with only the verse to veil the revelations. How much is heard of what he says? Perhaps, as Karl Shapiro remarks, "it is an audience that understands him even when they cannot understand his poetry." How deeply they do is a question, but for the poet the degree is unimportant compared with the feeling of acceptance that they give him and the replenishment in such assurance. • The kind of verse most avidly analyzed and revered in the classroom is of course least suited to reciting before people who hear it for the first time. Yet most recitals occur on college campuses. • Dylan Thomas: "It is impossible to be too clear. . . . I am

trying for more clarity now. At first I thought it enough to leave an impression of sound and feeling and let the meaning seep in later, but since I've been giving these broadcasts and readings of other men's poetry as well as my own, I find it better to have more meaning at first reading." Cited in John Press, *The Chequer'd Shade,* London, Oxford, 1958, p. 91.

9. That a listener can, on certain occasions, be strongly moved by an initial encounter, I know from my own experience at the Sorbonne when Prof. Fernand Baldensperger introduced, explained, and then recited a number of poems. As an almost unbroken rule, however, I cannot get much out of any poem when I hear it for the first time; nor can a number of other poets to whom I have confessed my weakness, including one who was supremely ear-minded (the late Dudley Fitts). • The Cummings explanation: Norman Friedman, *e.e.cummings,* Johns Hopkins, 1960, p. 123. Mark Van Doren, *Autobiography,* Harcourt, 1958, p. 290. • Barfield quotation from his *Poetic Diction,* p. 99. Stravinsky: interview, *N.Y. Review of Books,* March 14, 1968. • Jakobson gives a striking example of "the informational capacity of messages," in which an actor made 50 messages for a tape record, corresponding to 50 different "emotional situations." The listeners heard only the changes in the sound shape of the same two words. "Most of the messages were correctly and circumstantially decoded by the listeners."—Sebeok, *Style in Language,* pp. 354 f.

10. Henri Peyre, *The Failures of Criticism,* Cornell, 1967, p. 53. • "On most occasions when most adults are first conscious of something new they either attack or try to escape from it." This is W. H. George's "Attack-Escape Principle, *The Scientist in Action,* pp. 27-29. See also "the new" and "the essentially new," p. 281 below.

11. "The Function of Criticism," *Selected Essays,* pp. 18 ff. I think that this early essay, by its failure to clarify the misunderstandings fostered by its central terms, has done more than any other popular statement to obfuscate the subject of "conscious artistry" (see above pp. 56 ff.). • The editors quoted are Paul Engle and Warren Carrier in *Reading Modern Poetry,* Scott Foresman, 1955.

12. French New Criticism is a complex world of its own (see LeSage, *op. cit.*). For the tenets of American New Criticism: Cleanth Brooks, "Literary Criticism: Poet, Poem, and Reader," in *Varieties of Literary Experience.* For parody: Theodore Spencer, "How to Criticize a Poem (in the Manner of Certain Contemporary Critics)," *The New Republic,* Dec. 6, 1943, and *The Overwrought Urn,* Charles Kaplan, ed., Pegasus Press, 1969.

13. Ransom: *Southern Review,* Winter 1938; Harry Levin: *Contexts of Criticism,* Harvard, 1957, pp. 190 f.; Barzun: *The Griffin,* May 1955; Spender *N.Y. Times Book Review,* Jan. 15, 1956. The painter may be even worse off: "Art critics read into my paintings things about themselves that have nothing to do with me at all. The meaning is there

on canvas. If you don't get it, that's too bad" etc.—Georgia O'Keeffe. It is hardly necessary to show why an overconcentration on symbols, allegories, et al. will take a reader as far away from the poem itself as did the former overconcentration on sociological and other background elements.

14. Aristarchus, the scholar-critic-librarian of the original Alexandria (*c*.216-144 B.C.), made it quite evident, in his studies of Homer, that a work of art cannot be understood when it is cut off from the time and the world in which it had been born. • C. S. Lewis: *Studies in Words*, Cambridge, 1960.

15. "I fear going to other people's homes, and when I do, I leave as fast as I can, without seeming to be rude. It is not that I do not care deeply for my friends. . . . I dread unknowable disaster."—From one of the letters of Edward Dahlberg in his *Epitaphs of Our Times*, Braziller, 1967. Such a passage cannot distract or disturb a reader of Dahlberg's books, whereas the biographical information that Theodore Roethke "hated to touch animals" (A. Seager, *The Glass House*, McGraw-Hill, 1968, p. 244) almost forces itself into some relation with the quality of feeling in some of Roethke's poems; it may do so despite one's determined insistence on separating the private feeling-system of the artist-person from that embodied in work. • Ungaretti's note to the volume in which the poem first appeared supplied the biographical background. Depending exclusively on the text, one has only the reference to the "musico bimbo" (musical child), his characterization as "fiorrancino" (a European firecrest wren), and the auracaria tree. See *The Poem Itself*, pp. 31 ff. Brecht: English version in M. Hamburger and C. Middleton, *Modern German Poetry*, Grove, 1962, pp. 227 ff. (See also Apollinaire, "La Jolie Rousse," *The Poem Itself*, pp. 88 ff.) Rilke: *Sonnets to Orpheus*, M. D. Herter Norton, trans., Norton, 1942, pp. 46-47, notes p. 147.

16. "Se urgi fino al midollo i diàspori . . . / il tuo splendore è aperto." Literally: if you press the persimmons to the core, your splendor is open—which is to say: if you succeed in bringing the persimmons to ripen (by virtue of this power of love which is within you), your splendor will be open for all to see. I am quoting Luciano Rebay's account of his discussions with Montale in the spring of 1967. See also his "I diàspori di Montale," *Italica*, Spring 1969.

17. I discuss this practice in *Varieties of Literary Experience*, pp. 162 f.

18. Essay on Hardy's poem: Allen Tate, *On the Limits of Poetry*, New York, Swallow Press and William Morrow, 1948, pp. 185 ff.

19. Remy de Gourmont: "Nous devrons admettre autant d'esthétiques qu'il y a d'esprits originaux et les juger d'après ce qu'elles sont et non d'après ce qu'elles ne sont pas."—Preface to first *Livres des Masques*.

9 · Encounter

> I find in myself a tendency to take the images literally and seriously, to visualize them as completely as possible, as if they existed independent of whatever they may be intended to symbolize.
>
> —John Crowe Ransom

Anaxagoras' belief that everything is latently involved in everything else is confirmed by no phenomena more than poetry and discussions of poetry. The preceding chapter could as well have been called "Encounter I," the present one, "Encounter II." And despite the differing vantage points from which each of the Parts of this book proceeds, every page is involved with every other page. Similarly in this final chapter, which considers the reader when we present him with a poem, for what shall we see but the effects of our having replaced one type of wildness by another—as in Stevens' "Anecdote of the Jar"?[1]

> I placed a jar in Tennessee,
> And round it was, upon a hill,
> It made the slovenly wilderness
> Surround that hill.

The wilderness rose up to it,
And sprawled around, no longer wild.
The jar was round upon the ground
And tall and of a port in air.

It took dominion everywhere . . .

A poem is a vision of order in our worlds of chaos, for chaos is
what we know them to be despite certain contrary knowledge.
What does it matter to the body's response when we learn that they
actually move by laws of their own? That life in the wild can continue for thousands of years when left undisturbed? That every animal and plant in a biotic community, from microscopic bacterium
to massive tree, forms part of a thriving system of mutual dependence? Human senses, unable to perceive such order, reconstruct
whatever they encounter to the scale of human dimensions, powers,
and needs, making a truce by which survival is possible. Also, at
times, something more than a truce. Place a jar upon a hill and the
wilderness fills up with a new presence. Taking "dominion everywhere," it becomes "a port in air" radiant with significations of a
kind that cannot be explained yet are known and felt to be suddenly
true and mysteriously vast to those who see them. Response to a
poem fulfills itself in a wresting of safety from wildness. For if the
poem's significations were not "wonderfully in harmony with the
modes of our general being" (Valéry)—with the laws of our own
bodies and of the world's body—they could not bring on the true,
the serene, the inexplicable sense of completion. Creature-knowledge
could not flow from poem to reader out of mere assemblages of
words—ordinary words which speak with only fragments of themselves, which say ordinary things under the normative truce we make
with the chaos. But here in the poem they are released to regain their
possible powers. With their ordinary selves and with more, they
enter the reader. And there they are able to come to life in accordance with whatever his unique attunement to their possible
powers may be. In accordance not only with what these powers
denote and connote to his brain but also with what they lead his
body into *doing*.

The poem offers it even more than what we earlier observed
in the reader's encounter: notations for an internal dance (Colling-

wood's "psychical expression," Spire's "plaisir musculaire," Kafka's "I read sentences of Goethe as though my whole body were running down the stresses"). For a reader cannot help but read into the words images of his own body. "We interpret the entire outside world according to the expressive system with which we have become familiar from our own bodies," as Heinrich Wölfflin remarked; "we always project a corporeal state conforming to our own." If the reader inevitably tends to *feel himself into* the poem, there is nothing in the least extraordinary in this aspect of imagining.[2] Certain scientific minds, said Clerk Maxwell a century ago, in his presidential address on Mathematics and Physics,

are not content unless they can project their whole physical energies into the scene which they conjure up. They learn at what a rate the planets rush through space, and they experience a delightful feeling of exhilaration. They calculate the forces with which the heavenly bodies pull at one another, and they feel their own muscles straining with the effort.

Empathy, as Vernon Lee points out, "exists or tends to exist throughout our mental life. It is, indeed, one of our simpler . . . psychological processes." It "probably enters into both sympathy and intuition, and perhaps into all mental response," adds Suzanne Langer. Paul Schilder is yet more specific; for him all human perceptual reactions are to some extent influenced by the image of the organism. So the reader somehow tends, as it were, to bring his body to the poem, whatever may be said of the intent of the author of the words.

Very little, in fact, may be said. For a reader who has deeply responded to a poem, presumptions of what the author had "striven to achieve" become secondary. This is not to say that they cannot affect him. On the contrary, an author's comments may astonish the reader by the difference between his sense of the work and the poet's. Rarely can he fail to be troubled when the differences are wide. Lawrence's warning "Never trust the artist. Trust the tale" brings little comfort; Plato's none at all (who believes that "poets understand nothing that they say"?). Even the arguments against "the intentional fallacy," in the well-known essay by that name, do not cancel the reader's misgivings, for a critic always speaks from without, an author from within. Moreover, is it sane to assume that, once a poem has been given to the world, its maker automatically becomes just another outsider? Indeed, a number of poets would have it so—"if it is a good poem," says Robinson Jeffers, "then the author's own understanding of it has no more authority than any other competent person's." Other poets, however, cry out when a critic is "wrong." Naturally, whatever they say will impress a reader, regardless of contrary "proof."[3] But argument, public or private, cannot settle the question as to whether the ties that cling enable an author more than anyone else to know—and therefore to show—what his poem is saying.

For readers of Chapter 2, the answer lies clearly in the contexts of intent. ("A poet cannot know what he has to say until he has found the words; he does not know what he has to say until he has said it"—Eliot. Authors of poems "later wonder what they've done and look at it to see"—Ransom. "I have never started a poem yet whose end I knew"—Frost. Etc.) What the writer in the act of creating knows above all else is that he is borne along in a steady unfolding, a voyage of discovery. At some point, before or after the lines are written down, he begins to learn what it is that "he" has been "wanting" or "trying" to say and actually saying. Auden has asked:

How can I know what I think till I see what I say? A poet writes "The chestnut's comfortable root" and then changes this to "The chestnut's customary root." In this alteration there is no question of replacing one emotion by another, or of strengthening an emotion, but of discovering what the emotion is. The emotion is unchanged, but waiting to be identified. . . .

In the process of completion, short or long as the case may be, the words may lead the poem into saying what its author would not wish it to say: he will follow along, try to bend its course, or abandon it. In any event, only after it has found all its words will its maker be able to discover the *poem's achieved intent* and to call it his own.

Any other sense of the term brings a train of confusion, particularly when an author, in explaining what a passage, an allusion, an ellipsis was "designed" to do, refers to himself as the agent. To be sure, the achieved intent must have lain somewhere within him—

in the sense that his "creative self" was reaching toward expressing something that his "listening self" or "observing self" did not know till the words were found ("How can I know what I think till I see what I say"?). This is not, however, what a reader is told when a writer talks of his plan, his purpose, his design. The personal pronoun loses relevance once a work has become an object added to the landscape. And since its life, as a product of creative imagining, depends on its public power, the intent that concerns a reader is the poem's intent.

It cannot, however, always be found in its words alone.

The Poem's Intent

Whatever the poem conveys enters the brain and—as I need hardly repeat at this late page—whatever affects the brain affects the organism. Different elements, components, forces address themselves to different responsive capacities, irrespective of whether or not we can say what they are. Certain writings seem to work a spell on the reader more than to speak to him (*The Ancient Mariner*, Lorca's "Romance sonámbulo"). Others stir him yet leave him curiously troubled (Hardy's "Nature's Questioning," Unamuno's "En un cementerio de lugar castellano").[4] While remaining unable to explain its meaning, he may find himself responding to a poem with delight (Morris' "Blue Closet," Alberti's "El ángel bueno"). Still other poems whose setting and action mystify—which he never understands entirely (Frost's "Directive," George's "Denk nicht zuviel . . . ," Eluard's "Passer")—may affect him in ways that recall the experience of Jefferson when he heard the Cherokee Chief, Outassete, speaking his farewell to the warriors assembled at the campfires:

The moon was in full splendor, and to her he seemed to address himself in his prayers for his own safety on the voyage, and that of his people during his absence; his sounding voice, distinct articulation, animated action, and the solemn silence of his people at their several fires, filled me with awe and veneration, although I did not understand a word that he uttered.

It may be futile to try to learn more of the poem's intent in such instances than that the responding imagination is somehow totally freed. For reasons we cannot explain, the reader is "capable of being in uncertainties, mysteries, doubts, without any irritable reaching after fact and reason," to borrow the phrases of Keats. The experience brings the reader a sense of completion even though he does not draw from the words what is usually called understanding. Obscurity seems to form a part of fulfilled response.

Must such poems be considered exceptions? As a general rule a reader expects to know what the words of a poem are saying. When he cannot follow the courses of their ordinary meaning, he assumes the fault is the poem's; its author has knowingly allowed it to remain obscure.

The charge, of course, is not new; indeed, it would be hard to discover a single great poet at whom at some time it had not been thrown. In England, for example, as early as the 1600's, George Herbert could ask: "Must all be veiled, while he that reads divines,/ Catching the sense at two removes?" Ben Jonson was moved to sneer that "Nothing is fashionable till it be deform'd; and this is to write like a gentleman." Even while regarding Donne as "the first poet in the world in some things," he was convinced that "Donne himself, for not being understood would perish." The decisive question, however, was already recognized. Chapman had no patience with impenetrable passages which resulted from contriving, but he was careful to declare that where obscurity "shroudeth itself in the heart of the subject, uttered with fitness of figure, and expressive epithets; with that darkness will I still labour to be shadowed." Despite the immensity of changes in the writing of verse since the seventeenth century, a reader today asks exactly what Chapman had asked.[5]

How does he find the answer? Was Gérard de Nerval merely willful or could he not have done otherwise than to write as he did in allusions and symbols which cannot even be sought without recourse to his autobiographical prose and related materials. Is the title of his famous sonnet "El Desdichado" to be translated "The Unfortunate One," "The Outcast," "The Disinherited"? Whichever one is chosen will affect the first line in particular. The meaning of the second is the cause of yet another dispute:

> Je suis le Ténébreux,—le Veuf,—l'Inconsolé
> Le Prince d'Aquitaine à la Tour abolie. . . .

What of Blake and the quite ordinary words he often uses to denote extraordinary matters? And what of Yeats and the twenty-eight phases of his private system as described in *A Vision?* Scholarship provides much help, but readers' questioning persists. More usually than not, the French Symbolists are held responsible for the modern practice of using private images whose import a reader is likely to miss or misconstrue. "I alone have the key to this wild circus (*parade sauvage*)," cries Rimbaud at the close of one of his prose poems, making a proud virtue of what other poets may possess without awareness. But privacy of reference is not a strictly French aberration. In an essay on "The Literature of Primitive Peoples," Paul Radin reports that

One of the difficulties of understanding many short poems, particularly those of the American Indians, is that they are often so personal as to be unintelligible without commentary. [The poet] can use any image he wishes and he can be as personal in his allusions as he desires to be.

And—as one may suppose—like his civilized confrères, invite the risk of being misheard or ignored.

To leap from a private to the public domain is to move from darkness into light, yet allusions here may at times be quite as obscure. The great difference, of course, is that the referents can be identified by anyone who makes the effort required. Just how much effort is a poem "entitled" to require? "Words are only hard to those who do not understand them," said Samuel Johnson, who presumed to settle the remainder of the question by observing that "Every author does not write for every reader." Nobody throws the charge of obscurity at Cavafy's "Ithaka" or Haim Gury's "Odises," though neither poem—demotic Greek or contemporary Hebrew—could mean very much to a reader ignorant of the *Odyssey*. Every author, then—to put Johnson into the affirmative—has a "right" to allude to the Classics, surely also to the Bible: these are taken to comprise the common store. But why should the right end there? Why not also recent classics—such as Dante, Shakespeare, Milton, Cervantes, Racine, Montaigne—and why only creative literature? The question looms absurdly narrow within the range of contemporary allusions, when entire poems are written on Einstein, Freud, on Lyell's hypothesis; stanzas on Galileo, Engels, Wittgenstein, McTaggart; phrases on Gödel, Zen, the Kwakiutl, DNA, I Ching.

For whom, one may wonder, would Johnson's 20th-century poet be writing? And what is to be said of works in which meanings depend on allusions to public matters of the kind that only knowledgeable readers can grasp: the phrase lifted out of another's work and inserted without quotation marks? the passage playing against the unidentified text, event, or personage? Not even knowledgeable readers may be always aware when they meet with the first (in the title of Van Doren's "Down from the Waist They Are Centaurs," within Edith Sitwell's "Still Falls the Rain," throughout Kenneth Rexroth's "Un bel dí vedremo," to take but three of numerous examples) or the second (in many contemporary Hebrew poems). Unknowing readers will remain unknowing in such instances so long as poets continue to exclude from their books the clues they readily supply in conversation.

"Brevis esse laboro: obscurus fio," said Horace in his *Art of Poetry*. Every poet has reason to confess the same ("I strive to be concise: I become obscure"), since condensation is the mark of poetic speech. Though few would think to rival Nerval's ideal of compressing "years of anguish, dreams, and projects into a sentence, a word," all poets run the danger of analogous results, a danger which enlarged in the wake of the Symbolists' discovery of mystifying possibilities of power in the single word. For if "every word, being an idea," expands into more than idea, space must surround it: silence; and the space itself, the blanks, become part of the poem. Some of John Peale Bishop's aphorisms bear on this question:

Any poet may appear obscure to one who has not learned what his speech includes, what his silences intend.

But the contemporary poet, having learned the values of silences, almost at once begins to depend too much upon his blanks, upon what was not in his poem rather than upon what was there that could be transferred to the printed page. He is full of hints and innuendoes. But a disproportion remains between the reference and the thing referred to.

The disproportion does not necessarily come from omitted transitions. If, for a moment, the presences bodied forth in a poem be likened to still pictures, any order at all in which they appear will not fail to suggest a sequence—a meaning—of a kind. Difficulties result from compression within the stills. A reader of Tate's "The Meaning of Death" is bound to be stopped when he comes on the final line: "We are the eyelids of defeated caves." Here, says the critic (Cleanth Brooks), the speaker of the poem drops his ironical pretense of agreement with the "gentlemen" (the work is subtitled "An After-Dinner Speech"):

He shifts into another quality of irony, a deeper irony. . . . We are the generation that has broken with history, that has closed the mouth of the cave. ["Cave" is the last word of the "monologue" that precedes: a "twin poem" called "The Meaning of Life."] The word "eyelids" indicates the manner of the closing: the suggestion is that the motion is one of languor and weariness as one might close his eyelids in sleep. The vitality is gone.

To feel the force of the line, one must therefore also read the last words of the twin poem ("Longer than the arteries of a cave"), says the explication.

Instantly one thinks of the telescoped images of Hart Crane and his letter to the editor of *Poetry* (p. 93). As usual, the explication consumes more words than the image, a great many more when three or four images are fused together to produce—as the editor maintained—"not mystery but mystification." To which Crane replied that "plenty of people . . . will always have a perfect justifications for ignoring those lines and to claim them obscure, etc., until by some experience of their own the words accumulate the necessary connotations to complete their connection." Which is to say that the poet who violates expected patterns of expression counts on readers, few though they may be, who will understand or attempt to understand. He has to. And literary histories may tend to confirm his faith. If Crane is contemned as "difficult, unintelligible, obscure," so was Wordsworth by the leading critics of his day. Violations may turn into lawful conventions; many works that were once inaccessible, in time unfold or become unfolded. Many works but not all.

"O poet, you have always been proud," wrote Mallarmé at the close of his *Art for All*; "now be more than proud, be scornful." Yet the same effect of difficulty for the reader may arise out of no such desire to be hermetic. A writer of verse is often faced with an irreducible choice between "clarity" and "truth": he can retain one at the sacrifice of the other. Dare he allow the "understandable" phrasing to remain when it is not what he feels he must say?[6] If, faced with such a choice, he decided to keep the obscure version, it is only because the clearer one is unacceptable as untrue. The literature of the past is overladen with such troubled choices, and the responsibility all too often can be traced to the limits of language itself. Although comprehensibility is essentially a matter of such "choice," it is so only to a degree. Certain statements that are difficult for another person to follow may nevertheless continue to feel right to the poet; to alter them is to falsify. A writer of verse is likely to be compelled to let such an obscure passage stand, for poetry is feeling, and a poet, like everyone else in an uncertain situation, will act out of faith. Trusting his feelings, he must take the consequences: that his unaltered words will mean very little to most people or evoke even hostility and contempt. It is time that this much-argued problem were recognized in its context of struggle. In the last analysis, obscurity involves purely moral problems which only the poet can decide.

"Language is always bounded by a frontier of ineffability, by that which absolutely cannot be said in any language." Ortega's statement, jotted down at the close of a long life of thought, could hardly have been a late discovery. Young poets feel much the same —"there are not words enough" and those that exist are inadequate. Which does not, however, stop them from striving to use them. Most poets do what they can with the speech they inherit, but others, unable to bridle themselves, try to leap the frontiers of language. So *Paradise Lost* is *Syntax Regained*, regained and completely remade (as Aldous Huxley put it). But the verses of Mallarmé are *Syntax Abandoned*. Free the pure idea (*notion pure*) from its tie to appearances and things, the unruliness of time, chance, and circumstance. Scratch out such words (*Rature ta vague littérature*)! "To *name* an object is to suppress three quarters of the enjoyment of a poem; which is made up of gradual guessing; the dream is to *suggest* it." Focus on the words themselves in their relationships within the phrase, the clause, the sentence; for a grouping of syllables (*vocables*) can become a new and "total" word, new to the language from which it was drawn and charged with incantatory power.

"Le Tombeau d'Edgar Poe" can be easily followed in literal translation with interpolations that suggest, by square brackets, omitted transitions; by parentheses, simultaneous or alternative "equivalents." (Too much space would be required to indicate how the words "light up"—as Mallarmé hoped they would—"by mutual reflections.")

Tel qu'en Lui-même enfin l'éternité le change,
(*Such as into himself eternity at last changes him,*)

Le Poète suscite avec un glaive nu
(*The Poet arouses with a naked sword*)

Son siècle épouvanté de n'avoir pas connu
(*His century frightened* [aghast] *at not having recognized*)

Que la mort triomphait dans cette voix étrange!
(*That death triumphed* [was triumphant] *in that strange voice!*)

Eux, comme un vil sursaut d'hydre oyant jadis l'ange
(*They, like a vile start* [hideous twisting] *of a hydra* [headed
monster] *hearing of yore the angel* [the Poet: Poe])

Donner un sens plus pur aux mots de la tribu
(*Give a purer sense* [meaning] *to the words of the tribe*)

Proclamèrent très haut le sortilège bu
([*They*] *Proclaimed aloud* [that] *the magic* (charm) [*of his words
was*] *drunk* [*i.e., charged the angel* (Poe) *with being drunk*])

Dans le flot sans honneur de quelque noir mélange.
(*In the honorless flood of some black mixture.*)

Du sol et de la nue hostiles, ô grief!
(*Of the soil and the cloud* [earth and sky, which are] *enemies,
O* [grievous] *struggle!*)

Si notre idée avec ne sculpte un bas-relief
(*If with* [it] *our* [my] *idea does not* [fails to] *carve a bas-relief*)

Dont la tombe de Poe éblouissante s'orne,
(*With which Poe's dazzling tomb* [will, may] *be adorned,*)

Calme bloc ici-bas chu d'un désastre obscur,
(*Calm block fallen down here from a dim* [mysterious] *disaster*
[*Latin* dis + aster (star)],)

Que ce granit du moins montre à jamais sa borne
(*Let this granite at least forever show its limit* [impose a limit])

Aux noirs vols du Blasphème épars dans le futur.
(*To the black flights of Blasphemy scattered in the future.*)

Compared to Mallarmé's later poems, this one (1875-76) does not go to extremes in giving the reader's mind "the delicious joy of believing that it is creating." A poem presumably can give that joy by removing the clues, by stripping away the words that would present the thing "just as it is." Which is exactly what Mallarmé attempted to do, and with a dedication unmatched in the history of art. As his direct disciple Valéry observes, these efforts are directed toward creating *absolute poetry* which "should then be understood in the sense of a search for the effects resulting from the relations between words, or rather the relations of the overtones of words among themselves, which suggest, in short, *an exploration of that whole domain of sensibility which is governed by language.*"[7]

For readers the end-results of this type of creativity are usually too bewildering to draw them in. Mallarmé might be concerned with producing "an orphic explanation of the Earth," but readers are interested only in poems that will speak to them, which is what Mallarmé's most extreme achievements quite fail to do. When faced, for example, with his late sonnet "A la nue accablante tu," they must either apply themselves with immense and patient labor or throw up their hands. For the fourteen lines at first glance defy unriddling, with the subject (sepulchral shipwreck) delayed till line 5 and the main verb (abolishes) till line 8. And even after studying the explications, they may flounder forever in uncertainties. Despite the fascination of the artistry and its strangeness, readers will doubt that the game was worth the striving. It is the sort of poem that may offer no future for poetry as a whole: the beginning and the end of its own tradition.

Its legacy, however, is very much alive, having been adapted and refined by the disciple. Not the absolute poetry—Valéry believed it was impossible to achieve—but the enrichment of poetic expressiveness by detaching the image from the referent. A simple example is the first quatrain of "L'Abeille":

Quelle, et si fine, et si mortelle,
Que soit ta pointe, blonde abeille,
Je n'ai, sur ma tendre corbeille,
Jeté qu'un songe de dentelle.

[*However, so sharp and so deadly,/ Be your point, blond bee,/ I have, upon my tender basket,/ Thrown only a dream of lace.*]

To what does "tendre corbeille" refer? Valéry has left it unanchored; it floats free in the sentence. Therefore its meaning will have to depend on what the reader decides to attach to it; only he can do the attaching. And at once possibilities come to mind—roundness, flesh, soft curve of the body, fruit, ripeness, garden—but these are speculations; *the* meaning remains obscure: obscure in an unprecedented way, for the very indefiniteness of relation between image and referent produces varied reverberations. This vagueness thus contributes a special type of poetic pleasure which is further enriched by the resonances of such other words in the stanza as "fine," "mortelle," "blonde," "songe," "dentelle" (sharp, deadly, blond, dream, lace). One encounters such potentialities wherever indefiniteness is embodied as an end in itself: toward enrichment. Hence we remark paradoxically about this stanza—as we should about Valéry's "La Jeune Parque," whose emotionally colored words often can be taken to refer to a number of different objects at once—that if the images and the referents were more definite, the poetry would diminish in richness.

Here we have a new universe of relations where ties among the parts of the poem are merely suggested by images which condense a variety of meanings and hold them suspended upon others. A world in which the poem assumes that its readers will look for meanings because they feel they are there, both beneath and within the words, and therefore also between. Expected usage no longer matters—Cummings talks easily of "sames of am," "haves of give," "ropes of thing," a "white ago." Expected patterns of word arrangement give way to new modes of compression—César Vallejo defines a "Poetry of the purple cheek bone, between saying/and not saying" (Poesía del pómulo morado, entre el decirlo/y el callarlo). Rilke opens his fourth Duino elegy with the question "O trees life's, oh when winterly? (O Bäume Lebens, o wann winterlich?)" Though the reader can supply the omission between *Bäume* and *Lebens* (*des Lebens* = trees of life), he does not know the verb that belongs before the final word.[8] Something akin to these practices had occurred before, in the poems of Hölderlin (*circa* 1800). It went unheeded by his contemporaries; whereas the movement involving Nerval, Rimbaud, and Mallarmé created a revolution in expression which invested every subsequent poet with unprecedented rights.

But surprisingly few poets chose to make full use of the new freedom, despite the delusion that all obscurity should be laid at the Symbolists' door. If a century ago French writers came to feel that language had become corrupted and exhausted, the type of remedy they found was only one of a possible many. The living capacities of verbal language are always menaced by the stereotypes that its routine usage fosters. As Ernest G. Schachtel observes,

> in the course of later childhood, adolescence and adult life, perception and experience themselves develop increasingly into the rubber stamps of conventional clichés. The capacity to see and feel what is there gives way to the tendency to see and feel what one expects to see and feel, which, in turn, is what one is expected to see and feel because everybody else does. . . . Most of the time, when we listen to or read the written word, we neither perceive nor imagine the referent of the word but are in contact only with the words (or concepts). We behave as if the word were really all there is to the object which it designates. The label (sign) becomes a substitute for its referent, and thus, in listening or reading *we are divorced from any experience of that which the* words point to. (my italics)

Imaginative writers have always had to galvanize readers out of deadened responses. And of course one way of producing the shock, of restoring to words their evocative power, consists in breaking their ordinary patterns, their expected interrelations. But it is far from being the only way open to poets, as a number among them have shown in the last hundred years. The reminder is much in order. One easily forgets that language can spring into life with surprising freshness and power while adhering to the laws of conventional syntax, as Mallarmé adhered to the laws of conventional prosody.

One also forgets that much of the verse of the tradition is in fact elusive, difficult. "I know that some of the poetry to which I am most devoted," says Eliot, "is poetry which I am not sure I understand yet, for instance Shakespeare's." Hopkins said much the same thing: ". . . sometimes one enjoys and admires the very lines one cannot understand." My own experience with certain lines of Blake, Wordsworth, and Frost which everyone quotes and presumably "knows" is epitomized in Yeats's remark on one of his own poems: " 'Cap and Bells' has always meant a great deal to me . . . though it has not always meant quite the same thing" (p. 106). This type of obscurity, then, may be strangely desirable, forming part of a reader's fulfilled response while drawing him back again and again to the passage. At times it may seem about to dissolve into light. At other times (I am thinking especially of Dante and Shakespeare) certain lines of verse seem to stand at once both before and beyond the frontier of ineffability; they are "known" but not wholly known.

A poet is deeply aware of them. And much as he might wish to compose such lines of his own, he understands the futility of choosing or willing. An artist does what he "can," while keeping faith with his feelings; he is "fated" to be essentially what he "is." The quotation marks are important, in view of the fact that whenever he responds to a stimulus, reactions take place which alter his later response (even to the same stimulus). As I sought to explain in "The Body Makes the Minde," each human organism responds not with the full capacities with which it was born but with the functional remnant of its original capacities—the remnant made functional within the influences and accidents of all it encounters (p. 32). Each human being (in the phrase of Dubos) is unique, unprecedented, unrepeatable.[9] Each person does what he can. A poet may reach out in certain directions to subject himself to selected stimuli, but he cannot know what his reactions will be or how he may be altered.

That each poet speaks as he has to speak at the time of his speaking is no assurance that he will be heard. Nothing brings such assurance; not dedication, zeal, sensitivity, wisdom, or insight. He may well be ignored by most of the world he addresses. Yet if he speaks with a voice which is unmistakably his own, in time it may be heard. There is at least theoretical assurance in the principle the Remy de Gourmont proclaimed, that critics have the obligation to accept and acknowledge as many esthetics as there are original artists and to judge them according to what they are, not according to what they are not. By these terms—and who could reject them?—

the failures for which past criticism has been notorious can at least be remedied. For if the poet speaks with a voice that is his and his alone, even a reader who might dislike the shapes of its sound or substance will not be able to deny him the right to be heard or to hold an authentic place within the tradition.

It is possible, then, to identify "a true poet" and achieve consensus. Can one do the same with "greatness"? Distinguish major from minor artists without furthering the inanities of a pecking order? In *The Scientist in Action*, W. H. George distinguishes the "new" from the "essentially new." The simply new concerns the discoveries of something which may never have been known before or the formulations of a theory which modifies a previous one by adding some new consideration or factor. The *essentially new*, however, signifies an entirely fresh and different way of looking at things. For three decades the phenomena of atomic physics continued to be described in terms of a particle and then De Broglie introduced a completely different way of regarding an electron: in terms of a wave. Similarly, the cause of disease, which had always been attributed to something present in the body, as an outcome of observations by Gowland Hopkins, suddenly was seen as the result of something absent.[10] George's categories can be related as well to the arts. If Bosch and Picasso, Michelangelo and Lipchitz, repeople their respective new worlds, poets who create the essentially new do the same (albeit the "people" of Dante, Milton, or Blake strike the reader's eye as comparatively much more human). The respective worlds that all such creatures inhabit differ from any that the reader had entered before. Whereas a minor poet transfigures parts of the world, a major poet brings forth an entire creation, adding to the world a cosmos of his own.

Returning now from author to work, we face a number of curious difficulties which bear upon its intent or, rather, are brought to bear upon it by people with special predilections. No particular confusion occurs when a poem happens to be loosely likened to a parable or a ritual, for although such extra-literary comparisons tend to clutter more than clarify, they at least do not presume to equate the intent of a poem with morality or fixed ceremonial. Allegory, on the other hand, can become an obstacle, though a bearable one in the course of reading the *Divine Comedy*, *Everyman*, or *The Faerie Queene*. For the most part works of this kind obviously—perhaps easily—move forward on parallel tracks: the imaginative story or drama itself and the practical, everyday—historical, political, moral, doctrinal—events or ideas it refers to. The second no doubt tends to weaken the force of the first for a reader—as in La Fontaine's *Fables*, *Pilgrim's Progress*, *Absalom and Achitophel*: allegorical meaning is abstract and frequently single; poetic meaning, concrete and multiple. Too often, however, in other works a reader or a critic who is attracted to the possibilities of practical import may invest them with greater allegorical intent than the words support. And this kind of inspired interpretation, moreover, can flourish regardless of the nature of the work itself—as readily from *Hamlet* or *Macbeth* as from *Billy Budd*.

The distraction relates to critical tact, whose failure in instances of this sort takes us back to symbolic interpretation as a whole. It also takes us back to "Big Two-Hearted River" and the college students who found the work to be an allegory rather than a tale. Like many of their elders, they had been taught to ignore the story in favor of an extra-literary meaning. And of course there was no agreement as to the symbol, for any symbol might do. As Van Doren remarked of *The Tempest*, "Any set of symbols, moved close to the play, lights up as in an electric field." One has only to make a choice and the rest will follow. But "there is deeper trouble in the truth that any interpretation, even the wildest, is more or less plausible." At the time when this critical practice was beginning to come into favor, other poets also disclaimed its worth and attractions (for example, "The easiest interpretation of all poetry is the symbolic method: there are few poems that cannot be paraphrased into a kind of symbolism, which is usually false, being by no means the chief intention of the poet"—Tate). All these warnings are directly aimed at the allegorical fallacy, at the kind of symbolic interpreting that takes the reader away from the words to something outside, that reduces the poem itself into an illustration of a lesson, moral, event, idea, or doctrine. Jung adds a telling dimension to the basic distinction I am making when he says that an allegory "points to something all too familiar" in contrast to a symbol, which is "an expression that stands for something not clearly known yet profoundly alive." So the poet Jorge Guillén will observe that the verse of St. John of the Cross is "almost completely uncontaminated by allegory." Remarks of this kind unmistakably show how writers regard the "something else" that a poem must mean in addition to itself.

"Though I love symbolism," said Yeats, "I am for the most part bored by allegory." And so are a multitude of others—whereas for myth, the opposite holds true. In fact, a great many people speak with reverence about it, though most of them would, I believe, be hard pressed if asked to define what they mean. When carelessly used—as it generally is—myth may amount to no more than a term of endearment, at a far remove from its basic dictionary meaning. A myth is, of course, one tale or a system of tales common to members of a tribe, a race, or a nation, which explains in terms of the sacred or the supernatural some practice, belief, institution, or other phenomenon in the world of reality. According to Jung's psychoanalytic hypothesis, a myth expresses one of the many "primordial images" or "archetypes" imprinted on man's "collective unconscious" in the wake of certain recurrent experiences which were felt to have deep significance. Hence the inexplicable power with which we respond to the narratives and character-types that stir up these "psychic residua of numberless experiences." By Jung's archetypal extension, *Moby-Dick* embodies a myth of primal conflict. What, however, can be gained by regarding as a new mythology the referential system of Lawrence's *The Plumed Serpent*, which draws on the Quetzalcoatl legend and elements of Christian belief? Or that of *The Waste Land*, with its juxtaposition of anthropological lore, Hindu theory, Christian mysticism, Greek metaphysics, and so on? Yeats set out in *A Vision* to compound a new mythology of his own. A century before, Blake had declared "I must Create a System or be enslav'd by another man's"—at a time when Herder and Friedrich Schlegel had already assured their countrymen that a poet could not be great unless he possessed a mythology of his own.

To urge a poet to deliberately invent a mythology analogous to those of the primitive past is considerably worse than absurd—

one thinks of rephrasing Keats: if a mythology comes not as naturally as leaves to a tree it had better not come at all. Yet the same demand continues to be made, despite its wrongheaded uselessness, despite all the facts that have come into view from studies in the field by anthropologists together with those by literary and other scholars. A myth can no longer be confused with the wishful fantasy-spinning that produces a folktale. A myth is a serious story, a mythology is a system of stories which meet "the demands of incipient rationality . . . in an unfathomed world" (Whitehead).[11] It is a supremely serious attempt to understand this world's specific conditions of time, of place, of man: to "explain life and death, fate and nature, gods and cults" (Bethe). It is thus at once an amalgam of primitive science, theology, philosophy, metaphysics; and as each and all of these things, it addresses itself to the listener's assent and belief. Civilized myths of course must do the same thing, but the basis of the mythic explaining may distract the civilized reader from assent and belief; for example, that of Yeats's *A Vision*, formed as it is out of Irish folklore and gnostic philosophy, which the author felt to be essential in understanding his verse. Something more than Coleridge's willing suspension of disbelief must be found to cope with distractions of this kind, as our final pages make clear.

Meanwhile inherited worlds of myth course through the mind of a knowledgeable writer, and sometimes without his awareness one or more of their creatures enter his own compositions somehow disguised. At other times, he realizes how much his work may have drawn on their vibrant presences as materials shaping its thought. He may find himself reliving, much as Milton did in *Paradise Lost*, an ancient myth, from his time and place in the culture. Or the land of myth, the mythopoeic age, may seize his mind to become the very body of a poem—as in Perse's *Anabasis*, with its epic vision of the prehistoric human caravan, rooted in the earth and moving through the seasons' cycles, building its cities. Or in Yonatan Ratosh's lyric reconstruction of the Canaanite world in a litany for the dead, "El Niṣmát" (literally "The Soul of").[12] Another writer—in the manner of Joyce with *Ulysses*—turns to a single myth for an overall narrative structure. Yet another refers to incidents of numerous mythologies—as Dahlberg does in *Because I Was Flesh*—where they interfuse with the background of everyday life against which the figures move.

With instances of this kind, one tends to forget that a writer's materials, whatever their potentialities, do not stir a reader until they have been transfigured into art. One also tends to ignore how easy it can be for a critic to relate an imaginative work to some supposedly primordial image or psychic residuum. Finally, there is something equally fallacious in expecting the civilized culture to produce the kind of tale that is native to a mythopoeic age and that meets its "demand of incipient rationality." Obviously, if a civilized poet creates a new myth, it will be one imagined by a mind which functions in a civilized mode of creative thinking.

I believe that a limited number of myths of this kind exist, though not in a deliberately invented system nor necessarily as a part of a newly projected cosmos. At any rate, there is reason to think that a composition such as Pirandello's *Henry IV* or Kafka's *The Trial* contains and exerts an extraordinary power of representation: it achieves its explaining less as a series of practical events than as a symbol which overshadows one's immediate sense of the work. This is to say that the something else that every literary creation means in addition to itself has by far the greater residual import and memorableness in these particular instances. I am speaking of course of what the reader feels once he is out of their spell, when he is able to follow the thoughts as they float on the surface of his mind and to see where it is that they gather. A parallel may even exist between literary works of this unusual type and totemic phenomena if, as Durkheim remarks in comparing the images of totemic beings with the beings they stand for, "The representations of the totem are more actively powerful than the totem itself."[13]

The representation of Brecht's *Mother Courage*, for example, has greater import and purport than its words, at least for myself as a reader. Out of the spell of the drama, my mind watches something beyond the pedlar woman dragging her cart from European battleground to battleground: her persistence against the frustrations, tragedies, losses, hopelessness that assault her; her fighting to stay alive out of bodily will. All around her, people are caught up in the business of victory, armies, political boundaries, battles, defeats;

concerned with her creature needs, she cares only vaguely about such things. I cannot of course know what the woman-as-presented becomes in the minds of other readers, but for me, dragging her cart away at the close of the drama, she becomes the life-bearing, life-protecting human organism driving on and across the surface of the planet, at best only dimly aware of where she is going but knowing above all else that the truth for her and her children is simply survival.

This entirely personal account can at best only hint at the difference; I am quite aware of the danger and futility of trying to fix the meaning of any symbol, great or small. The search for intent in a literary work steadily founders upon the obstacles that inhere in language-thinking, some of which have already been noted in connection with poetry's ways of speaking (Chap. 3). Henri Peyre speaks of "the very considerable, and often unfathomable, obscurity which persists in most great works of the past." Metaphor itself, as J. Middleton Murry and others have discovered, "cannot be pursued very far without our being led to the borderline of sanity." Similarly with analyses of sound-and-sense: they invariably end in reporting inexplicable facts. Arthur H. Hallam, for one, contemplating his own response to Dante, Petrarch, and the "clear searching notes of Tuscan song," dwells on a single aspect:

These mighty masters produced two-thirds of their effect by *sound.* Not that they sacrifice sense to sound, but that sound conveys their meaning where words would not. There are innumerable shades of fine emotion in the human heart, especially when the senses are keen and vigilant, which are too subtle and too rapid to admit of corresponding phrases. The understanding takes no definite note of them; but then can they leave signatures in language? Yet they exist; in plenitude of being and beauty they exist. . . .[14]

Valéry emphasizes another aspect in the course of one of his many definitions of poetry as "The attempt to represent or restore, by means of articulate language, those things or that thing that cries, tears, caresses, kisses, sighs obscurely attempt to express, and that objects seem to wish to express insofar as they seem to live or have a presumed purpose." Reading remarks of this kind, one is inclined to point out that descriptions are not explanations, as I have done before in this book. But the demurring statement itself must be questioned for implying, as it does in some measure, both a misconception of the ways by which poetry speaks and a possible equivalence it denies by asserting their difference. What Whitehead remarked in another context may apply with exactness here: "We have to search whether nature does not in its very being show itself as self-explanatory. By this I mean, that the sheer statement of what things are, may contain elements explanatory of why things are."

Many Meanings and One

To a person who thinks that esthetic response proceeds by discrete stages—that nothing else can enter a reader's mind until it clearly knows what the poem is "about"—the discussion of the last few pages must seem out of order. But a reader is engaged with a total work in an indivisible experience. It is afterwards only, when he moves outside it, that he is able to see where the words have taken his mind. This is not to say that he will necessarily have perceived the totality. More often than not in an initial encounter, if he cannot make some immediate sense of the words, his mind may close up to everything else they embody. Fortunately, language tends to produce some species of meaning, not to mention the fact that no more than an intuitive feeling for what the poem is about may be sufficient to give a reader his bearings and admit him into the poem. Once there, he will—in our manner of speaking—make up his mind to remain or to leave. The decision may have nothing at all to do with the merit of the poem *qua* poem, since with art (as with everything else) the characteristics of human responses are determined as much by the peculiarities of the person involved as by the nature of the stimulus. Assuming, however, that the poem is good in itself and attracts him deeply, we may expect that in time he will gain a satisfying sense of its meaning. And as likely as not, it will differ from the one or the ones discovered by others, for, as everyone knows, a great many poems of the past and the present are able to sustain a number of alternative interpretations.

Does it follow, however, that each is equally "true," "dominant"?

that a reader has only to select the one that to him seems "best"? In our time, when people have been made to assume that every work must possess several different meanings each of which is authentic, it is startling to be told the opposite—and to hear it declared in connection with Mallarmé: a poet whose "words and the images they delineate (symbols) reach out," as his critic says, "in all directions toward other words and images;" "richly connotative, fluid, ambiguous, suggestive" words, which "saturate the air with overtones"; etc. Robert Greer Cohn's declaration, however, includes all poets. "There is only *one* meaning to a Mallarmé poem, or any other authentic poem," he writes in the preface to his book which applies the thesis to twenty-nine typically hermetic Mallarmé poems.[15] Fifteen years following the author's death the first full study appeared (by Thibaudet), but the critic, for all his brilliance, succeeded better in stirring admiration for the verse than in clearing its mysteries. And as more and more explanatory essays were published, readers began to wonder if the poems would ever be accessible. Some of their doubt was diminished by the appearance of a remarkable biography in 1941 and of the poet's correspondence eight years later. With these doors thrown open, many new interpretations became possible; some of which demanded attention if only for their glimmers of useable light or for showing where light would not be found. Meanwhile the zealous reader had come to wonder how not to stumble in a critical wilderness which contains, along with plausible thoughts, the proposal (for example) that all the hermetic poems are enciphered eroticism addressed to a mistress, and another which makes of a Mallarmé sonnet a description of a bidet.

Cohn, equipped as he is, can be sure of his way. Faithful to his author, he believes that the meaning at the core of an authentic poem can be approached only through its concrete words and all they suggest. What guides his search through each poetic work is its relationship to everything else of its author's writing, including lectures, letters, critical articles, and other poetic works. In a sense, this amounts to applying in the large the "method" of the words and images which "reach out in all directions toward other words and images" in the Mallarméan universe. Although at first it may seem paradoxical, such searching for "only *one* meaning" must draw on everything of valid relevance—ambiguities, insights (of his own and of others), "levels" of meaning, correspondences, phonetic and pictorial symbols, as well as statements from the author.

Does the last show Cohn to be guilty of looking for the meaning of a poem in a writer's "conscious intention"? In view of all that we know of the creative process, there cannot be the slightest doubt that this scholar-critic brings to bear more elements—echoes, clues, anticipations, and other interrelationships—in the totality of Mallarmé's writing than the author himself could have possibly been aware of or have consciously intended, even after brooding endlessly over every facet of these poems—these "preparatory exercises" for the Great Work that he longed to compose. Relying neither on author-intent nor on anything-goes permissiveness, Cohn moreover all but asserts that conflicting interpretations have no actual reason for existence. One has only to understand fully the relation of an individual poem to the whole of the author's production and the part it plays there, even when the whole is inconsistent or unfulfilled as a system.

One instantly asks: Is this relation always discoverable? What, for example, can be done with Yeats's "The Second Coming," a poem of 1921? That its beginning refers to the chaos in the wake of World War I was declared by the author himself. "If you have my poems by you," runs a later letter, "look up a poem called 'The Second Coming.' It was written some sixteen or seventeen years ago & fortold what is happening."

> Turning and turning in the widening gyre
> The falcon cannot hear the falconer;
> Things fall apart; the centre cannot hold;
> Mere anarchy is loosed upon the world,
> The blood-dimmed tide is loosed, and everywhere
> The ceremony of innocence is drowned;
> The best lack all conviction, while the worst
> Are full of passionate intensity.
>
> Surely some revelation is at hand;
> Surely the Second Coming is at hand.
> The Second Coming! Hardly are those words out
> When a vast image out of *Spiritus Mundi*

Troubles my sight: somewhere in sands of the desert
A shape with lion body and the head of a man,
A gaze blank and pitiless as the sun,
Is moving its slow thighs, while all about it
Reel shadows of the indignant desert birds.
The darkness drops again; but now I know
That twenty centuries of stony sleep
Were vexed to nightmare by a rocking cradle,
And what rough beast, its hour come round at last,
Slouches towards Bethlehem to be born?

For Charles G. Bell, the lines that follow the opening description of "the dissolution of our time, the fall of the West" affirm the coming of some Revelation or mystical faith such as is sometimes supposed to succeed upon civilizations in decay. Here it is "the projected return . . . where a late-cycle material culture seemed on the point of destroying itself." "The prototype was the *savingly destructive coming* of Christianity into Rome" (italics added). So obvious did this seem to Bell that when he happened to talk with T. S. Eliot about culture cycles and mentioned the poem, he was startled to hear that Eliot "had assumed it was a negative work, describing an age of decay and the coming of the Antichrist."[16]

I think Cohn would have to approach this dilemma by asking what the poem *must* be saying in its simplest terms as a representative part of Yeats's total vision. Then, with all the sympathy, insight, and intelligence at his command, he would study everything relevant in everything Yeats had written and had said—in other poems, in *A Vision*, in the *Letters*, in conversation (including, for example, the remark once made to Horace Gregory: "I am Blake's disciple, not Hegel's; 'contraries are positive. A negation is not a contrary' ").

The next step is harder to follow but it would seem to consist in relating the self of the poet as a human being-with-a-private-history, as a man living among men, to the ineffable "something" at the core of the poem. What lies there, according to Cohn, is felt as a type of truth or insight which cannot be articulated; hence it is concealed from readers. But for the poet who, as it were, placed it there, it is vibrantly alive. And readers can see its effects upon him in the language of the poem, characteristically in the original images and symbols. Cohn calls them "crystallizations" because they form out of great pressure between two "selves" of a poet: between the poet-as-visionary with ineffable feelings-intuitions that demand expression and the poet-as-human-being who responds to them with language. But the crucial work has only begun. That the original images and symbols reflect the poem's true meaning does not show which among them hold the key. Cohn sends us back to the poet's vision, which readers have to reconstruct. And if they succeed, they will relate its elements to both the concrete particulars of the poet's language and his everyday experiences as a man.

Cohn's procedure ends by insisting on what every reader and critic will admit to himself whether or not he admits it to the world, for is anyone actually able to accept both Bell's and Eliot's views, to rest content with both? The mind is by its nature impelled to make synchronous knowledge out of all the elements in a poem, however elusive or disparate they may be. And it does not rest till it arrives at a sense of the whole, which subsumes the multiple meanings that words and images, with their heightened aliveness, assert. So the reader finds himself borne toward a self-fulfilling response. I emphasize direction, for some works are marked by a type of obscurity which draws the reader back again and again. As noted before, certain lines of verse seem to stand at once both before and beyond the frontier of ineffability—they are "known" but not wholly known. And they constitute part of a reader's fulfilled response. Perhaps this type of obscurity is exemplified by the vision in Yeats's poem. If so: there could be no point in hoping that any scholarly method could arrive at the "one true" meaning of "The Second Coming" which would alter the one it has had for a Bell or an Eliot. On the other hand, if not: the one true meaning might turn out to include yet also somehow to subsume their discordant views.

Towards the Poems of Mallarmé has changed my own mind about the intent of many of the works it discusses; not about all. Here disagreement has little relevance. Far more significant than any score of success and failure with an isolated reader is a scholar-critic's direction. And I think there can be no denying that "meaning" as used by Cohn—many meanings *and* the one that subsumes the many—is what ultimately demands to be sought, especially in poems so resistant as those of Mallarmé. Difficulty, of course, is not a measure of esthetic excellence, yet at times the two are inseparable—as are also, at times, in matters of intent, the poet as a visionary-language-thinker and as a man living as a man.

Assent and Disbelief

Through most of this book, to facilitate discussion, we have followed a type of encounter in which all that a poem embodies is more or less able to speak to a reader. Here, however, impedances ask for attention. And the rather perfect paradigm must be abandoned although not as an outcome of failures caused by obscurity. Many excellent poems cannot fully speak to a reader because he is simply not able to believe what they say or suggest as a whole or in part. For him the viability of the work, as noted before, will be qualified not only by the associated meanings of its words but also by its evocations of dissent or belief; which, in turn, depend on the history of the respondent. At this late page it would appear as needless to restate the fact that all the perceptions and apprehensions of his mind were translated into organic processes as to review the physiological reasons why the same event can be so differently perceived that it forms a different truth for each of the persons who perceived it.[17] The implications, however, bear directly on the problem of belief in poetry. In fact, it cannot be directly faced except in relation to this variability of perception. Every reader brings to his encounter with any poem a unique responsive capacity. We know it is fixed yet alterable. We also know that it makes for strong variations in the constitutional ability of individuals to accept certain things proposed to them as valid. This is not, of course, to deny that "universality" of response is frequently possible. It is only to add that the opposite also exists and, at times, can stand as a block between a poem and a reader.

For beliefs exist at all levels of awareness, including those from which they might never emerge except in response to a challenge. Indeed, a great mass of any person's beliefs lies within him not as ideas so much as feelings which he seldom if ever has occasion to form into words. A great many others will have entered him as ideas received from the culture at separated times. And unless some event should bring them to the surface of his mind, they may influence his response through the rest of his days entirely without his awareness. Facts of this kind are self-evident, and also another: that some of his beliefs are likely to be in conflict and that the conflicts will go on unrecognized—by the person himself or by others —unless they manifest themselves in overt behavior or for other reasons bring about his concern for reconciling differences. Needless to stress, though belief is fixed yet capable of alteration, here as elsewhere established structures of response strongly resist any force that tries to unmake them.

That the "problem" of belief is complicated most scholars and critics acknowledge; yet they also hold (in the phrase of Abrams) "that in appreciating literature as literature, the skilled reader in some fashion suspends his disbelief so as to go along in imagination with express judgments and doctrines from which he would ordinarily dissent." He is able "in some fashion" to do this for one of two reasons or both: (1) "a central and essential ethical humanity . . . transcends particular creeds" or man's "essential humanity . . . transcends the innumerable differences that set apart individual men and women of various cultures and periods of history"; (2) a poem speaks "a special language" or "constitutes an autonomous world of its own" and is therefore "immune from the criteria of valid reference, as well as from the claims on our belief, appropriate to the language of science." In theory either explanation or both ought long ago to have disposed of the problem, whereas they fail whenever either assumption turns out to have claimed much more than its practice warrants—which is often indeed. Three sentences of Levin have especial relevance. More often than either theory could allow, a literary work

is ultimately looked upon as a vehicle, not as an article, of belief whether of Anglicanism for T. S. Eliot or of Thomism for Jacques Maritain. All critics [and readers], to be sure are sooner or later confronted with works based upon beliefs they do not share. To what extent is suspension of disbelief possible?. . . . Can doctrines be taken—along with poems— as "pseudo-statements," and tested by emotive or formal criteria rather than by correspondence with reality?

—by correspondence, that is, with what a reader holds to be reality.[18]

With poems of a supra-reality no such questions arise. They

do not call for suspension of disbelief—ordinary belief has nothing to do with the worlds they project. Their irrelation to criteria of actuality makes them immune from any test of validity except in respect to art. We accept the events of an *Ancient Mariner* essentially because they are true by their own implicit premises. Similarly with other cosmologic creations whose existence does not depend on "valid reference" but sustains itself by coherent forces of its own. For example, I have no problem with the lofty conceptions of Mallarmé's system so long as I do not pull them down from their mythic plane and attempt to apply them to the one on which I live (when I do, they may seem insane). Similarly also with other assumptive supra-realities whose effect is not to challenge my notions of the factual but to bring to life certain aspects of the marvelous. So an ancient poem of prayer to the Sungod of Egypt has no bearing whatever on what I believe—or I take it as having no bearing—for distance and time have fringed its expression of faith with an aura of make-believe. I respond in this way to its dramatized speaking not because I transcend its particular creed but because my plane of belief and that of the poem's can never meet. I am able to take whatever it assumes so long as they never meet.

These are of course the exceptions if Levin is right in asserting that a work of art is ultimately regarded as a carrier of belief. Nevertheless as a practical matter there is small interference with the process of reader response when the force of the implicit assertion is feeble enough to be overlooked or dismissed—in effect denied. One may think in terms of a reader's threshold of tolerance. One may think of the force of many beliefs as provoking no greater disturbance than does a stereotyped thesis or proposition which the reader neglects as his mind is drawn and held by compelling elements within the poem.[19] Passages of this passive sort have no deeper effect on response than a proverb which he takes in his stride along with another which upholds an opposing truth. The lofty declaration in *The Ancient Mariner*

> "He prayeth best, who loveth best
> All things both great and small;
> For the dear God who loveth us,
> He made and loveth all."

for all its possible structural fitness makes no more impact on the mind than a moral cliché. Excellent poems are not always excellent in every aspect nor necessarily in all their parts. Often a single passage is enough to bring a reader a profound response. Indeed most memorable verse stands in fragments, rarely throughout entire poems. And although the fragments cannot do without the settings, the settings themselves may fade into a species of blankness. Blake's prophetic works as a whole make the obvious example, for what does a reader retain but a number of memorable passages?

None of the foregoing examples solicits the reader's active assent; with those that seem to do so, the claim can be ignored without any serious loss. At any rate, here belief differs from the impedance it sometimes forms when a poem requires not suspension of disbelief but affirmation of what it holds to be true. Coleridge recoils from the grand exaltation of a six-year-old in Wordsworth's *Ode*:

> Thou best philosopher, who yet dost keep
> Thy heritage! Thou eye among the blind,
> That, deaf and silent, read'st the eternal deep,
> Haunted for ever by the Eternal Mind,—
> Mighty Prophet! Seer blest! . . .[20]

I find myself stopped for other—factual—reasons by Van Doren's quiet exaltation of "those bones/ Of permanence, the unalterable stones." Ransom rejects as absurd the shape of the thought in Donne's famous sonnet "Death be not proud." Meanwhile a dozen critics continue to look for ways of accepting "Beauty is truth, truth beauty—that is all/ Ye know on earth, and all ye need to know." Coming at the climax of Keats's Ode, its claim on belief is crucial. But though the "special language" and "autonomous world" apologists "shift the emphasis from truth of correspondence to truth of coherence" or to "primary structural relationship," they cannot, of course, alter the response of any reader who is unable to grasp the proposition or who regards it as quite untrue.

It is helpful here to remind ourselves of the ways by which poetry speaks; that is makes both common and uncommon sense together; that both ordinary and extraordinary meanings are present simultaneously. I need not again discuss the effect of contextual forces in orchestrating the stress upon various kinds of meaning or show how the reader's mind takes part in the action. Rather what must be emphasized here is the influence of highly sensitized areas in the reader's mind which are indisseverable from belief. Even the most imaginative passages always retain, in addition to their utterly unparaphraseable import, irrepressible forces of ordinary signification. So Coleridge has to explain at complex length his own inability to suspend disbelief with the "best philosopher" passages. So Tate, in examining "coherence" among the various types of meaning in "Nature's Questioning," finally applies the criteria of ordinary meaning. Hardy's portrayal of the deity in one passage as a schoolmaster, in another as an automaton, and so on will not hold.

Even in the magnificent image of the "Godhead dying downwards" we get a certain degree of contradiction between tenor and vehicle: in order to say that God has left the universe to chance after setting it in motion, Hardy can merely present us with the theistic God as blind and imbecile.[21]

It does not seem to occur to Tate that this particular configuration of attributes is precisely what Hardy's poem conceives the deity to be. Assent becomes out of the question for other readers as well who cannot accept as possibly valid any divinity whose combination of attributes violates their own harmonious and lofty picture of a God omniscient.

One cannot pursue the subject of belief without also considering the role of dramatic fitness in producing conviction in the reader. While experiencing a play, one accepts whatever a speaker will utter or do provided it is "in character" and the world in which he moves is convincingly real by the terms of its own premises. To the extent that every poem is a dramatized form of speaking, the same must also hold for a lyric, a descriptive, a narrative poem. Nevertheless, full contextual appropriateness cannot always assure assent, even when a reader is convinced of the "drama's" own reality; for its theme has also the force of an issue upon which the work as a whole implies a judgment or choice—some type of assertion that everything which its world portrays is true.[22]

So one who believes all that occurs in Beckett's *Endgame* may also disbelieve in its "judgments," in what its vision of man's existence implies. Surely the same also must be admitted of Dante's incomparably greater work of art which justifies the necessity for terrible suffering by taking for granted the presence of a divine will and love which are humanly comprehensible only by faith. To explain away this belief-disbelief by insisting that the *Commedia* needs to be read purely as fictive art or unsignificant fantasy cannot be done, for, as anyone familiar with the *Letter to Can Grande* knows, Dante assumed both his readers' assent to all the events in the poem and a consequent practical change in their earthly behavior as well. But over and above the poet's purpose, the intent of the poem does not allow itself to be taken as disinterested or esthetic speculation: its dramatic structure rules out such a view because of what the speaker as one of the drama's characters declares in forthright words. To read the *Commedia* as a fantasy, as a work of amoral art, is to read not the author's poem but one of our own remaking—and not out of innocent ignorance, as in the instances noted by Lewis (p. 258), but of willful bowdlerization.[23]

No one, so far as I know, would seriously suggest that Beckett's play be read as supernal vision. It is plainly a work of this world. So, of course, is *The Waste Land*, which has become a kind of scripture for countless students (as well as for those of their elders who "follow" modern poetry). But, scripture or quasi-scripture, for many readers it represents, in the words of Herbert J. Muller,

a very feeble and sentimental view of the modern world—a view of unqualified sordidness, barrenness, futility, in a society without the dignity even of evil because without knowledge of good and evil. I should myself say at least that it is as crudely "oversimplified" as any vision of the youthful Shelley.[24]

For all its heresy, such a statement can sound only reasonable to a reader familiar with the author's well-known *The Uses of the Past, Freedom in the Western World*, and *The Loom of History*. Moreover—and quite apart from Muller's judgment on its vision—*The Waste Land* demands reader assent by a peculiar explicitness of ordinary and extraordinary thought: its presences tend to argue much as propositions tend to assert in frankly didactic works.

A good many readers, then, cannot respond to Dante's, Eliot's, and other noted poems without reservations. An obstacle stands in the way whose presence, here as elsewhere, depends on the relative importance for the particular reader of the matter requiring assent. And, as noted before, with numerous poems the "matter" creates no larger disturbance than a proverb.[25] Indeed the preponderant number of literary works do not bring up provocative issues or make a reader take sides. The challenges raised in poems are not often of theme. Moreover, an analogous sort of neutrality appears on the other side of the encounter.[26] Many readers simply do not have firm views on an issue. They may be "of two minds," they may have "mixed feelings," about the existence or nature of God, about man's present, about his future—for them the *Commedia*, *The Waste Land*, "The Second Coming" create no obstacle at all.

In fact, belief is a problem only when a poem exacerbates areas of thought-and-feeling which are highly sensitive at a particular time in the reader's life. Powerful "views" may continue powerful yet change in "position" (communist into anti-communist, etc.). They may also subside into apathy, as other issues spread over the sensitive zones. Compare the responses at varied intervals of middle-aged Americans, Britons, Frenchmen, to say nothing of Spaniards, to César Vallejo's impassioned requiem for a Loyalist hero: "Poesía del pómulo morado, entre el decirlo/ y el callarlo,/ poesía en la carta moral que accompañara/ a su corazon." (Poetry of the purple cheek bone, [a poetry that is half way] between saying/ and not saying,/ poetry in the moral message that had accompanied/ his heart). Or make a test—for clashing views and apathy, even—with the "Todesfuge" ("Fugue of Death") of Paul Celan, with its vision of wartime Germany:

Schwarze Milch der Frühe wir trinken dich nachts
　　(*Black milk of daybreak we drink you at night*)

wir trinken dich morgens und mittags wir trinken dich abends
　　(*we drink in the mornings at noon we drink you at nightfall*)

wir trinken und trinken
　　(*drink you and drink you*)

Ein Mann wohnt im Haus der spielt mit den Schlangen der schreibt
　　(*A man in the house he plays with the serpents he writes*)

der schreibt wenn es dunkelt nach Deutschland dein goldenes Haar Margarete
　　(*he writes when the night falls to Germany your golden hair Margarete*)

Dein aschenes Haar Sulamith wir schaufeln ein Grab in den Lüften da
  liegt man nicht eng . . .
  (*Your ashen hair Shulamith we are digging a grave in the sky it
  is ample to lie there. . . .*)[27]

These examples are not exceptions. Topicality merely reveals in
spectacular ways the types of response that follow naturally when
the highly sensitized zones of a reader's belief are stirred as well as
how they may alter with time. Time, one must recognize also,
may work in another manner, when the distance it brings tends to
convert an otherwise immediate object of issue into what is almost
an artifact. Cultural distance alone, if sufficiently great, can do the
same. A non-believer accepts the poem-prayer to the Sungod of
Egypt but recoils from a Soviet Asia folkpoem which has changed
the name of a traditional deity to "Lenin."

A poem simply assumes assent to the truth of the world it
images, whether by suggestion, as in Celan's "Todesfuge," or bold
assertion, as in Edith Sitwell's "How Many Heavens. . . ." Here the
opening quatrain gives the setting for the thoughts of three succeeding dramatic characters—

> The flame of the first blade
> Is an angel piercing through the earth to sing
> "God is everything!
> The grass within the grass, the angel in the angel, flame
> Within the flame, and He is the green shade that came
> To be the heart of shade."   [Stanza 2]

—which are reaffirmed in a final stanza bare of quotation marks.
The poem stands as the embodiment of a clearly painted vision,
hence also, as Yeats might have said, as a "revelation of the speaker's
life." Whether the reader spurn or share its attitudes, the poem
presents him with a dramatization of experience to participate in
as he *can*.

Hence, to regard belief in literature as a "problem which is
probably quite insoluble"[28] is to take an irrelevant stand: there is
no occasion for seeking the "problem's" "solution." Reader-reactions
of assent and of dissent exist. Belief exists. Given the nature of
works of art and of readers, it has to—I am tempted to add, that
it should, for people without any "minds of their own" would
scarcely be worth addressing. The "problem," however, is ultimately

irrelevant for the writer. He cannot choose what he believes, any more than can anyone else. Stirred as he is from time to time by his own particular vision, he does what any organism does when seized by this burden. "He" does what he can. "He" unburdens his mind. And it tells its truth or as much of its truth as the words it uses will bear.

NOTES AND COMMENTS

1. Epigraph: Ransom, *American Scholar*, vol. 12, p. 59. Wallace Stevens, *Harmonium*, Knopf, 1923.

2. Heinrich Wölfflin, *Renaissance and Baroque*, Cornell, 1962. Vernon Lee, *The Beautiful*, Cambridge, 1913. P. Schilder, *The Image and Appearance in the Human Body*, International Universities, 1935. Titchener's views, as summarized by F. H. Allport: "As the organism faces the situation, it adopts an attitude toward it, and the kinaesthetic sensations resulting from this attitude [assuming it to be a muscular tension or reaction] give the context and meaning of the object to which the organism is reacting."—S. Fischer and S. E. Cleveland, *Body Image and Personality*, Dover, 1968. • "The influence of the image of the body on artistic productions," says Kris, referring to L. Münz and V. Loewenfeld, *Plastische Arbeiten Blinder*, Brunn, 1934, "is dramatically illustrated by the highly impressive sculptural creations of the blind child."—*Psychoanalytic Explorations in Art*, p. 56n.

3. See Stevens' poem "Mr. Burnshaw and the Statue" and my "Wallace Stevens and the Statue," *Sewanee Review*, Summer 1961. "The Intentional Fallacy," by W. K. Wimsatt, Jr., and M. C. Beardsley, in Wimsatt, *The Verbal Icon*, University of Kentucky Press, 1954. Jeffers, *Letters to F. I. Carpenter*, 1939. W. H. Auden in *Poets at Work*, C. D. Abbott, ed., Harcourt, 1948, pp. 171-81.

4. Poems referred to may be found in *The Poem Itself*: Lorca, p. 237; Unamuno, p. 166; George, p. 131; in *Caged in an Animal's Mind*: Alberti, p. 95; Eluard, p. 99. • *The Writings of Thomas Jefferson*, P. L. Ford, ed., 1892-1899, G. P. Putnam's Sons, vol. IX, p. 358.

5. See *Varieties of Literary Experience*, pp. 154-164. Paul Radin, *Diogenes*, Winter 1955, p. 4. Cavafy: *Six Poets of Modern Greece*, ed./trans. Edmund Keeley and Philip Sherrard, Knopf, 1960, p. 42; Gury: *Modern Hebrew Poem Itself*, p. 154; Rexroth, "On Lyell's Hypothesis," *Collected Shorter Poems*, New Directions, 1968, p. 180. Bishop, *Western Review*, *Winter* 1948. Brooks, *Modern Poetry and the Tradition*, University of North Carolina Press, 1939, p. 108.

6. See my *Early and Late Testament*, preface. See also Calvin S. Brown, Chap. 8, note 4 above. Relevant to the "conscious artistry" of

Mallarmé are these sentences of his: "I think the healthy thing for man—for reflective nature—is to think with his whole body; then you get a full harmonious thought, like the violin strings vibrating in unison with the hollow wooden box. But I think that when thoughts come from the brain alone (the brain I abused so much last summer and part of last winter) they are like tunes played on the squeaky part of the first string—which isn't much comfort for the box; they come and go without ever being *created*, without leaving any trace. For example, I can't recall a single one of those sudden *ideas* I had last year. . . . Ever since then, whenever the crucial hour of synthesis approaches, I say to myself: 'I am going to work with my heart'; and then I feel my heart (at those times my whole life is undoubtedly centered in it), and the rest of my body is forgotten, except for the hand that is writing and the living heart, and my poem is begun—*begins itself*."—Letter to Eugène Lefébure, May 17, 1867, in Bradford Cook, *Mallarmé*, p. 95.

7. Valéry, *The Art of Poetry*, pp. 184-192. See Herbert Read, *Poetry and Experience*, Horizon, 1967, pp. 120-131. I have quoted (p. 273 above) "every word, being an idea" from Rimbaud's letter to Paul Demeny, May 15, 1871. As Read observes, Rimbaud's revolution of the word arose independently of Mallarmé's; at least Mallarmé's own direction had been firmly taken (mid-1860's) long before he had heard of Rimbaud's work (*c.* 1883). • Hölderlin: "In his late hymns and fragments all is vivid, sensuous, and specific to a degree that explains the impact of these poems on writers of the Symbolist, Expressionist, and Imagist schools."—Michael Hamburger, *Hölderlin*, Penguin, 1961, p. xxiv.

8. O Bäume Lebens, o wann winterlich?
Wir sind nicht einig. Sind nicht wie die Zug-
vögel

O trees [of] life, oh when [are you? will it be?] winterly?
We are not in accord. [We] do not, like migratory
birds, receive [the] signals.

In his first Duino elegy, Rilke writes of the figure of Night as the "sanft enttäuschende" (tender-mild disillusioning-disappointing) one who is "mühsam bevorsteht" (painfully-wearily-laboriously still in store for us). • Schachtel quotation, from his *Metamorphosis*, pp. 288 and 189.

9. "Throughout life, the constitution becomes modified and enriched by the responses that the body and the mind make to environmental stimuli and that become incorporated in the physical and mental being of the person—incarnated in his being. At any given time, the constitution of a particular person includes the potentialities that his experiences have made functional; its limits are determined by his genetic endowment."—Dubos, *So Human an Animal*, pp. 100 f. Remy de Gourmont: note 19, preceding chapter.

10. W. H. George, *The Scientist in Action*, pp. 23-29. Wordsworth defined genius as "the introduction of a new element into the intellectual

universe." • Allegorical meanings: "The political allegory in Dante is a part of the multiple poetic meaning, properly and ideally, but (1) there is so much other and more interesting (to us) poetic meaning in the work that we can let it go without too much loss; and (2) it cannot become a real part of the *poetic* meaning until we understand it so well and intimately that we take it in without much effort as we read. This last observation applies to all special knowledge which the poet assumes in his audience."—Letter to me from Calvin S. Brown, May 16, 1969. • Guillén: J. F. Nims, *The Poems of St. John of the Cross*, rev. ed., Grove, 1968, p. 132.

11. *A. N. Whitehead, An Anthology*, F. S. C. Northrop and Mason Gross, eds., Cambridge, 1953, p. 475. See especially Suzanne K. Langer, *Philosophy in a New Key*, 3rd ed., Harvard, 1960, Chaps. 6, 7. E. Bethe: as cited by Langer, p. 177n. See also Ernst Cassirer, *The Myth of the State*, Yale, 1946; Maud Bodkin, *Archetypal Patterns in Poetry*, Oxford, 1934. ("Gorgons, and Hydras, and Chimæras, dire stories of Celæno and the Harpies—may reproduce themselves in the brain of superstition—but they were there before. They are transcripts, types—the archetypes are in us, and eternal."—Charles Lamb, "Witches and Other Night Fears.")

12. St.-John Perse, *Anabasis*, T. S. Eliot, trans., Harcourt, 1949. Yonatan Ratosh: *The Modern Hebrew Poem Itself*, pp. 96 ff.

13. Emile Durkheim, *The Elementary Forms of the Religious Life*, Free Press, 1965, pp. 156, 217; but see contrary view of Lévi-Strauss, *The Savage Mind*, pp. 162, 238 f.

14. Unsigned review of Tennyson's *Poems, Chiefly Lyrical* (1830) in *Moxon's Englishman's Magazine*, Aug. 1831. (Cf. Mendelssohn: ". . . what a piece of music expresses is not too vague a thought to be put into words, but too precise a thought.") • Valéry quoted by E. Roditi, *Kenyon Review*, Summer 1944, p. 406. A. N. Whitehead, *Science and the Modern World*, Mentor, 1948, p. 94 (quoted in part above, p. 103).

15. Robert Greer Cohn, *Towards the Poems of Mallarmé*, California, 1965. See also his *Mallarmé's "Un Coup de Dés": an exegesis*, Yale French Studies, 1949. Yeats, *Letters*, London, Rupert Hart-Davis, 1954, p. 850.

16. Charles G. Bell, "Modern Poetry and the Pursuit of Sense," *Diogenes*, No. 10, 1955. Implicit in Cohn's approach are such questions as: At what point do personal biography and literary criticism merge? Or should they never merge? And as for autonomy, to what extent is the principle actually obeyed when critics and readers are struggling with a difficult work? How much of it, in the search for such a work's inclusive meaning, is in fact desired?

17. George gives striking examples in discussing eye-witness responses. including one incident reported at the Congress of Psychology in Göttingen: "Yet in spite of these favourable conditions only 6 of the 40 reports were admissible as approximately correct accounts of the facts" (*op. cit.*, pp. 78 f.).

18. Almost instantaneous alteration of profound belief by single events has been observed frequently in the last four decades among professors of faith in the U.S.S.R. and all its works. • See *Literature and Belief*, Meyer H. Abrams, ed., Columbia, 1958, pp. vii-xiii, 1-80 *passim*. Levin, *Contexts of Criticism*, p. 258. His paragraph concludes: "And if they cannot, must not the critic brave the winds of doctrine, seeking his particular version of truth? And when he applies what he finds, then will he be just to anything that conflicts with his assumptions?" • Pseudo-statements: scientifically unverifiable statements typical of poetry, hence "untrue" yet of some use, according to Richards, who invented the term.

19. Yeats, however, "was careful not to require knowledge of his prose from the reader of his verse. . . . For the most part, then, the *Vision* supplies only additional connotations for the symbols in Yeats's verse."—R. B. Ellmann, *Yeats*, Macmillan, 1948, pp. 233 f. For Yeats's own —contrary—view, see p. 284 above.

20. Coleridge, *Biographia Literaria*, vol. 2, esp. pp. 107, 111-114. Mark Van Doren, "A Winter Diary," in *Selected Poems*, Holt, 1955, p. 40. Ransom: "Donne sets up a figure, a metaphor, proceeds to go through an argument and as a result of the argument—which applies in reality only to the figure—calmly informs death that it's dead."—quoted by Donald A. Stauffer, *American Scholar*, vol. 12, pp. 59 ff. Keats's *Ode:* for varying reactions, see Abrams, *ibid.*; also Burrow, *Literature and Belief, Preconscious Foundations of Human Experience*, p. 48.

21. Allen Tate, *On the Limits of Poetry*, p. 194. • "Pretend what we may, the whole man within us is at work when we form our philosophical opinions. Intellect, will, taste, and passion cooperate just as they do in practical affairs; . . . It is almost incredible that men who are themselves working philosophers should pretend that any philosophy can be or ever has been constructed without the help of personal preference, belief or divination."—William James, "The Sentiment of Rationality."

22. "Poetry is not substitute-philosophy; it has its own justification and aim. Poetry of ideas is like other poetry, not to be judged by the value of the material but by its degree of integration and artistic intensity."—Wellek and Warren, *Theory of Literature*, p. 124.

23. Of the four types of meaning in literary works, as specified in Dante's *Convivio*—literal, allegorical, moral, anagogic—only the last required explanation ("supermeaning" [*sovrasenso*], which is attained "when we interpret a Scripture spiritually, a Scripture which, besides being literally true, bears witnesses through its literal meaning to the eternal glory of supernal things . . .").

24. Herbert J. Muller: *Southern Review*, Spring 1941, p. 825.

25. By referring to a proverb here, I intend to suggest a large range of tolerance as being typical of readers of verse. The range, however, depends in each instance on the "constitution" of the reader. For most people such lines as Shakespeare's "From fairest creatures we desire

increase" and Frost's "The fact is the sweetest dream that labor knows" are "true enough" to be taken in stride. But what of the implications for certain readers of Valéry's "Il faut tenter de vivre!" ("One must try to live!"), in the last stanza of "Le Cimetière marin"—which the poet dismissed as "really of no account, almost a cliché"—or Rilke's concluding command "Du musst dein Leben ändern." ("You must change your life.") in his "Archäischer Torso Apollos"? I suppose the ideal approach—theoretically, that is—would be, rather than a negative suspension of disbelief, an open acceptance of unlimited possibility.

26. George Eliot, for example, was not interested in changing or educating people. Nevertheless she recognized that the effect of her published writings had been to make her into an "aesthetic teacher" (her words). So indeed is every other writer in some degree, whether willing or not, from the preceptor who composes a *Commedia* to the author of a ballad or a lyric which does no more than reflect a commonplace belief.

27. Vallejo: *The Poem Itself*, pp. 226 f. Celan: *Modern German Poetry*, p. 319 (stanza 2, Christopher Middleton's translation).

28. Eliot, *Selected Essays*, p. 138. Sitwell, *Collected Poems*, Vanguard Press, 1954.

CODA

Conflict and Truce

Coda:

Conflict and Truce

That my view of poetry as art experience issues from the chapters which preceded must, I believe, be apparent to a careful reader; or so, at least, I have assumed. Hence rather than burdening the last hundred pages with every relevant cross-reference, I have limited them to the few that appeared essential. But here we must follow certain points of connection which lead beyond the implicitness of relationship that binds the three Parts of this book. For a poem, however regarded—in itself, as related to the reader, or within their encounter—testifies to a conflict and a truce between the two main forces in the human mind.

Anatomical names serve no better here than terms which suggest their nature, function, and behavior. So I prefer to speak not of the "diencephalon" and "cerebral cortex" but of the "primal" as opposed to the "civilized" forces of thought that interpret and control.[1] The former is of course by far the more ancient of the two, lying as it does roughly in the middle of the brain, where it *strives* to translate at once into physical action all that we mean by impulsive, animal drive. The italicized word is crucial, for the messages sent by this "lower" process into the cortex remain subject to the "higher" controlling centers of thought. And whatever the stage of societal advance, cortical reason bears down on spontaneous impulse in the interest of creature survival. Cortical processes of thinking monitor, censor, control. Increasingly they tend to overcontrol, to stifle the innermost tendencies of the organism, to ignore the dictates of biological necessity.

What matters for poetry—and, by extension, for all the arts—is the steadily harsher relationship between these powers in the mind. The more the civilized process strives for dominion and the more it tends to bear down, the firmer the counterthrust of the primal process. Thus conflict becomes a normative part of existence for a mind in which neither force can wholly subdue the other: conflict leading to conflict-resolved—resolved through innumerable modes of erstwhile truce, to enable the host to survive. And, needless to stress, one type of the conflict-resolved appears in the truce that is art, as certain innermost needs of the organism fulfill themselves through imaginative creations.

That a compromise composes every such truce must be taken for granted, since the cortical centers re-form the primal demands. So a diencephalic "instinct" will emerge in the shape of a culturally acceptable "emotion," thanks to the civilized process of thought with its countless ways for transforming: its veils, disguises, symbols, and other procedures for distancing importunacy and directness. Some awareness of this truce-like action of art can be read into forthright statements by artists and critics. I have earlier cited a few in other contexts—Aristotle, on the "esthetic distance" that detaches a member of an audience from the immediacy of the passions evoked in a drama; Wordsworth, on the need for accompanying the "most pathetic scenes" "with an overbalance of pleasure" by employing "harmonious metrical language" and similar resources; Carlyle, on the verbal symbol as "concealment yet revelation." But no one, so far as I know, save the much neglected Keble, has regarded a work of art as a conflict-resolved in an act which preserves its maker "from actual madness," or has taken such care to explain that if poetry "reveals the fervent emotions of the mind," it can do so "*only* under certain veils and disguises."[2]

The indirectness that marks all creative expression could father a book of its own. Mindful of all the cortical ways of transforming, one could look for the source of a number of critical axioms in the compromise imposed by the act of truce. Must every poem be an unparaphraseable totality? Must it always seem to be trying to express something beyond itself? The concealments that follow the conflict-resolved between primal and civilized thinking illuminate these questions as well as the cause of those matters which beset a reader as he looks for a poem's intent and its resonance-meaning.

Similarly with another phase of the truce, with the tenseness that develops from the pressure of the "fervent emotions" against the veils and disguises. Neither process of thought completely surrenders. The poem that results pulses with the thinking of each, yet it holds together despite this contradiction. In fact, such contradiction forms part of its binding force, enabling the work to have many different meanings as well as the one which subsumes the many and making it both an autonomous work and an object which is tied by its words to a time and a place in the culture. Similarly with the numerous unifications that pervade the shapes of sound, the choreographic shapes of the poem's substance, and the patterned rhythms of both which resound and reverberate in the reader's body as it comes to relive the feeling of creature-knowledge.

All we have learned in the foregoing pages of this book has been drawn from seeking the answer to a twofold question: What manner of persons are these that compose a work of art and respond to its speaking?[3] A poem, we have found, is something that is done to a poet. It is also something that is done to a reader from the moment its voices have seized his ear. The opening lines give him the clue, the key to its total rhythm and texture of sound, to be followed as both evolve toward the closing silence.[4] The poem is heard, and the one who hears it "scans," not as a metrist does to mark off feet but to know the pulse of the whole. And to know, further, so far as he can, all that is said in its language of thinking song.

Yet—"Song aspires to silence":[5] the act of singing for the poet; the song, for the listener. The poem ceases to exist as the object of words that it was, once it has been incorporated by the reader. The words themselves fade and with them a part of the creature-knowledge they offered, as the change they fostered emerges in the silenced poem.

"Poetry begins with the body and ends with the body": it begins in one and ends in another. The sentence that opened this book, having made a voyage, closes it now.

NOTES AND COMMENTS

1. "It is into the diencephalon [the higher brain stem] that the currents of sensory information come. Patterns of traveling potentials that produce voluntary activity originate here and move out through the motor cortex on either side to the muscles. From here, different areas of cerebral cortex are called into action and carry out their function by means of back-and-forth neuronal activity with the diencephalon. Thus, the different processes of the mind are made possible through combined functional activity in diencephalon and cerebral cortex, not within diencephalon alone."—Wilder Penfield in Eccles, *Brain and Conscious Experience*, p. 235. • "In the millions of years spent in the trees, the diencephalon had learned to serve superbly the most timid of mammals and to protect it from making wrong and dangerous decisions. In this it could rely implicitly on the perfect cooperation from the cortex [p. 53]. . . . Animals have cortical control over their instincts, but they differ from modern man in that their control is directed exclusively to biological and not to artificial requirements. Moreover, man not only controls his instincts, but also represses them, together with the emotions they engender. . . . [p. 46]"—A. T. W. Simeons, *Man's Presumptuous Brain*, Dutton, 1962.

2. Keble, *Lectures on Poetry*, vol. 1, pp. 2, 22, 47, 55. • In animals "the instincts can pass without further cortical embellishment into consciousness. In early primitive man many raw instincts were still consciously acceptable, but in urban man this is no longer so. When a raw instinct such as fear, rage or sex breaks through all cortical barriers, it is usually interpreted as insanity or crime, because raw instincts threaten the cortical authority with which man runs his artificial world." Simeons, *op. cit.*, pp. 45-6.

3. An overconcern with tact may produce obfuscation. I have assumed that the reader has perceived, for example, that the "holisticity" of the organism (Chap. 1) is related to the fact that in creativity the mind acts upon the totality of all its processes (Chap. 2), and that Chap. 3 is a

mirror-image of Chap. 2. At this stage, is it desirable to connect by specific detail the conflict-and-truce of these concluding pages to both Chaps. 2 and 3—and to Chaps. 4, 5, and 6 as well? Need I also bear down on the implications of, for example, the "tenseness" that characterizes the conflict-resolved for the critical "questions" and "problems" discussed in Chaps. 7, 8, 9? And what of the relation between the primal and the civilized processes of mind and "The 'Incompatible' Forces" of Chap. 3 (pp. 106 ff.)? Where does a writer's overconcern with reader-sensitivity result in omitting too much?

4. In discussing his "Bells for John Whiteside's Daughter," Ransom says: ". . . we just count the number of accented or stressed syllables in the line and let the unstressed syllables take care of themselves. So that sometimes you get two stresses coming together, and sometimes you run over two or three, or maybe even four, unstressed syllables at once—which was against the rule of the old poets—but the moderns have done that a good deal."—Brooks and Warren, *Conversations on the Craft of Poetry*, p. 22.

5. Burnshaw, *Caged in an Animal's Mind*, p. 143.

Index

311